W9-AAY-491

PRAISE FOR

In the Shadow of a Saint

A BEST BOOK OF 2000, *The Globe and Mail* and *Ottawa Citizen*

"Wiwa leaves no holds barred in his account of his father's remarkable life and appalling death. It's a searing personal and political document." Harold Pinter

"Wiwa honours his father's memory with this book, transforming Ken Saro-Wiwa the martyr into a real multidimensional man—more complex and interesting than his myth could ever be…. Exceptionally—sometimes bracingly—frank." *Toronto Life*

"Ken Wiwa does not spare himself in this story. He reveals self-truths he is not proud of. You feel for him. You feel for his father. His elegantly written book is a weave of Nigerian and family history, both turbulent, both tragic, neither without hope. The book is also a song of the Ogoni people, a tribute to their struggle, their endurance." *The Guardian* (UK)

"[This is] no mere biography or polemic, but a book which marries the political and the personal, a technique which illustrates certain universal dilemmas which haunt fathers and sons worldwide….Wiwa's even hand, honesty, powers of description and even humour deliver a poignant account that never abandons heart and hope to the sulphur of despair….This is the kind of book that people have been killed for writing, even reading." *Calgary Straight*

"This book delicately exposes and explores the most personal and most sensitive areas of relationships in a family that was together under one roof in London but was apart in the variety of the involvements of the head of that family…. A wise book indeed." Kole Omotoso, *The Guardian* (Nigeria)

"Sparkling, real and often heart-rending…. *In the Shadow of a Saint* is a morality tale for the 21st century, a time in history when no country, people or individual can avoid the all-pervasive impact of global capitalism." Movement for a Socialist Future website

"Marvellously written, this memoir offers both exploration and expiation." *The Mail and Guardian* (Johannesburg)

PAPA   JEJE   NENE

In the Shadow of a Saint

▼

Ken Wiwa

TEDUM TAMBARI
SARO-WIWA

AT MY
FATHER'S GRAVE

FELIX
SARO-WIWA

Vintage Canada

A Division of Random House of Canada Limited

VINTAGE CANADA EDITION, 2001

Copyright © 2000 by Ken Wiwa

All rights reserved under International and Pan-American Copyright
Conventions. Published in Canada by Vintage Canada, a division of
Random House of Canada Limited, in 2001. First published in hardcover
in Canada by Alfred A. Knopf Canada, Toronto, in 2000. Distributed by
Random House of Canada Limited, Toronto.

Vintage Canada and colophon are registered trademarks of
Random House of Canada Limited.

1. Poems, excerpts, letters and lyrics by Ken Saro-Wiwa © The Ken Saro-
Wiwa Estate. All rights administered and represented by Westwood Creative
Artists, 94 Harbord St., Toronto, Ontario, M5S 1G6, Canada. 2. *The Four
Quartets* by T. S. Eliot. Reprinted by permission. 3. "One" Lyrics by U2. ©
Blue Mountain Music Ltd. Reprinted by permission. 4. "Solitude" Lyrics
by Geoffrey Oryema. Reprinted by permission.

National Library of Canada Cataloguing in Publication Data

Wiwa, Ken, 1968–
  In the shadow of a saint

ISBN 0-676-97310-8

1. Saro-Wiwa, Ken, 1941-1995. 2. Saro-Wiwa, Ken 1941-1995—Political
and social views. 3. Ogoni (African people)—Government relations. 4.
Environmentalists—Nigeria—Biography. 5. Wiwa, Ken, 1968- . I. Title.

DT515.45.O33W58 2001   966.905'3'092   C2001-930773-X

www.randomhouse.ca

Printed and bound in the United States of America

10 9 7 6 5 4 3 2 1

For Nene

CONTENTS

There are at least two stories here. One about forgiving. One about forgetting. Very different stories seeming to need to be told at once. Time is what links them and distinguishes them and blurs the space of one into the other. Time and my father.

John Edgar Wideman

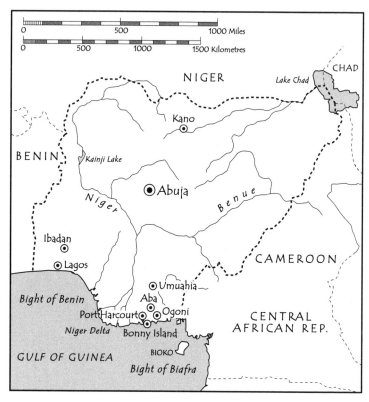

NIGERIA

Preface

▼

What we call the beginning is often the end / And to make an end is to make a beginning. The end is where we start from.
—T.S. ELIOT, *Four Quartets*

M y father. Where does he end and where do I begin? I seem to have spent my whole life chasing his shadow, trying to answer the questions that so many fathers pose to their sons. Is my life predetermined by his? My future defined by my past? Is his story repeating itself through me, or am I the author of my own fate? Is he my father, or am I his son? Where does he end and where do I begin?

I was always my father's son. His influence was visible in just about everything I did: my career, the woman I chose to marry, why I shortened my name, the books I read, the way I speak, the way I write, my politics. I used to fantasize about his death, imagining it as the moment when I would finally be free to be my own man, to make my own way in life without having to consider how he would react.

He was hanged in Nigeria on November 10, 1995. On the morning of his execution, he was taken from his prison cell in a military camp in Port Harcourt, on the southern coast of Nigeria, and driven under armed escort to a nearby prison. It took five attempts to hang him. His corpse was dumped in an unmarked grave; acid was poured on his remains and soldiers posted outside the cemetery.

Ken Saro-Wiwa's execution triggered a tidal wave of outrage that swept around the world. John Major, then British prime minister, described my father's execution as "judicial murder" and the military tribunal that sentenced him to death as a "fraudulent trial, a bad verdict, an unjust sentence." Nelson Mandela declared that "this heinous act by the Nigerian authorities flies in the face of appeals by the world community for a stay of execution." World figures, including Bill Clinton and the Queen, joined the worldwide condemnation of Nigeria's military dictator, General Sani Abacha. Nigeria was suspended from the Commonwealth; countries recalled their diplomats, and there were widespread calls for economic sanctions. There were candlelit vigils and demonstrations outside Nigerian embassies and at Shell Oil stations and offices. My father's death was front-page news around the world. Letters and tributes poured in from every continent, and Ken Saro-Wiwa was canonized in hastily prepared obituaries that were often littered with errors. A man whom few people had heard of twenty-four hours earlier was suddenly invested with a mythic quality, and his campaign against Shell Oil and a ruthless military regime was being touted as a morality tale for the late twentieth century.

But there were ugly footnotes to the saga. The quicklime had barely calcified around my father's bones when dissenting voices began to question the public's perception of Ken Saro-Wiwa. In *The Times,* one commentator wrote, "People are comparing Ken Saro-Wiwa to Steve Biko, which of course he isn't." A society columnist in *The Sunday Times* insisted that "Ken Saro-Wiwa may have got the short end of the stick but he was no angel." Shell Oil, the company my father had accused of devastating the environment and abusing the human rights of our people, responded to questions about its role in the affair by launching a public-relations campaign that spread doubts about his character and his reputation. The multinational distanced itself from the execution, insisting that it was being used as a scapegoat to deflect attention from the real issues in the trial. In a television interview, the head of its Nigerian operations claimed that Ken Saro-Wiwa had been executed for murder.

General Abacha declared war against Ken Saro-Wiwa, spending $10 million to counter the negative publicity his regime was attracting because of the execution. Washington lobbyists and public-relations consultants were hired to sell the line that Ken Saro-Wiwa had incited his followers to commit murder. An advertisement in the *Washington Post* graphically illustrated the sequence of events leading up to the trial and the execution. In London, the Nigerian High Commission took space in *The Times* to explain "the truth about Ken Saro-Wiwa." Newspaper editors were pressed to report "the other side of the story," and in *The Guardian*, where I was working at the time, one of my father's former associates described him as a "habitual liar." *Punch* magazine claimed that Ken Saro-Wiwa had duped gullible liberals and had used his friends in the media to "fool the world."

The ideas and ideals that my father had championed were almost relegated to the side as his name, his life and his death were manipulated to service all kinds of agendas. Depending on where you stood, Ken Saro-Wiwa was either a devil or a saint.

Ken Saro-Wiwa was best known in Nigeria as a fearless newspaper columnist who won admirers and attracted powerful enemies for his trenchant criticisms of the country's military dictators and power-brokers. He was a prodigious writer with twenty-five books to his name, and he also wrote, produced and directed the country's most popular sitcom. He was a successful businessman too, developing an extensive property portfolio and building a retail business from nothing. He was a man of many parts, and was variously described as a poet, a writer, an environmentalist, a businessman and a Nobel Prize nominee. He left behind a complicated personal and political legacy, and I, his first son and namesake, was expected to carry on from where he had left off.

I once wrote to him complaining about how his life had restricted my choices. He had just been arrested for what turned out to be the final time, and I was venting my resentment at having to give up my life to try to save his. He wrote back suggesting it was a shame that children couldn't choose their parents. I didn't understand what he meant by that, and it was only after he was executed that I began to appreciate what he had tried to tell me.

▼

Nigeria should be God's own country in Africa. Spread over a million square kilometres in West Africa, it is richly endowed with mineral and human resources. It is the sixth-largest producer of crude oil in the world, and it has one of the largest deposits of natural gas—which will be the prime energy source for the twenty-first century. With a population of more than 100 million, it is the largest country in Africa. One in six Africans and one in ten blacks are Nigerian. It ought to be the pride of the black man, but despite earning an estimated $600 billion from oil since 1960, Nigeria has one of the lowest per capita incomes in the world and external debts of $40 billion. Most depressing of all is that unlike many oil-rich nations, Nigeria has little to show for its wealth. Its infrastructure is prehistoric, overwhelmed and poorly maintained. Many of the roads are potholed death traps, and the telephone system is notoriously inefficient, almost useless by Western standards. There are frequent power shortages and virtually no running water. Public services are chronically inefficient and undercapitalized. Schools and universities are underfunded and in a state of permanent neglect; teachers and lecturers are poorly paid, if on time. Nigerians routinely die of treatable diseases like malaria and tuberculosis, while AIDS and stress-related illnesses stalk the collective health of the nation. Most hospitals would be best described as mortuaries; simple and routine operations are often a matter of life and death. Infant mortality is among the highest in the world, and life expectancy is only fifty-four and falling. Life in Nigeria is nasty, brutish and short, as my father often used to say (paraphrasing Hobbes).

Nigeria is a deeply troubled country, a volatile land divided along ethnic, economic, political and religious fault lines and tottering, as the title of one of my father's collection of essays describes, "on the brink of disaster."

Since gaining independence in 1960, Nigeria has been in the tight grip of a clique of religious leaders, traditional rulers; ruthless military despots; corrupt, grasping and nepotistic businessmen; greedy multinationals and influential foreigners. This untouchable elite of multi-millionaires and -billionaires, almost exclusively male, has profited from a system that falls somewhere between a feudal, conservative system of patronage and the unregulated opportunism of the Wild West. This system, which has been variously described as a lootocracy or a kleptocracy, guaranteed its beneficiaries fast and easy returns; 99 per cent of the country's wealth is in the hands of a minority. The elites have grown fat on the lack of accountability in government and in the absence of an ethos or understanding of public service. The private immorality of the few has crushed the notion of public morality in its remorseless maw, stripping the country of its assets and bleeding it dry. Unborn generations of Nigerians have been saddled with the burden of a huge external debt, the country's future mortgaged to foreign banks by leaders who were too preoccupied with amassing their own wealth to care about the costs and consequences for the people.

When my father founded the Movement for the Survival of the Ogoni People (MOSOP) in 1990, he saw it as a vehicle to "mobilize the Ogoni people and empower them to protest against the devastation of their environment by Shell, and their denigration and dehumanisation by Nigeria's military dictators." He had modest expectations of what he conceived as a non-violent, grass-roots organization, but MOSOP so caught the popular imagination that 300,000 of our people, three out of every five Ogoni, came out in support of the aims and ideals of the movement during a protest march on January 4, 1993. That day, in what was a peaceful demonstration, the Ogoni declared Shell *persona non grata* until it paid back rents and cleaned up the environment. A people who had a reputation for being lazy and docile had rediscovered its voice, and my father saw that as the greatest achievement of his life. He maintained that if he had died that day, he would have died a happy man.

Less than two years later, he was dead.

▼

On May 21, 1994, four chiefs, including my uncle and a founding member of MOSOP, were brutally murdered during a riot in Ogoni. That night, my father was arrested at his home in Port Harcourt. The following day, the military administrator of Rivers State, Lt. Col. Dauda Komo, held a press conference blaming the riot and the murders on MOSOP. Hundreds of MOSOP activists were hunted down and rounded up. Many fled underground and went into exile. My father was detained without charge for nine months. He was chained, routinely tortured, and denied access to his family, his doctor and a lawyer. When he was finally charged in January 1995, he was arraigned before a military tribunal and accused of inciting the youth wing of MOSOP to eliminate the four chiefs, including his own brother-in-law.

On October 31, 1995, eight months after the trial began, the presiding judge, Chief Justice Ibrahim Auta, sentenced my father and eight other Ogoni men to death. Ten days later, the nine men were hanged.

I was in New Zealand when I heard the news. I had gone there to lobby Nelson Mandela and the heads of state of the Commonwealth countries, who were meeting in Auckland for their biennial summit. I had already spent the best part of a year travelling around the world, trying to raise public awareness of my father's predicament. I was aware that the Commonwealth summit was our last chance to save him. But despite intense lobbying and the heavy media coverage of my father's story, the Commonwealth's leaders decided to ignore my insistence that only a strong, concerted message from the organization would stop General Abacha from executing my father. They decided to pursue a policy of "constructive engagement" instead.

That policy exploded in their faces on the opening day of the summit, and I left Auckland disillusioned and disturbed by my experiences there. But instead of giving myself the chance to grieve, I was swept along on a tidal wave of anger and sympathy. My father's supporters were willing me to carry on his struggle, to lead the demonstrations against the huge multinational oil company and to provide a focus for opposition to the embattled military dictator. I was twenty-six years old and found myself on a world stage, blinking in the spotlight and bewildered by the strength of the forces and passions that my father's death had unleashed. It had the ingredients of a Shakespearean drama: Ken Saro-Wiwa was dead, and his son and namesake was primed to avenge his death. But like Hamlet, I hesitated, then left the stage altogether, pleading political naïveté and the need for time and space to deal with losing my father.

But even as I retreated from the public arena, I was conscious that I would have to return to deal with his political legacy. A week after my father was executed, Morley Safer, the veteran CBS journalist, flew into London from New York to cover the story. When he interviewed me, the first question Safer asked was: "Why Ken Saro-Wiwa?"

He wanted to know why my father's death had attracted so much attention when many other human-rights activists were periodically killed or imprisoned for speaking out against brutal regimes and big business interests.

I knew part of the answer, but I couldn't find the words to express it, couldn't squeeze it into a nice, neat sound bite. Though I realized I would have to provide a comprehensive answer to Safer's question one day, it was too soon after the "funeral" and I desperately needed to sort through the complicated, conflicting emotions I was feeling about my father.

I was angry with him, resentful at having been handed such a complicated personal and political legacy. While I resented having to atone for my father's sins, I was also proud to be the son of a man who had refused to compromise his principles and had sacrificed his life for them. I spent two years struggling to make sense of the dilemmas of being Ken Saro-Wiwa's son. I was tormented by a nagging feeling that I hadn't done enough to save his life. I was convinced he would have been disappointed that I had refused to carry on a struggle he'd lived and died for. I felt I wasn't doing enough to counter the propaganda and the lies that his critics and enemies were spreading about him, and I kept wondering whether the publicity I had whipped up during his trial might have panicked the Abacha regime into executing him. And did I drive my father into a suicidal confrontation with the military and Shell? Had I been so hostile to him at home that he had sought refuge in the unquestioned adulation he received as the father of our people? As my confusion and guilt deepened, I began to feel that I had betrayed him, that I was somehow responsible for his death.

When I decided to confront my feelings about my father, he had been dead two years, but in many respects, not least in my mind, he was still very much alive. I spent the next three years writing this memoir, trying to unravel the complexities of our relationship, trying to come to terms with his death and trying to establish whether I was trapped in his story or whether I could escape my father's legacy.

In one of his last letters, he had urged me to write, and I took that as my cue. I felt it was my duty to set the record straight about Ken Saro-Wiwa, to expose his critics and accuse his killers. I imagined that this book would be my contribution to the struggle—my opportunity to right the wrongs done to my father and to our people.

I mounted my high horse and set off, taking the moral high ground. I threw all my anger and confusion onto the page until I came up against the bitter truth that for all I knew about Ken Saro-Wiwa, I really had no idea who my father was.

▼

I had a difficult and troubled relationship with my father, and although he was rarely around, I grew up in awe of him, intimidated by his achievements and haunted by the passions he stirred in both men and women.

I never forgot the day he decided to let me in on the meaning of his *and* my life. We were driving around Port Harcourt and he was showing me around his business empire. Everything, he revealed, was for one purpose: to secure justice for our people. His books, the properties, the businesses—everything was subservient to his hopes and ambitions for our people. As we drove along the main road in the city, he outlined his vision of the future, and I sank lower and lower in the passenger seat. He was in the driving seat, his eyes firmly fixed on the road ahead, his horizons expanding as he outlined his vision. When he had mapped out my future, he glanced over and saw me looking grim-faced, my chin buried in my chest.

"You know you won't inherit my enemies," he said, trying to reassure me with a thin, unconvincing smile.

I was fourteen years old and I had no idea what he was talking about or which enemies he was referring to, but those words planted the notion in my mind that being Ken Saro-Wiwa's first son and namesake was a complicated and heavy burden.

As I brooded, fourteen years later, on how to handle his enemies, it occurred to me that it was time to find out a little more about this man, a man of stark contrasts and inexplicable contradictions. I needed to reconcile the two faces of the man I barely knew as my father. Ken Saro-Wiwa was generous to a fault, a charismatic man who fought injustice armed only with his wit and an engaging smile. And then there was my father, the brooding, irascible and sometimes volatile presence who was physically distant, and emotionally demanding. I found it hard to feel anything more than respect for Ken Saro-Wiwa. When he died, I didn't have that deep, inconsolable sense of loss I should have felt. All I experienced was the cycle of anger, resentment and guilt. And I was tired of the conflicting emotions I felt, or was supposed to feel, about Ken Saro-Wiwa and my father.

But once I decided to face up to the truth about him, I began to see this book as an opportunity to finish a process that had begun when we exchanged long, heartfelt letters while he was in detention. We had tried to reconcile our differences then but had come to a tacit agreement to finish the process after he was released, when we could sit down and talk face to face. Man to man. Because the hangman had cheated us of our reconciliation, I saw this book as our chance to finish those conversations. So I set off on a different tack—to reconcile the bitter memories with the recollections of a man I had idolized and adored as a boy.

But how do you separate the man from the myth, my father from Ken Saro-Wiwa, without compromising the innocence of the struggle?

That was the dilemma I had to face when it dawned on me that by revealing the private man I might find my father, but I might also devalue the currency of the Ken Saro-Wiwa legend. In exposing our heroes as ordinary, flawed individuals, we also run the risk of reducing them. The legends that were already growing up around my father's life and death were meant to inspire not just future generations of Ogoni, but also the millions of people around the world who are struggling for social justice and human rights. Ken Saro-Wiwa's life and death had been invested with a sacred weight, and the sanctity of his story carried an enormous burden. It was a crucial chapter of Ogoni history, a story that was supposed to be told and retold, embellished and mystified with every retelling.

I had two choices; I could either take the path of self-indulgence or sacrifice my father on the altar of the higher cause. It seemed like a straight choice between my personal needs and the political demands—in essence, the story of my life.

I shrank from making a choice initially. I convinced myself that there was no point dragging the past into the light. I was uncomfortable with the prospect of exposing myself in public too, because in confronting my father I would also have to reveal, if I was honest, some of my own shortcomings. I couldn't see how I would ever resolve the dilemmas and all the competing claims to my father. I decided to let it lie.

But the memories, the questions, the conflicting emotions wouldn't release me. I *had* to tell his story. I was his first son and namesake, and it was my duty to honour my father, to protect his legacy. I had to be his witness.

I would love to say that my decision to carry on was inspired by some noble quest to keep his memory alive, but I have to confess that there was an element of self-preservation in it: I was a desperate man. I had committed myself to writing something, and I couldn't turn back. I was tired and there was nowhere left to hide from him.

I hope you find something of value in all of this, because I have lived a political life, which means that this story, though personal, is also a political statement. For me, for us, the personal *is* political, and I hope my efforts to find my father leaves you, as it did me, with a rounded picture of a man who was far more complicated and more courageous than the one-dimensional figure that his critics and supporters presented to the world in November 1995.

But there is more to this story than Ken Saro-Wiwa. As I uncovered the circumstances that shaped my father, as I peeled back the layers of misunderstandings and hostility between us, I discovered universal truths about fathers and sons, about families, about people, about what it really means to stand and die for your beliefs. As I gained a new perspective on the tensions and passions that competed for one man's love for his family, his people and his country, I arrived at a richer understanding of sacrifice and its impact on families caught up in a struggle for social justice.

And once I had made an accommodation with my father's life, I set off on another quest, this time to understand the meaning of his death. The second part of this memoir is the story of my experiences in conversations with the Nobel laureate Aung San Suu Kyi—herself the daughter of a martyred parent—Zindzi Mandela and Nkosinathi Biko, the oldest son of the anti-apartheid martyr Steve Biko. It was through these conversations that I managed to find some answers to the riddle of what it means to be Ken Saro-Wiwa's son.

So where does Ken Saro-Wiwa end and Ken Wiwa begin?

I don't know. I have no idea where he ends, but I'm learning to accept and appreciate that I am my father's son. My life is bound up in his; we are one, but not the same. Our lives feed into and out of each other's narrative like the chapters of an endless book. My story, his story, our story will continue beyond this book. But there is a story here, with a beginning, a middle and an end. And if the narrative sometimes seems circular, then that is because the journey, as they say, is the destination, and to make an end is to make a beginning.

I trust you are a visionary reader, though, and hope we will arrive at the same conclusion, because writing this book took me to places I never imagined existed. I learned a great deal along the way, including the rather exciting discovery that you can set out to write a book and the book ends up writing you. But the simplest and most profound truth I have learned is that you can never truly know who you are until you know your father.

Ken Wiwa
Toronto
July 2000

1

Home

▼

Just because he [Ken Wiwa] speaks the Queen's English everyone applauds, but he's just a spoilt child who wouldn't know the way to his own village.

—LT. COL. DAUDA KOMO

I ran into him one afternoon two years after he was murdered. He was in his house in the village, sitting in a chair at the far end of a long rectangular room. He was smoking his pipe and listening to a group of elders who were animatedly discussing MOSOP business.

I was five thousand kilometres away, in London, trying to find a way into this story. As soon as that picture of him popped up in my head, I decided to retrace my steps to find out why that particular image, out of all the ones I have of him, had become my abiding memory of my father.

The story begins in March 1992, when he came over to London and gave me an ultimatum.

I had graduated from university two years earlier, and had been drifting in and out of temporary jobs in London. I was unsure of what I wanted to do with my life and was trying to break into journalism, though deep down all I really wanted to do was play professional sports. I was good at games—football, cricket, rugby—but I had never dedicated myself to any of them because I knew my father would never approve. Although he loved sports, he felt they were a part of the "entertainment industry," and as he later told me in one of his letters from detention, the best black minds had no business playing sport for a living.

Although I wanted to pursue my own ambitions, that was easier thought than done, especially as he had given me the kind of opportunities that few people, let alone Ogonis, even dream of. I could never shake the feeling that I owed him, that he had worked so hard to give me a head start in life and I had an obligation to repay the faith he had invested in me. Whenever I thought of going my own way, a little voice would pull me back, reminding me that I'd been given, as he used to say, "the best education that money could buy . . . the best opportunities in life."

He wanted me to return to Nigeria. That was why he had sent his children—three boys and two girls—to private schools in England. He hoped, he *expected*, that we would all return to Nigeria at the end of our studies and apply our expensively educated minds to the resolution of the problems facing our people.

But if there was one thing I was sure of in March 1992, it was that I didn't want to return to Nigeria. There were all kinds of complicated reasons for this but the only one I could articulate at the time was that it was what my father wanted me to do. I wanted to make my own choices, and I needed time to work things out for myself. But he was impatient. He couldn't see the point of me "loitering around the fringes of British society" when there was so much to do at home. He wanted me to help him run the business, or better still, to apply my skills to the cause that was just starting to fire our people's imagination.

But what, I argued, was the point of going back to a place that most people were desperate to leave? There was nothing to entice me back there. Nigeria was a frustrating place to live—the constant power shortages, the oppressive heat, the mosquitoes, the sandflies. The prospect of working for my father was hardly a selling point, and since I was firmly apolitical I didn't want to sign up to the struggle. (When you grow up in a political home you either toe the party line or you want to get as far away from politics as possible.)

If there was one thing my father hated it was procrastination. You had to have a positive reason for *not* wanting to do something. And since I couldn't find a decent excuse for remaining in England, I tended to avoid him whenever he came to London.

Facing my father was like taking a hard look at myself in an unforgiving mirror. Each time I stood before him, I saw the man I was meant to become. I saw the man I would always be compared to. He was ambitious and worked hard. He relished and sought out challenges. He was careful with his money. He was meticulous and religious in his attention to detail. He was confident in himself, and he was successful. He was, I was certain, everything I wasn't.

It was hard to avoid him, though, and even if I only saw him three times a year, he was never far from my mind. I could never completely relax and live my life on my own terms. Even if I managed to convince myself that most of my peers in Nigeria were looking to leave the country, or that the struggle to make the country a better place was a thankless task, I could never shake the thought that it was a thankless task to which my father had dedicated his life. I could argue the toss, convince myself that I would rather be a black man in a white man's country than endure the daily aggravations and frustrations of living in Nigeria. I could argue that I just wanted to live in a place where I could get a job that paid a decent wage, where I had a roof over my head, with running water and a constant supply of electricity. But just as I was getting comfortable with my decision to give up on Nigeria, just when I had satisfied myself that the country could never offer me a reasonable life, and just when I had forgotten about Nigeria—that was when he usually came back to remind me of my obligations.

When he came over, he was rarely in the same place for very long. He was always rushing around, hustling for business, cultivating his contacts, dropping in on old friends and looking up his girlfriends. You never knew when he would turn up. You would be lounging in the house watching television, enjoying your holiday, and he would suddenly burst through the door. Once you recovered from the shock, the games would begin. I would hide in my room, trying to figure out how long he was going to stay. I would listen for clues as he boomed down the telephone, barking orders to his offices in Nigeria. If he didn't reveal his travel plans, I would bide my time and wait until he had left the house before going downstairs to rummage through the papers scattered on the dining-room table.

In my father's house, there was never any clear distinction between home and office—at least not at our London home. He treated the place like a warehouse. Cartons of unsold copies of his books were piled in the corridors and crammed on the bookshelves in his bedroom and in the garage. A big, red, ugly filing cabinet filled with letters and documents all meticulously catalogued sat in the middle of the house. He kept strict records on everything, including detailed accounts of how much he had spent on my education. There was nothing lavish about the house. It was an unremarkable, modest four-bedroom home in a lower-middleclass suburb of London. If anything, it was a relatively small house for a family of seven, especially as half of it was commandeered as a warehouse. Home comforts were not high on my father's list of priorities—especially in England. As far as he was concerned, his children were in England to get an education. His attitude to the house was probably meant to reinforce that message.

If I didn't find his plane ticket among his papers, I would search through his notebooks, where he scribbled his plans and thoughts. I often came across outlines for novels, screenplays and rough drafts of poems jostling with reminders to pay bills and obscure calculations and estimates of his fortune. If I didn't get an idea from the notebooks of when he was due to fly back, I would second-guess him anyway—he rarely spent more than a month away from Nigeria.

He always returned home, though I could not understand why. He was forever moaning about the situation in Nigeria, and I would wonder why, when he had the means, he didn't just walk away and leave it all behind. But all he ever did was complain and then go back. It was almost as if he actually relished the challenges of living there. Most reasonable men had long since given up or been forced to compromise their principles out of the sheer frustration of trying to survive in a society that "rewarded theft and penalized graft," as he used to say with a perverse grin.

I would usually wait until the night before he was due to fly back to Nigeria, when he was too tired or too busy tying up the loose ends of his trip to pin me down, to raise the issue of my future. My timing always aggravated him. "Why do you always wait until I am just about to leave before you come and trouble me with your problems?" he would groan.

When we found a mutually inconvenient moment to talk, he would sit on the edge of the large sofa opposite the fireplace in the lounge, filling his pipe with tobacco. He would pack the tobacco tightly with his thumbs. It always took him two or three attempts to light it, but once he got it going, he would ease back into the sofa and puff away, popping his lips contentedly. He always had a puzzled frown on his face as the smoke curled out of his pipe, filling the room with a thick cloud of a rich, woody aroma. I usually sat in an armchair next to the fireplace, staring ahead in nervous silence, conscious of the intense expression on his face.

Once he'd collected his thoughts, he would take three short puffs, yank the pipe out of his mouth, lick his lips and swallow loudly.

"How are your studies going?" he would bark at me.

"Fine," I would reply tersely.

He usually took the hint and switched to a less sensitive topic. I would still bat his questions back at him, responding with monosyllabic, guarded answers. Whenever we attempted to talk about anything other than politics or school, the conversation usually ended in an awkward, embarrassed silence, but once we gave up the pretence that we could manage anything as complicated as small talk, and reverted to the familiar parameters of our relationship, the conversation would flow. He usually opened the proceedings, droning on about his politics, trying to drill his values into me, sprinkling the lecture with his favourite phrases: "You can't always sleep on a full stomach"; "Hard work doesn't kill"; "To whom much is given, much is expected"; "In Nigeria, the only wrongdoers are those who do no wrong"; "To live a day in Nigeria is to die many times." He usually ended with the clincher that the ball was in my court, or with the reminder that he had given me the best opportunities in life.

I would listen patiently, waiting to sneak my own items onto his agenda. I rarely questioned his politics—they had a seductive logic that was hard to deny. If I offered any thoughts of my own, it was usually to placate him so that he would be more malleable when it was time to extract some money out of him. Getting money out of my father was a tricky business. The man had deep pockets but very short arms. If the money was for furthering your education, he would gladly cough up. If not, you had to be circumspect, pick your moment. If you allowed him to get too far ahead of himself, he would talk you into a corner; you had to dance around him, wait for a gap in his sermon, for that moment when it was okay to ask for money without feeling that you had to mortgage your future to him.

He was quite indulgent, given how I must have taxed his patience. Although he had an extremely short fuse, he rarely lost his temper with me. He could be caustic and brusque, but he was quite philosophical whenever we discussed my future. I was always wary of his temper, though. Underneath the calm, the mercury was bubbling.

Anything could set him off, from the thought of how much he was paying for my school fees or the incoherence of my latest career plans to the state of my hair. If I showed up in dreadlocks he would stare at them, trying to figure out what was going on under that "load of hair." Stuffing his pipe between gritted teeth he would puff away, popping his lips loudly, trying to stem the red mist rising.

We tiptoed around each other for years, avoiding the question of when I was going to go back to Nigeria. Neither of us was prepared to negotiate, and we had a tacit agreement not to talk about it.

"You know you have to return home once you've finished your studies," he once snapped at me.

We were facing each other, sitting in the armchairs on either side of the fireplace. There was an uncomfortable silence as the significance of what he had just said sank in. His face froze in anticipation of my answer; the eyebrows arched, as if caught between making a statement and asking a question. He knew he had strayed into the no-man's land between us, and he must have read my murderous thoughts, because his face suddenly collapsed into a pained look.

"You have no choice," he muttered weakly.

I sidestepped the question with my usual claim that I wanted to "concentrate on my studies before making up my mind," and watched him choke back his disappointment. He didn't bring it up again until I had finished those studies.

After I graduated from university, it became harder to avoid the issue. I did my worst, drifting in confused circles until his patience snapped. That was when he came over to London and cut to the chase. "What are you going to do with your life? When are you going to start living?" he demanded.

I started telling him about my plans to go to journalism school. As he listened to what must have sounded like yet another one of my elaborate schemes to avoid having to go back home, he glowered at me. Whenever he gave you that look—eyes blazing, mouth open and lips quivering—you knew it was better to save the cock-and-bull stories for another time. Suitably intimidated, I clammed up and stared at him plaintively.

"If you don't know what to do with yourself, why don't you just come home and make yourself useful? There's plenty for you to do there."

It was the tone that threw me. It was restrained, almost pleading. Even more devastating was the logic behind the suggestion. I was vaguely aware that MOSOP had begun to restore the individual and collective pride of our people. Women were being empowered. Everyone was getting involved in the movement—professionals, traditional rulers and priests, even unemployed and unemployable youths. Every Ogoni was in MOSOP because MOSOP was in every Ogoni, as the saying went. No one could opt out. The struggle was defining our people, giving Ogoni a renewed sense of purpose.

I could hardly resist. I owed it to myself, to him and to our people to return home and lend my weight to the cause. He took my silence as a tacit acknowledgement that I had finally come round to *his* side of our struggle. He rose up from the sofa and walked over to the dining table. He opened his briefcase, pulled out an airline ticket and tossed it onto the table.

"There's a ticket to Lagos for you there," he said, nodding in the direction of the ticket.

I got up from my seat and examined it.

"Nobody will know if it is for you or me," he snapped, closing my last loophole.

Not for the first time, I cursed my luck at having the same name as my father. I made a mental note that it was time I did something about changing it. Meanwhile, he snapped his briefcase shut and gave me a brief pep talk. He left for the airport the next day and I flew out to join him a week later, travelling, once again, on my father's name.

▼

The first thing you notice, even before you leave the aircraft, is the heat. It is so humid in Lagos, even at six in the evening. It's like stepping into a sauna. A film of air wraps around your skin like Cellophane. It has that unmistakably tropical, musty smell, and it tastes so thick that when you take your first breath you panic, thinking you're going to suffocate. While you're busy gasping for air, the mosquitoes and sandflies home in to extract their dues. I was born and raised in Nigeria, but England made me. England softened my skin and thickened my blood, which was good for keeping out the cold but made me an easy target for every parasite in Nigeria.

As I emerged into the arrival hall, I was met by a sea of faces. The glazed, cold expressions always unnerved me, stripping me of my pretensions. I shuffled along, anxiously scanning the crowd for a friendly face.

I'd been dreading that moment as the aircraft started its final descent into Lagos. As soon as the city's streetlights appeared below, I began to fret, wondering if someone would be at the airport to meet me. I had missed my flight, and when I phoned my father's office in Lagos to explain that I would be on a later one, he exploded. "Look, my friend," he bellowed down the phone, "you better buck up your ideas and pull yourself together. Just make sure you're on the next flight down here, because if you miss that one, there won't be anyone to meet you at the airport."

I could never be sure whether he was serious or not, because he was always trying to find out whether I could stand on my own two feet in Nigeria. Although I was born in Lagos and had passed through it many times on my way to and from England, I always felt out of place there. I have never known how to get around the vast, intimidating sprawl of the city.

"Junior!"

I stopped and peered into the crowd. The faces blurred until I saw Sonny, my father's driver, with his reassuringly familiar gap-toothed smile beaming back at me. He was as relieved to see me as I was to see him. I imagine he wouldn't have relished the prospect of having to tell my father that I hadn't arrived.

As I waited for Sonny to fetch the car, I watched the crowds milling around me in the arrival hall. Languid Muslims in white flowing robes ghosted across the concourse like tall ships in a crowded harbour. Soldiers swaggered back and forth, waving their guns around with a casualness that was disconcerting. Expensively dressed and haughty-looking women strutted around, avoiding predatory eyes and catcalls with practised indifference. Large families with children trailing in convoy crabbed across the terminal, dragging the entire contents of their homes behind them. Hustlers worked the rich seam: middlemen, pickpockets, officials and unofficial officials. Beggars harassed travellers; clerics and priests swished past in starched robes while pasty-faced white men in sweat-stained khaki shirts scuttled to and from gleaming new cars.

The hustle was a good barometer of the state of the country. But that's the paradox of Nigeria: it might look chaotic but there is method to the madness. You just have to think on your feet—be smart, as they say in Nigeria. You have to know the unwritten rules. And even if you do know the rules you still have to assume that your friend is your enemy and that the vice is versa, because in Nigeria the only wrongdoers are those who do no wrong. Our Nobel laureate, Wole Soyinka, once declared that what Nigeria needed was therapy, not democracy. If that was the trouble with the country, then Murtala Muhammad International Airport was, in March 1992, the waiting-room to the madhouse.

When Sonny returned with the car, we headed for my father's office, where he was waiting. Once you hit the ground, the order that you see from the aircraft turns out to be an ad hoc, unplanned mess; Lagos is a sprawling, hectic, overcrowded, overpopulated, disorganized city. As you drive past its busy evening markets, you can just about make out the shadows of people flickering in and out of the night. The atmosphere is thick with the smell of petrol fumes and the heavy bass line of music blasting from huge roadside speakers. Something about being in Lagos always gets my heart pumping a little faster, bringing on an anxiety that is strangely reassuring. Going home is always a troubling reminder that I do and don't belong there.

Somewhere in the middle of the liquid heat of a Lagos night is a district called Surulere, where my father had an office. Surulere wasn't the kind of place where you would expect to find the country's most famous satirist, a man who was rumoured to be one of Nigeria's super-rich. That was one of the paradoxes of my father: he lived "a peripatetic life," but once he settled somewhere he rarely moved house. When I once asked why he chose to have an office in Surulere, why he didn't move to somewhere a little more salubrious, his face lit up. We were sitting in his private office, a cool, windowless back room sparsely furnished with a large desk and filing cabinets. The only extravagance was the chair, an expensive, high-backed leather affair. He leaned back and pointed in the direction of the street. "Look out there," he said, "you only have to stand on those streets to find all the stories a writer needs."

It was late by the time Sonny and I reached my father's office, and he had already left. He had been summoned to Abuja to meet the president. There was a message for me. I was instructed to meet him at the office first thing in the morning so that we could travel to the airport and catch the first flight to Port Harcourt.

I left the office and took a taxi to my uncle's house, where I always stayed when I was in Lagos. When I returned to the office the next morning, however, my father had already left for the airport. I found my own way to the airport and caught a flight to Port Harcourt. I was happy to fly on my own because I never enjoyed travelling with my father: I was too nervous and self-conscious around him.

When I arrived at Semaseng Place, the family home in Port Harcourt, the night-watchman informed me that my father had been expecting me but had just left for the village. I gave my taxi driver a large tip and told him to drive as fast as he could to the village. I wanted to give my father a little surprise.

It took him only thirty minutes to cover the first forty-eight kilometres from Port Harcourt to Bori, the main town and capital of Ogoni. As we approached the last row of houses before the market, I ordered him to pull up at number 103 Hospital Road, a brick bungalow with a rusting corrugated aluminium roof. The front door was wide open, but it didn't look as if anyone was home. I stamped my feet on the veranda and tapped on the door. There was no answer. I peered inside. It was dark in the front room, but I saw the outline of an old man lying on the sofa.

"Papa?"

The figure stirred. The old man wheezed as he woke up, rubbing the sleep out of his eyes.

"*Me naa wah?*" he asked in a slow, deep baritone as he glanced up at the shadow silhouetted in his doorway.

"Papa! *Nda-eh. Junior naa lu-aah,*" I replied.

"Eh! Junior! *Ndaago? Olo naa wah?*" he said in a thick Nigerian accent. When did you come?

"*Aba yahn-woah nam lu-ah,*" I replied slowly, searching for the right words in Khana.

I walked in and shook my grandfather's hand as he sat up. He was wearing a cloth around his waist and his feet were jammed into an old pair of black brogues. His eyes were bloodshot and set back in his skull. There was a pungent whiff of palm wine and snuff in a room that was furnished only by two sofas separated by a long, low, Formica-topped wooden table.

Papa is my father's father, and he is reputed to be the oldest man in the village. As long as I have known him, he has always had the same hangdog expression and rheumy, doleful eyes.

I sat down on the sofa opposite him. A young girl emerged from the bedroom, scraping her feet and smiling as she sashayed past. She didn't look much older than I was. I sat back and settled in for a long talk because you never passed through Bori without paying your respects to Papa. He was eighty-eight then, but he was still working his soft drinks business, buying and reselling crates of Coke, Fanta and Sprite from his house-cum-store in Bori. Chief Jim Wiwa is the patriarch of the Gbenedorbi clan. He is a great-great-grandfather, and his youngest child, Gibson, was born in 1993, when Papa was ninety years old. You can't pass through Bori without paying your respects to Papa.

We have a ritual whenever we meet. He scolds me in fluent English for not writing, and I respond, offering lame excuses in my ugly but functional Khana.

"You mus"—he slurred with a slight lisp—"work harder. Show more respec for your seniorrrs. You mus never forget your home."

Papa spoke slowly, stopping from time to time to catch his breath and stare out at the road, where cars were flashing past at insane speeds on their way to and from Port Harcourt. When he had finished reminding me of my obligations, he disappeared into his bedroom. I could hear him rooting around, cursing cantankerously. He returned with a bottle of Kaikai, a triumphant, toothless grin and a twinkle in his eye. He fetched two shot glasses from a cabinet, arranged them on the table and filled them to the brim without spilling a drop. He picked up one of the glasses, held it up in front of his face, toasted our ancestors for delivering me back home safely and sprinkled the colourless drink onto the concrete floor with a flourish. He glanced at me, and I picked up my glass at the silent invitation. I held my breath and downed it, the gin settling in the pit of my stomach, a pleasant, warm sensation swirling around my chest.

We sat staring at each other. After a few minutes of awkward silence, I estimated that I had paid my respects. I made my excuses and got up to leave. I asked Papa if he had seen my father. He waved his hands in the air and smiled.

About thirteen kilometres east of Bori, you turn off the main road and head north down a side road that snakes through the forest into my home village. I've made that journey so many times it is etched in my memory. There is only one way to get to the village by car, although you can cut through the forests and farms that flank the road by foot, or get there along the rivers and streams that criss-cross Ogoni. But those journeys require the kind of intricate knowledge of the place that I have never had. In and around the main road are the oil wells, pipelines and gas flares that have helped to enrich Nigeria but have jeopardized the viability of village communities that once made a simple living from farming and fishing. The dense forests on either side of the main road hold the secrets of our culture. The giant iroko, the palm trees swaying and sighing in the wind, the vultures circling above the dark green canopy—all these have been witnesses to our story, providing the symbols of our myths and traditions, silently observing the conflicts that have scarred our history. You can never fully understand our people until you persuade the rain forest to give up its secrets.

Although I'd abandoned my fantasy of beating my father back to the village, I still got a thrill when I saw his blue Toyota Crown sitting on the grass verge in front of his bungalow.

Gbor compound in Bane is the spiritual home of the Gbenedorbi clan. The psychological clues, the origins of the passions that rule my family, are hidden in the layout of the compound. The houses are arranged in a pattern that is filled with nuances and history. The imposing, two-storey brick building that Papa built back in the 1950s, long before he moved to the Ogoni Delta capital of Bori, still dominates the compound, facing the west. On the eastern border are three concrete bungalows. They belong to the first three of my grandfather's wives. He has recently added another bungalow for his latest wife. The newest addition sits behind the original three and is not technically within the bounds of the Gbenedorbi compound. The last available space in the compound was taken when my father built his own village home there in 1983.

I don't know whether there is any significance to the fact that my father chose to build a bungalow—whether he was opting to defer to Papa's status—but his house sits on the edge of the compound and looks across Papa's house. My father rarely spent any time in there anyway. In Nigeria, people tend to build a house in their ancestral village either as a sign of achievement or as a retirement home. I can't imagine my father ever saw himself living out his days in Bane, without light or electricity, without his books, an old man passing time, waiting to die or for his children and grandchildren to visit him once in a while. And I never asked him why he built a house he never spent any time in. But even though he rarely spent time in the village, he kept one foot there. He was anchored there, and it took me a while to work out why.

Taking the path between my father's and grandfather's houses, I headed for my grandmother's bungalow. Mama almost fainted when she saw me. She obviously hadn't been told that I was coming. My grandmother is tiny, not much above four feet tall, but like most Ogoni women she's resilient and resourceful. I hadn't seen her for two years, and she must have thought I hadn't eaten since I last saw her because I had barely sat down before a mountain of fried plantains and thick goat stew was placed on the table in front of me. And almost as soon as I finished with the plantains, a large bowl of steaming pepper soup filled with fresh fish was brought for my attention. The old women's grapevine had begun to hum from the moment I set foot in the compound, and even while I was struggling with the second course, delegations of Mama's friends began arriving at the bungalow. They arrived as if they were just dropping by for a casual visit. When they saw me, they would break into a little jig, ululating and waving their hands in the air. The faces looked vaguely familiar but I couldn't put a name to many—which amazed and even offended some of them. Each time I stood to greet one of the women, she would hug me, then pull away and stare at me, praising the Lord, wondering aloud if it was really me standing before her, repeating my name, my second name, my nicknames or any local variations of my names:

"*Jenior? o lo naa wan?*"

"*Zunior? Zunior? Bari a me dem. Meso nor weh luu-ah?*"

"*Bornale? Aaatio!*"

"*Ndago? Owa ara? Ndaawin?*"

The names were repeated questioningly at first, then with greater insistence and amazement—as if I'd come back from the dead.

Children flocked to Mama's bungalow, crowding the entrance and jabbering among themselves. I doubt there would have been as much fuss if an alien had landed right there in the village. One of the children kept up a running commentary, describing how I was eating, what I was wearing. He didn't realize I understood Khana. I humoured him for a while, then asked him a question in Khana. There was pandemonium in the house. The children looked at each other, surprised. Two of my grandmother's friends leapt out of their seats, threw their arms in the air and started dancing around the room, offering praises to God, to our ancestors, to my parents and to my grandmother. Mama sat in her chair, beaming with pride.

When I finally finished the feast—it would have been an insult to leave anything, and I still had Dada's (my maternal grandmother) meal to deal with—I washed my hands, thanked everyone and waddled off to my father's house.

I walked into the long, rectangular sitting room and interrupted a meeting my father was having with some village elders. The elders turned to acknowledge me, and I greeted them individually before glancing over to the far end of the room, where my father was sitting. There wasn't a flicker of emotion on his face. He took his pipe from his mouth and waved his hands in the air, motioning me to take a seat beside him. That was the scene, the moment that has become my abiding image of my father.

I had walked into a meeting my father had called to consult the elders about the struggle. He was doing his duty as MOSOP's publicity secretary, and he had called the meeting to impress upon the elders that the time was ripe for our people to embrace MOSOP's vision of the future.

When I think of him holding court before those old men, I see him as the link between the past and the future. I imagine him sitting there, listening to the elders, collating their thoughts, computing them in his modern, educated mind, using the wisdom of the past to conceive of a vision of the future. As he motioned me to his side, I imagine he was probably hoping that his son had finally arrived to take his place in that struggle.

He hoped. But he probably knew what I knew—that I wasn't ready.

It is clear now why that image remains so vivid in my mind: I never did catch up with my father that day in the village. He never stood still long enough for me to get near him. He was always one step ahead, always moving, pulling me along in his slipstream as I wondered whether I should be following him or trying to find my own way.

Our paths were just crossing that day in Bane. The next day, before I left, I persuaded him to give me more time to myself to determine where my future lay—in England or by his side in the political struggle. He agreed to let me go and I returned to England, where I had decided to become a journalist.

2

Who's Afraid of Ken Saro-Wiwa?

▼

If a man of my upbringing, education, cultivation and demonstrated achievement in various areas of life cannot conduct an argument for rights peacefully and in a civilised manner, then no one else can do so.

—KEN SARO-WIWA

They say my father was born five times. Each time, they gave him up for dead, he clung to life. He was born on October 10, 1941 and there is a curious symmetry in that it took five attempts to bring him into the world and five attempts to take him out of it fifty-four years later.

My grandfather was cursed with stillborn children before my father was born. His first wife couldn't bear him any children, his second kept miscarrying and his third wife, my grandmother, had two miscarriages before my father was born, clinging to life.

My father was seen as a child prodigy; he walked at seven months, and his parents doted on him because he was, for the first seven years of his life, their only child.

When he was thirteen, he won a scholarship to Government College in Umuahia, a small town 125 kilometres north of Bori. Umuahia was one of the best secondary schools in Nigeria; it was modelled on an English public school and run by expatriate teachers. Umuahians were taught the same curriculum as an Etonian, and my father enjoyed Latin and French, excelled at history and geography, and fell in love with literature. He flirted with the French and Russian classics, but his passion was English literature. He devoured Dickens, Matthew Arnold and Shakespeare. He adored the English way of life and particularly enjoyed cricket, a game he saw as representing quintessential English values of fair play and decency. He was a model pupil in a model school designed to produce model colonials to serve as a loyal elite in the British Empire.

When he left Umuahia, he took another scholarship to University of Ibadan. As a freshman English undergraduate in 1961, he walked onto a campus that was the hotbed of intellectual and political activity in the newly independent country. Nigeria was still suffering a hangover from the year of wild parties following our independence from Britain in 1960, and we were waking up to the task of nation building. Now that we were finally in charge of our destiny, everyone was anxious to throw off the yoke of our imperial past and forge a collective identity for the new country. It was the perfect climate for a young man anxious to cast off the mould of an identity that had been constructed by a classical, colonial education.

He had ambitions to become a writer, and he was drawn and influenced, like Chinua Achebe before him (himself a graduate of Umuahia and Ibadan), to writers of the Irish Revival. His first novel, *Sozaboy*, published when he was forty-four, was written in the vernacular style that he had experimented with as an undergraduate at Ibadan, when he was influenced by James Joyce's experiments with language.

And no aspiring writer or intellectual of the time could escape the influence of the black power and black consciousness movements of the 1960s. The success of the civil-rights struggle in America had its echoes in Africa and the Caribbean. As black people around the world began to reassert themselves and reclaim their political identity, writers and artists reflected these struggles in and through their work, trying to construct a black aesthetic to feed off or inspire the process of political liberation.

When my father graduated from Ibadan in 1965, the world should have been his oyster. He was a member of the intellectual elite that was filling the leading positions in society with young graduates like him. Whenever I read accounts of Nigeria in the early 1960s, it seems that all you needed in those days was a degree and a vague plan, and the government would hand you a plum job or offer you a juicy scholarship to study abroad—that is, if you were from the right tribe and had the right connections.

Despite all the optimism of the emerging nation's propaganda about building a federal, detribalized character, however, ethnicity mattered more than qualifications when it came to distributing the best jobs and scholarships. When he went up to Umuahia, "there were hardly more than ten Ogoni boys and girls in secondary schools," as he later recollected in a political pamphlet.

Eastern Nigeria was seen as the preserve of the Igbo, who used their influence as the majority ethnic group in the region to secure the best jobs. They looked down on minority ethnic groups like the Ogoni, and while many of our people resented their influence, most accepted and felt that to get ahead in eastern Nigeria, you had to have influential contacts among the Igbo.

By the time he left university, my father was already aware that despite his efforts to present himself as an educated, detribalized Nigerian, his ethnic origin mattered, especially when it was time to go out into the world to look for a job.

What always intrigues me about my father's life—or at least his accounts of it—is that it reads like a seamless progression from one triumph to another. There are few grey areas, few moments when he stumbles, unsure of himself and what to do next. But I suspect that he struggled to find his feet after he graduated.

Years later, in his column for *The Nigerian Sunday Times*, he let slip this uncertainty about his post-university future when he recalled an interview that changed the course of his life, my life and much else besides.

"I met him [Bobby Reid, then head of Shell in Nigeria] shortly after I graduated from the University of Ibadan and applied for a job in Shell-BP," he wrote. He interviewed me at some stage and told me he did not quite see why I wanted to work in Shell-BP. You will not be surprised to hear that I ended up being offered a scholarship by Shell-BP to study whatever I wanted in any University in the United Kingdom. I was not able to take up the offer. The Civil War intervened, Bobby left Nigeria and I went to the war-front."

The Nigerian civil war had a profound and lasting effect on the course of both my father's life and Nigerian history. So much of this story hinges on that war. Everything flows in and out of that conflict.

The Biafran War was, with the benefit of hindsight, an inevitable consequence of Nigeria's colonial legacy. The idea of Nigeria is an artificial construct that would probably never have materialized but for the British presence in Africa. Nigeria was created from the remains of the Niger River Trading Company, a British conglomerate that operated the concession of land that was ceded to the British after the Europeans helped themselves to vast tracts of Africa through the Treaty of Berlin in 1884.

With the help of a handful of native soldiers and a small contingent of officers, the British managed to win control of and maintain their authority over a vast area of land that stretched from the fringes of the Sahara Desert in the north to the rain forests of the Niger Delta and the Atlantic Ocean in the south. The concession was populated by peoples as diverse as the landscape. In the north, the mainly Muslim Hausa-Fulani ethnic group was ruled by emirs who ran a feudal and nomadic community. The British controlled what became known as northern Nigeria by allying themselves with these politically sophisticated and astute emirs. The feudal, quasi-religious leaders were allowed a measure of autonomy in their regions in exchange for committing to lucrative trading arrangements with the British. Controlling the southern portion of the concession proved to be a different proposition altogether, however. Many of the ethnic groups in southern Nigeria were fiercely democratic in character and tradition, and had long and proud histories. The land was hostile and often impenetrable, and the people were far more difficult to control, especially as there was not the same unifying religious structure or homogenous character that made the north much more coherent. To impose their authority over southern Nigeria, the British resorted to a judicious mixture of religion, bribery and the gun. Christian missionaries led the way, converting the heathen and softening them up for soldiers, tax collectors and district officers. When the locals were difficult, the order was reversed—soldiers first, then tax collectors, district officers and missionaries.

There is an old African joke that says that before the white man came to Africa, we had the land and the white man had the Bible. But now we have the Bible and the white man has the land.

In 1914, the British decided to merge northern Nigeria with what they euphemistically called the southern protectorate. Northern Nigeria was proving to be a financial drain on the empire's resources, and although the British acknowledged that the two parts of the concession were very different in character and outlook, they needed to streamline their operations and cut costs. This cost-cutting determined the borders that later came to be known as Nigeria. But this stew of economically unequal, multi-ethnic identities sowed the seeds of the troubles that have plagued Nigeria since its independence in October 1960.

With so many distinct and unrelated peoples with such different histories, religions and temperaments, nation building was not easy. Nigeria has only ever made sense as an economic enterprise, and so the interests of the country only ever meant the vested interests of the business and economic elites.

Behind Nigerians' political desire for independence was an economic imperative—to take control of our resources from the colonialists. The British had kept the independence aspirations in check with good, old-fashioned divide and rule. So the majority ethnic groups—the Hausa-Fulani in the north, the Yoruba in the west and the Igbo in the east—competed with each other for favours from the imperial master. After the British decided to sail with the winds of change that were sweeping through Africa in the late 1950s and 1960s (by granting us our independence), the majority ethnic groups, popularly known in Nigeria as Wazobia, carried on their pre-independence rivalry, competing with each other for control of economic power and political privileges. The three major ethnic groups contrived to make nonsense of the pre-independence dream of Nigeria as a federation of multi-ethnic nations united for the commonwealth of all its peoples.

Between 1960 and 1965, the Igbo, a hard-working and commercially astute people, often came off third best in that struggle. When they decided to take their destiny into their own hands and secede from Nigeria, declaring eastern Nigeria the republic of Biafra in 1967, the rest of the country went to war to preserve the unity of the nation. That, at least, was the language the federalists used to justify the war. For their part, the Biafrans spoke of discrimination and victimization by the Hausa and the Yoruba. You can make a strong case for both sides of the argument, but the reality was complicated and the truth was that the

Nigerian civil war was a battle for control of the vast and largely untapped oilfields of the Delta.

My father sided with the federalists. He was one of few Ogoni intellectuals and leaders to declare for Nigeria. He felt that the Ogoni had better prospects for economic development within Nigeria than in an Igbo-dominated Biafra. He had experienced enough discrimination at the hands of the Igbo to fear for our fortunes within a putative Biafra. As a graduate assistant at the University of Nsukka, he was at the front when the war started, and he saw what he described as the "empty triumphalism" of the Biafrans. He thought they would be easily routed. Many of the Ogoni elite sided with the Biafrans, however, and the personal and political consequences of my father's decision would follow him until his death. There are suggestions even today that his execution was the revenge of the Igbo for his siding with the federalists. I'm not so sure about this, but my father was never their favourite Ogoni.

An immediate consequence of my father's choice was that he was drawn into politics. When federal troops captured Bonny Island—a strategically important oil terminal on the south coast of Nigeria—my father was appointed the federal administrator in charge. But his appointment would not have been possible had he not taken a decision that also had a profound effect on his personal life.

When the civil war broke out, the Biafrans tried to take control of the oilfields of the Delta by securing not only Bonny Island but also Port Harcourt. The war raged around Port Harcourt as federal forces fought to prevent the Biafrans from gaining an outlet to the sea. Ogoni was in the eye of the storm, and in late 1966 and early 1967, my father was there, observing the fighting and hoping that federal troops would soon liberate his region from the marauding Biafran militia. But after cooling his heels for a year, my father decided, as was his wont, to take control of his destiny. In his memoir of the civil war, *On a Darkling*

Plain, he recalls his decision to leave Ogoni: "I took my mother in confidence. I had made up my mind. It did not seem right, I said, that I should be pottering around doing nothing while my friends were making progress in their studies and in their careers. The way the war was dragging on, it might take a long time before it would end. I proposed to leave to seek my fortunes in the wider world. I might return to Ibadan to complete my second degree or go abroad."

My grandmother gave her approval, and on September 23, 1967, my parents escaped from Bane in a hired canoe, travelling in the middle of the night to take advantage of the tide and to avoid the Biafran militia. "It was a remarkably unemotional parting," my father recalls in *On a Darkling Plain*. "Although I was not overly worried, I was disturbed. It looked as though I was leaving my mother to face an uncertain future with the burden of five children ranging in age from seven to seventeen."

My parents negotiated a maze of creeks and rivers, crossing the front line to Bonny Island, where they boarded a ship to Lagos. They arrived on October 2, but I imagine that the night the canoe left Bane, my father anchored himself to the village for the rest of his life. His conscience would never allow him to forget that he had left his family to the mercy of rampaging Biafran militiamen who terrorized them, especially after Biafran radio denounced him as the "Lagos-based puppet administrator for Bonny."

The civil war ended in 1970, and my father remained in politics to begin the lonely task of easing his conscience and repaying his dues to his people and his family. As the Rivers State commissioner of education, he tried to ensure that our people were given access to government scholarships and educational programs. He tried to set up Ogoni in business, and he made sure that those who had fought on the side of the Biafrans were rehabilitated. He tried to put into practise the federalist magnanimous concession that there were to be "no victors and no vanquished."

But politics and my father never mixed well. And civil wars are always more devastating than international conflicts because they are never won or lost. Whatever my father did and wherever he went, he was dogged by controversy. He was accused of profiteering, of buying properties abandoned by Igbo in Port Harcourt during the war. He was accused of favouring the Ogoni when it came to awarding scholarships. Many Ogoni who had fought on the side of Biafra conducted a campaign to have him removed from office. But my father rarely bothered to reply to allegations of impropriety. In his civil war memoir, he dismisses the allegations as "dishonest" and "boring." Many of the accusations, in fact, were made in retaliation to his public revelations of corruption in the state administration.

My father has been described as naïve or a second-rate politician because he appeared to be blind to the consequences of openly criticizing an administration of which he was part. But he felt he had a duty to speak his mind, given that he was supposed to be serving the interests of the people. When he later reflected on his time in government, he wrote it off as experience. He was shocked when the governor, Admiral Diette Spiff, sacked him. He heard the news on the radio. What must have really stuck in his craw, however, was the fact that he had already tendered his resignation twice before but had been persuaded to reconsider. Politics is a dirty game, especially in Nigeria.

My father had been in government for five years, and he was suddenly faced with the prospect of having to earn a living in the private sector for the first time in his life. He was thirty-two years old, and he had a wife and two children to support.

▼

"Where in the world can you buy milk at these prices?" was a jingo frequently heard on the radio in Port Harcourt in 1974.

"At Gold Coast Stores . . ." came the answer.

When he opened a store on 24 Aggrey Road in Port Harcourt, my father dispatched my uncle Owens to every shop in the neighbourhood to find out the price of milk.

"I had just come back from my school holidays and thought I had done something wrong. I thought it was some kind of punishment," Owens later recalled. It was only when he saw the queues outside 24 Aggrey Road that my uncle realized why my father had sent him to research his rivals.

My father introduced the concept of competition to the retail business in Port Harcourt. Up until then, customer loyalty was taken for granted: you named your price and haggled for it if you couldn't reach an agreement. And unlike most of the shop owners on the street, my father also worked long hours and stayed open late. The business took off.

Gold Coast Stores was eventually renamed Dorbi & Sons to reflect his pride in family. The rise in oil prices after the Arab-Israeli War in 1973 buoyed the Nigerian economy, and Dorbi & Sons cashed in. In time the shop became Khana & Sons, as my father's philosphy and vision extended from family to tribe. Guided by my father's sound instincts and good contacts, Khana & Sons eventually became Saros International, the holding company of a conglomerate that had interests in land and property management, traded palm oil, imported rice and other foodstuffs. Saros also eventually published my father's books and produced one of the most popular sitcoms in Nigerian television history.

So much nonsense, much of it lies, has been written about his wealth. In an article that appeared in *The Independent* on the first anniversary of my father's death, Richard D. North alleged that he had "feathered his nest when managing the Niger Delta oil port of Bonny during the [Nigerian] civil war," and suggested that "if he was a crook, it is no more than Nigerians expect of each other." There are always people ready to imply without any evidence that he used his contacts and influential friends in the military to fatten himself on government contracts.

My father was not rich—at least not by the standards of Nigeria's super-rich multi-millionaires and billionaires, which is how he was often perceived—but he was not poor. He made enough money to take care of his obligations and priorities, which were, in no particular order, to educate his children to the same standard of schooling that he had received, to put a roof over his head, to take care of his immediate and extended family, and to make his contribution to the community. He lived comfortably, but his philosophy was simple: be frugal and save. He could at any time have called any one of his influential friends and become one of the country's super-rich. But he never did, because his political conscience would not allow it. And besides, while my father's rich friends enjoyed his company, they were wary of his reputation as a conscientious man who valued his reputation above all else. So while Nigeria's elite milked their position, my father kept his nose clean and worked hard for every kobo he earned. The reality was that his finances were always stretched. He had so many responsibilities and obligations, and he often skirted with disaster, but something kept him from tipping over the edge. Such was the case when he was introduced to the foreign-exchange markets in the 1980s.

Gilbert Chagouri was a businessman who "knew his onions around Nigeria and Nigerian leaders," as my father once said. He was one of a number of wealthy Lebanese businessmen who have their fingers in every pie in Nigeria. Chagouri was even reputed to be one of General Abacha's bankers. When Chagouri introduced him to the financial money markets in 1986, my father invested in a couple of how-to books, did his homework, studied the markets for a few months, then took the field. He opened a stop-loss account and traded the margins of minimal shifts in the value of the American dollar against the yen, the Deutschmark and the pound. My father was not a gambler by nature, but he needed the money—the value of the naira had began to plummet by then, and rising school fees in England had pushed him to the brink of disaster. His investment strategy was simple: he would listen to his broker's advice, then take a contrary position. He once told me that Ronald Reagan liked to jack up the dollar during the summer to give Americans cheap holidays. He would buy dollars based on this devastating piece of knowledge, watch the value of the currency rise over the summer and sell once the Americans returned from their holidays. He made a healthy profit on his early trades and carried on confounding his broker until his luck ran out in the late 1980s. He never got carried away by his success, though, and had the foresight to quit while he was ahead.

My father was coy about revealing how much he was worth. He knew that Nigeria is the kind of society where money gives a man the sort of status that he couldn't buy anywhere else, and he cultivated a mystique about his fortune. Whenever journalists inquired, he would reply that he was a man of simple tastes who couldn't be bought. When they intimated that he was milking the system, he would wearily point out that a man who had made his name on an anti-corruption platform, who had made powerful enemies by calling the corrupt to account, had to be cleaner than clean. Accordingly, he kept strict records. He was a stickler for documentation. He kept receipts for everything. He pored over his books with a Micawbish relish and was always quick to challenge anyone who accused him of impropriety to a mutual inspection of each other's books. My father often said that he held a mirror to society, and I suspect that many of those who reacted against him didn't like what they saw in that mirror. Though it may be hard for his critics to swallow, the bottom line is that Ken Saro-Wiwa was a simple man who went a long way on a little. As the leading character in his sitcom liked to say, "To be a millionaire, think like a millionaire." "Basi and Company" lampooned Nigeria's get-rich-quick mentality.

In the character of Basi, a con man who was always dreaming of the next scam, my father satirized the Nigerian's fondness for quick, easy solutions. I suspect he had an ironic chuckle to himself each time Basi trotted out his catch-phrase.

Despite my father's success, business never particularly excited him. He was always hankering after a return to politics, or better still to his first love—writing. After a failed attempt to get back into politics in 1977, he did finally return to his literary ambitions.

He had already been contributing the odd piece to newspapers, and when an old friend invited him to write a column in 1977, he reinvented himself as the trenchant and engaging columnist who enjoyed tweaking the nose of Nigeria's elite and laughing along with the masses. Once writing had reclaimed him, my father dusted off some old manuscripts and started hawking them around publishing houses in Nigeria and Europe. He was dismayed to discover that despite his popularity as a columnist, publishers were generally unwilling to take a chance with him. Publishing in Nigeria was in a parlous state because of the high rates of illiteracy and cost of producing books, which made them a luxury item and a high-risk, low-return investment. European publishers dismissed his manuscripts as "too parochial" and of little interest to the general reader outside Nigeria. In the end, he decided to publish his own books. He was often accused of vanity publishing, but he argued that in a society that was emerging from oral to written literatures, self-publishing was the rule and not the exception.

My father also ventured into television, and between 1985 and 1988 he wrote, produced and even acted in his own sitcom. Thirty million Nigerians tuned in to "Basi and Company" every week, but he never made any money from the show. In fact, he lost money on it because he had to use his own resources, especially after the television authorities refused to sponsor the show despite its high ratings. He couldn't find a commercial sponsor for "Basi" because in Nigeria the usual laws of economics do not apply; a hit show with a large audience ought to be an easy sell, but by the time the lack of a sponsor forced the show off the airwaves in 1990, anything attached to Ken Saro-Wiwa had to overcome all kinds of hidden agendas. My father had rubbed so many powerful people the wrong way with his outspokenness that his targets were already lining him up in their sights.

He never imagined he could make a living out of writing. He used to joke that in Nigeria, a freelance writer is someone who writes for free. For him writing was a political act, the pen was his sword. He made few concessions to artistic sensibilities and matters of style. He once had a public spat with Wole Soyinka that was ostensibly about the role of the writer in Nigerian society. He accused Soyinka of pandering to a European audience with literary pyrotechnics that left the average Nigerian reader groping for the meaning of his work. I have to admit that Soyinka is my favourite author, and I suspect my father envied Soyinka's literary profile and fame outside Nigeria. Writers are notoriously insecure, cantankerous and competitive, and my father was no exception. But they did at least kiss and make up—when my father was arrested, Soyinka was, and still is, one of his staunchest defenders.

He once told me that he bothered with only one draft of a manuscript. His production-line approach to writing partly explains how he managed, despite a late start, to produce those "25 books in all genres of literature, from pamphlets and poetry to children's stories and novels" (as the blurb on his books boasted). He once wrote and published seven books in one year. And while he was churning out all those words, he was also producing his television show, managing his businesses, maintaining five children at boarding schools in England and keeping up a weekly newspaper column. Ken Saro-Wiwa was a busy man, and he didn't have the time or the inclination to hone his craft. His writing, like everything else, had to serve a higher, communal purpose. And that meant keeping it simple and relevant to the masses.

In a lecture he delivered to the Association of Nigerian Authors in 1993, he declared that "the writer cannot be a mere storyteller; he cannot be a mere teacher; he cannot merely X-ray society's weaknesses, its ills, its perils. He or she must be actively involved in shaping its present and its future."

He went on to describe himself as following in the ancient Ogoni tradition of the Wiayor. The Wiayor are ordinary members of society who, when a spirit descends on them, acquire unusual powers of clairvoyance that make people accept their judgement and views. When the spirit deserts him, a Wiayor has to return to society and live up to its laws and mores, but he also has to accept the conditions under which his special powers were given. A Wiayor loses his power if he betrays the vision he was sent to tell.

"A writer," he concluded, "is a Wiayor, forced to live in the society but yet apart from it; critical of society and himself being critically watched by society."

3

My Father's House

▼

It's a poor sort of memory that only works backwards.
—LEWIS CARROLL, *Through the Looking-Glass*

The first thing I remember is lying on the floor, distraught, as my father's car pulls out of our long driveway one morning. I can almost feel the cool, hard concrete of the veranda as his cream-coloured Mercedes turns onto the road and disappears into the early morning traffic.

I was born in 1968, in Lagos during the civil war, but my earliest memories are of Port Harcourt, where my parents returned after the war ended in 1970. We lived at 11 Nzimiro Street, a colonial mansion in the middle of the city. Nzimiro Street is in an area of Port Harcourt that, for some reason, is known as Amadi Flats. Most of the homes on the street were the kind of palaces that expats had built to cocoon themselves from the realities of living in Africa. Number 11 was a two-storey building with large verandas, spacious rooms and high ceilings. A vigorous ivy creeper covered the outside walls, and in my mind's eye the house is an island surrounded by a sea of gardens that are filled with magnolias and bougainvillaea, and guava, orange, coconut, mango and palm trees.

Amadi Flats was an exclusive area that housed the families of expats, army officers, wealthy businessmen and government officials. As a commissioner in the state government, my father enjoyed the privileges of office: a chauffeur-driven Mercedes, the house and a pampered lifestyle with servants.

Every now and again, I catch myself day-dreaming that I have woken up one morning in my old bed at 11 Nzimiro. My parents are chatting and laughing, listening to music in the lounge along the corridor. Outside in the gardens, the chickens and peacocks are strutting around, foraging for food, and the goats are congregating under a tree while the household staff goes about their work.

My parents were a glamourous couple in Port Harcourt society in the early 1970s. He was well connected, a power-broker whose views and opinions were often sought by the country's political elites, especially after he stood by the idea of Nigeria during the civil war. She was his beautiful young wife, courted by modelling agencies. My parents were always throwing lavish parties. Pictures of my father show a handsome, confident dandy, a twenty-something minister who, when he wasn't wearing extravagant hipsters and colourful shirts with collars that had the wingspan of a Boeing 737, was invariably photographed in smart Italian suits. His friends were always dropping by to make recordings from his eclectic and comprehensive record collection. He had everything from the Beatles to Beethoven. If I close my eyes, I can almost hear the soundtrack of my childhood; Jimmy Cliff's "Remake the World" and Marvin Gaye's "Let's Get It On" were favourite turns on the state-of-the-art stereo system that he kept until his death. He had all the popular artists, such as Stevie Wonder, Fela and Bob Marley, but he also had records by people like PP Arnold, Andy Williams, the Troubadours and Bread—music that very few people in Nigeria had heard of or were listening to. Two songs in particular always remind me of my childhood, though: Procol Harum's "Whiter

Shade of Pale" and "Woyaya" by a Ghanaian band called Osibisa. Whenever I hear Alan Price's organ introduction to "A Whiter Shade of Pale," I'm transported back to our large living room, where my parents are dancing cheek to cheek, my mother, tall and slim, her hair in a head scarf, a Nubian queen with her wide, beautiful smile, her high cheekbones and a childlike innocence in her eyes, towers over my father. As I watch my parents dancing, my younger brother Gian is sitting next to me. Everyone is happy, everything in its rightful place, as Gary Brooker's voice wanders lazily into my reverie.

Life was relatively uncomplicated back then. Everyone doted on Gian and me—my sisters, the twins Zina and Noo, were not born until 1976, and my youngest brother, Tedum, came two years after them. Before they arrived on the scene, Gian and I were the only children. We were treated like little princes because my father was the favoured son, the first son who had made good and thus who carried the hopes of his extended family. His younger brothers and sisters called him Deede, which is a title of respect usually reserved for elders and respected members of the Ogoni community. One of my uncles once told me that when I tried to say Deede, it came out as Jeje, which is what all my father's children called—and still call—him.

My mother once told a journalist that although I didn't like to be pushed around, I "never gave much trouble." This is not quite true, because I was actually a handful. The cook, my nanny (Kpedume), the gardeners and the chauffeur all had their work cut out trying to keep me under control.

Kpedume could probably offer a more accurate testimony of the kind of trouble I was. She lived in the boys' quarters (a row of one-storey buildings at the back of 11 Nzimiro). When I wasn't chasing the goats and chickens around the gardens, I would loiter there, pestering the servants, especially in the evenings when it was time for bed.

Gian and I would hide in a tree or a bush. Kpedume rarely bothered looking for us. She would report us to the cook, Akpan, a short, stocky old man whose family lived back in his village. Akpan was having an affair with Kpedume, and I once caught them at it. I would often threaten to tell my father, and Akpan was itching for an excuse to give me a piece of his mind. But he could never lay a hand on me. He was too old and too fat to catch me; I ran rings around him. One night, after Gian and I had run him into the ground, he stood in the early evening light, panting heavily. "Why na dis peking dey cause dis kind palava, ehn?" he cursed. "Eehhffiong!" He shouted in frustration.

Effiong was the gardener. He couldn't have been much more than fifteen or sixteen years old, but he was tall and had huge rippling muscles. He had a permanent frown on his face and no one messed with him. I once saw him beat up three grown men, a fact I related to my father. "Jeje?" I wondered. "Are you stronger than Effiong?" My father laughed without reassuring me that he was in fact the most powerful man in the world. When I asked Josiah, the chauffeur, he doubled up, sucking his teeth loudly. Everyone refused to confirm what I knew to be true, and I worried about it for days. Eventually I decided that if it ever came down to it, my father could still beat up Effiong.

When Akpan called for Effiong that night, I steeled myself. I was hiding behind a bush by the boys' quarters, and I saw him emerge from his room. His muscles were glistening from the sweat of hard day's work cutting grass, and he looked as tall as a palm tree. I pictured him as Power Mike, the champion wrestler we used to watch on television every Saturday afternoon. He stood in the early evening gloom of the boys' quarters, fuming. I ran out of the bush, screaming. Effiong wasn't quick, but he was loyal and very hard-working. He never stopped until the job was done. He lumbered after me, moving with the agility of a buffalo, until Gian came running out of his hiding spot. Effiong stopped and watched us buzzing around him like flies, then plodded after Gian. After catching my brother, Effiong tossed Gian over his shoulder, then came lumbering after me. Gian wriggled around on his shoulder, trying to escape, but Effiong barely broke either sweat or stride as he cornered me. When he caught me, he pinned my wrists together in one of his giant paws and flicked me over his other shoulder. When Akpan saw that our fun was over for the night, he came running towards us, cursing in seven languages. "Effiong, holam, ah dey come!" he hollered.

While Gian pulled Effiong's neatly groomed Afro, I sank my teeth into the nape of his neck, but he didn't flinch. Then Akpan scuttled towards us with two red peppers in his hand. There was a gleeful, almost spiteful look in his eyes as he approached, grinding a thumb into the core of the peppers. When he finally got his hands on me, he smeared a coarse, fat thumb across my eyelids. I fell to the ground and rolled around, clutching my head as a red mist burned my eyes.

"You ye-ye man. Blokkus," I screamed in pidgin. "You will see. When Jeje comes back, he will beat you up," I promised, resorting to English to emphasize the threat.

I wasn't always a nuisance, though. The house at 11 Nzimiro was a busy place and I used to help out from time to time, feeding the chickens, helping my grandmother with her little plot of yams, sweet corn and sugar cane at the back of the house. I also remember the unforgettable nights I spent watching Akpan making the preparations for one of my parents' parties. I would sit around a fire in front of the boys' quarters as a goat roasted on a spit. The crackle of the logs and the smell of roasting goat would fill the air as Josiah, Akpan and Effiong swapped jokes and told us ghost stories. Somewhere in the village beyond the house, hi-life music would be blaring from a radio as crickets and frogs added to the unmistakable sounds of an African night.

In the intermittent silences, you could hear distant voices echoing into and out of the darkness, like the sandflies that flickered across the sky while mosquitoes mingled silently, looking for a juicy arm to feast on.

My memories of those soft, warm nights are so clear and so vivid, and yet I sometimes wonder about them because I'm not altogether sure that my childhood memories are that reliable.

When I returned to Nigeria to bury my father, I went back to our old house on Amadi Flats. It was much smaller than I remembered. I had anticipated that, but I was shocked at exactly *how* small it looked. The driveway was much shorter than I had expected, and I was convinced that the road had been moved. I couldn't find the little inlet where I used to go fishing with my friends—a new bridge and residential area had been built over it. There was no ivy on the walls at 11 Nzimiro either. No peacocks or goats or chickens on the gardens. But what really upset me was that a house was being built on the field where I had spent hours trying to emulate my hero, Adokiye Amesimaka. He was the winger on the Green Eagles, Nigeria's national team, and my ambition was to be like him and play for them myself one day. Amesimaka was a lawyer in his spare time and his family rented a flat from my father. After he retired, he went back to the law and eventually became the attorney general of Rivers State. He was the minister who was responsible for overseeing the tribunal that convicted my father.

Eleven Nzimiro was still painted in the same blue and yellow colours but the paint had faded and was peeling off. The house probably hadn't been painted since we left, and everything looked shabbier, older and sadder. It was and it wasn't the house I grew up in, and I was desperately disappointed.

Going back to your childhood can be a treacherous and distressing journey. Although you never really forget the way back, when you get there you're never quite sure that you've arrived at the right place, even though everything looks familiar.

My father's house was a happy place, though, and he was the central figure, the axis on which my world turned. He was the man who would look over my shoulders, ready with all the answers as I cast my inquisitive eyes over the map of the world in my treasured atlas. My father was the man who nursed me through the trauma of a broken arm when I fell out of a tree. He would come home from work and I would fold myself into his lap as he massaged my fingers, explaining why the cast was called plaster of Paris. The world, its wonders and all its terrors were always reassuringly explained. He knew everything, and the world made sense to me through his eyes.

What troubles me about my childhood is that some memories stubbornly refuse to confirm the impressions, the myths perhaps, that I have constructed of my father. I have, for instance, a very vivid memory of him trying to clown around with us on the veranda. In this scene I am annoyed with him. He had brought me and Gian a Frisbee, and he wanted to throw it around one morning after breakfast. I was annoyed because we were late for school, and I just couldn't understand why he was insisting that we had to play right there and then. Only now, with the benefit of hindsight and my experience as an itinerant father of a young boy, do I understand the significance of that scene.

My father was hardly around during the early part of my childhood. He was often away on government business. On his passport there are visas for Cuba, Brazil, America and just about every country in West Africa. He always claimed on his c.v. that he had visited "over fifty countries." He loved travelling—he had caught the bug when, as a commissioner, he travelled on several diplomatic missions. Gian and I were always being dressed up to go and welcome him back at the airport. I imagine that's why I had the tantrum that has become my earliest memory—when he left, I was never sure whether he would be gone for the day or longer.

My mother was hardly around either. Although she wanted,

as she later told me, to have a go at modelling, my father persuaded her that it was not a suitable career. He was, even then, a firm believer in the "cultivation of self-development until the individual can realize all of her or his potential." He insisted that she finish the education that had been interrupted by the civil war, and so, soon after Gian was born in September 1970, she left for boarding school. That's why, I imagine, I don't have many outstanding early memories of my mother.

Although my parents were rarely around, I wasn't exactly traumatized by their absence. I'm told I would cry for a while after they were gone, then quickly forget about them. I had a few phobias that may or may not be linked to the fact that they were always coming and going. I was afraid of the dark, for example, and I wet my bed—especially when they were both away. But on balance, I felt safe and secure in that house. My childhood days *were* the happiest of my life, and there were always plenty of relatives—uncles, aunts, cousins—looking out for me.

Still, although I wasn't overly conscious of it, there was always a cloud hanging over my father's house. I do remember the atmosphere around 11 Nzimiro when he was sacked from government. I felt my father's humiliation and I was worried about the future—especially when they took the Mercedes away. There was talk that we would have to leave Amadi Flats. I went around asking people why my father, my all-powerful father, had been sacked. I was told that there had been a difference of opinion over a budget that was two pence short. That's the explanation I remember. I was only four years old at the time.

I was teased at school—especially after his sacking was announced on the radio—but I got busy defending his honour. After several hot-headed scuffles and heated arguments on the playground, I was reported to the headmaster and sent home to cool off. It was a rehearsal for the role I would play years later, when I again had to stand up for my father's honour, but back in 1973 I had no idea why he was in trouble. I stood up for him anyway, of course, because I loved him unconditionally. When I had to defend him twenty years later, I understood all the political arguments, but my reasons for standing up for him were much more complicated.

▼

My childhood ended in 1977. I came back from playing football one afternoon and saw my grandmother sitting on the veranda. I had a feeling that something was wrong because Mama only came to Port Harcourt to work on her garden plot or be cared for when she was sick. The yams were not ready and she didn't look sick but she seemed unhappy. She invited me to sit next to her. She pulled me close to her, took out the little tin of Vicks VapoRub that contained her snuff and offered me some. I decided to accept because I had a feeling that my grandmother was about to tell me something important. I felt grown up as I tipped my head back and stuffed a pinch of snuff in my nostrils. My grandmother took a pinch of the fine black ash and snorted it off her thumb. She pressed a finger against the side of her nose and exhaled, sending a mixture of mucus and snuff flying across the veranda. She stared into the distance, cleared her throat and started rambling away in Khana, telling me that I mustn't leave, that I must stay. I nodded impatiently, wondering when she was going to get to the point. When she asked me to promise her that I wouldn't leave, I assured her that I wasn't going anywhere. She told me to tell my father, and I promised I would do so, but she seemed unconvinced when she finally shuffled off slowly, looking as if the world had just collapsed on her shoulders.

"What did Mama want to talk to you about?" my father asked when he came home.

"Oh, she told me to stay," I replied casually.

He smiled. "You're going to England," he said, chuckling to himself. I looked at him, confused. "I'm sending you to school in England," he explained.

I was so excited I forgot the promise I had made to my grandmother.

▼

There was a sense that something was coming to an end around Amadi Flats in 1977. We were preparing to move out of 11 Nzimiro; my childhood friends Tombari and Edward had already left, and I had started to hang around with Suleiman and Ibrahim, who lived next door at 9 Nzimiro. I lost touch with Suleiman and Ibrahim after we moved, but my memory of those childhood friendships would return to haunt me.

If I pause the tape of my life in the middle of 1977 and fast-forward to the night of May 21, 1994, it is the night my father was arrested after the riot in which four Ogoni were killed. One of the murdered men is Chief Edward Kobani, the father of Edward and Tombari. And General Sani Abacha, the man who would later authorize my father's execution for his alleged role in the chiefs' murders, is Ibrahim's father.

Nineteen seventy-seven was the year that something died in my father. That year, the head of state, General Obasanjo, decided to end ten years of military rule by returning the country to a civilian government. Elections to a constituent assembly that was to draw up a constitution for the new republic were held as part of the transition process. My father stood as the Ogoni candidate but was defeated by one vote. There were bitter accusations of election fraud, and in the recriminations my father fell out with his friend Edward Kobani.

I remember watching the news as the results came in. When my father's defeat was announced, he turned to me with tears in his eyes. "What do you think about that?" he asked.

I didn't know what to say. I was stunned, not just that he had lost but because it was the first time I had seen my father cry. I shrugged and he returned to the news. He had expected to win, and the disappointment of losing that election left him with an abiding distaste for conventional politics.

When we left 11 Nzimiro, we moved across the city to Simaseng Place, which is still our home in Port Harcourt. But we were in our new home for only a few months before we moved to England in January 1978. My father left me Simaseng Place in his will. I appreciate the symbolism of the gesture, but it probably never occurred to him that my memories of that house are not particularly happy ones. Simaseng Place reminds me of the changes in our relationship.

After he lost the election, he became the critical, demanding man that haunted my adolescence. He would sit at the dining table, shaking his head and warning us about what to expect in England; we would be teased because we ate with our mouths open, because I still wet my bed, because we didn't know how to hold a knife and fork properly, because of our accent . . . The man who had always found time to explain the wonders of the world to me suddenly became the man who seemed to take pleasure in telling me that the world was a harsh place and that not everyone in it loved me.

My father never sat us down to explain why he was sending us to England. It was just presented as a *fait accompli*, a great adventure that promised everything and nothing. I became quite apprehensive about the trip, especially after I misheard him say that we would be flying to England via Swaziland.

Swaziland! I thought. I consulted my atlas. Why were we going all the way down there? I wondered. I couldn't understand why we would have to fly so far south before heading to England. I would normally have asked my father to clear up my confusion, but since something had changed between us I kept my fears to myself. I stared at my atlas, trying to work it out, trying to make sense of the inexplicable changes that were happening in my life.

I remember waking up in the plane at Zurich airport. I looked out the window and saw snow for the first time. I was amazed at how the white flakes seemed to float to the ground. There was a strange, dreamy music playing in the cabin, and each time I hear Johann Strauss's *Blue Danube*, it reminds me of falling snow at Zurich airport.

And the pungent stench of ammonia. I was mortified when I looked down between my legs and saw a familiar damp patch on my trousers. I looked up to see an air hostess staring at me, trying but failing to hide her contempt behind a frosty smile. I was relieved when she decided not to make a scene about it and I managed to keep my guilty secret from my parents until my mother spotted the stain on my trousers as we wandered around Oxford Street, looking for Harrods on a bitterly cold evening in London.

4

On a Darkling Plain

▼

The flares of Shell are flames of hell.
—KEN SARO-WIWA

The Niger is the longest river in West Africa. It rises in the foothills of the Tingi Mountains, on the border between Guinea and Sierra Leone, and empties, 4,200 kilometres later, into the Bight of Benin. The Niger River Delta is the largest in Africa, 240 kilometres long north to south, and spreading along a 320-kilometre stretch of the southern coast of Nigeria. It extends over an area of dense rainforest covered by an intricate pattern of tributaries, streams, rivers, creeks and mangrove swamps that is rich in minerals—timber, coal, palm oil and crude oil. It is one of the most densely populated parts of the world, and one of the world's great ecosystems and it is often described as the heart and lungs of Nigeria.

▼

Scattered across 1,046 square kilometres of the northeastern fringes of the Delta are the mud huts of the 128 or so villages of the Ogoni. Although there are an estimated 500,000 Ogoni, we are one of the smallest of the 250 ethnic groups in the Niger Delta. We have lived on a gently sloping, heavily forested and fertile plateau for anything from eternity to four hundred years, depending on whose history—oral or written—you subscribe to.

Although much of my father's writing reflected his obsession with Nigeria's political dysfunction, his underlying concern was always with the social and economic problems facing the minority ethnic groups in the oil-bearing areas of the Niger Delta. The focus of his bracing jeremiads was Nigeria's dependence on oil, which, he felt, was the root of the country's social, political and economic problems.

Oil accounts for 90 per cent of its foreign-exchange earnings. Most of that oil is found in the Niger Delta. And since oil plays such a preponderant role in Nigeria's economy, the struggle for control of that resource is the main preoccupation of the country's politicians and power-brokers. My father never wasted any opportunity to point out that Nigeria's three largest ethnic groups have controlled the power and the resources of the country since independence, and have managed to squander and loot the nation's inheritance. He argued that the minorities of the Delta were subsidizing and underwriting a system he described as a lootocracy.

Despite earning an annual average income of $30 billion from its oil in the past ten years, Nigeria has somehow managed to amass an external debt of $40 billion without much capital investment or infrastructure to show for it. The sum of money held by Nigerian nationals in foreign bank accounts around the world is suspected to be equal to Nigeria's foreign debt.

What pained my father about Nigeria was the lack of accountability in government. He argued that this affected every aspect of life in the country, corrupting private and public morality. The easy access to oil money created an "easy come easy go" attitude, breeding a "collective failure to think," as he once wrote. That careless attitude was the reason why Nigeria's lawmakers refused to enforce environmental regulations, preferring to turn a blind eye to the oil companies that were destroying our environment. It especially pained him that an area like Ogoni, which should have been as rich as a small Gulf State, was one of the poorest corners of Africa. He argued for a fairer distribution of the revenues from the oil resources, pointing out that successive constitutional fiats and decrees had whittled down our share of our own resources. Nigeria's constitution has a revenue-allocation formula, a derivation fund, which is supposed to redistribute revenue to the places of origin. Before independence, regional governments had an equal share of revenue with the federal government. By 1990, the derivation fund returned a miserly 1.5 per cent of revenue to the regions. My father argued that outlying regions, places like Ogoni, were being stripped of their natural resources to feed the greed of insolvent governments and profit-hungry multinationals.

In article after article, book after book, he preached his gospel, rounding on the oil companies and the major ethnic groups, accusing them of genocide, of human-rights abuses, of theft, of greed. He was a tireless advocate, but he became increasingly disillusioned with the efficacy of his writing. By 1990, he was dismayed at the thought that he had written prolifically for ten years about the problems of the oil-bearing communities, but the situation had, in that time, deteriorated. He came to the conclusion that in a country with 60 per cent illiteracy, where books were a luxury item, writers and writing could not change or move society.

After he lost a manuscript at Lagos airport in 1992, he took it as an omen that it wasn't his destiny to be a writer. The book was to have been a love story. He had decided to write a novel with universal themes to introduce his name to a Western audience. He had hoped that the book would raise his profile outside Nigeria, and thereafter sneak his political concerns onto a wider, global stage. But when he lost the manuscript, he decided to take "the word to the streets." Once he trained his mind on the problem of how to mobilize the Ogoni to stand up against the oil industry and the military, he set himself on a collision course with powerful and ruthless opponents.

Few people had any idea of the scale of my father's ambitions for MOSOP. Few people took much notice when he announced his intention to set up MOSOP. Nigerians love their acronyms. If you travel around the country, read the newspapers, listen to the radio, you will come across a plethora of them—NICON, NAFCON, NITEL, NEPA. Political parties, electoral commissions, church organizations, quangos—everything has to have an acronym. Some of them, such as the beleaguered NEPA (Nigerian Electrical Ports Authority), are national institutions but most of them are anonymous, shadowy oranizations with impressive looking initials that signify nothing. Few people would have raised an eyebrow when Ken Saro-Wiwa announced yet another acronym, but my father had done his homework while everyone else enjoyed the joke that his new baby sounded like Mossad.

Oil was discovered in Ogoni in 1958, but after thirty years of exploration, after an estimated 900 million barrels with an estimated $100 billion had been extracted from the land, the region had very little to show for it. There was little electricity or pipeborne water in the community; schools and hospitals were chronically underfunded, poorly staffed and badly maintained. A community of fishermen and subsistence farmers was threatened by the effects of the oil industry.

Six thousand kilometres of pipelines criss-cross the Niger Delta. Many of the pipes were old, had been laid without community consultation and leaked oil onto farmlands and into the water table. According to Shell's own figures, the incidence of oil spills in the Delta is among the highest in its global operations. By the early 1990s, Ogoni fishermen were complaining that the streams and creeks they used to fish had become so polluted that they had to go farther and farther out to sea to make a living. Frequent blow-outs and twenty-four-hour gas flaring scarred the land and polluted the air. A recent World Bank report indicated that conditions in the Niger Delta were a significant contribution to global warming and the rise in respiratory diseases among the local people.

Like most of the minority groups in Nigeria, the Ogoni suffered from the discrimination and chauvinism of the larger ethnic groups. There were few Ogoni in key government positions or within the management structure of the same oil industry that derived such rich rewards from our land. Seventy per cent of Ogoni university graduates were unemployed, and many of them had to leave the country in search of opportunities. While one generation was being forced out of the community, another was left behind to suffer the consequences of hosting oil companies that seemed hell-bent on exploiting the resource without any regard to the health and safety of the indigenous people.

My father felt it was intolerable that the oil companies were reaping fantastic profits at the expense of our land and our people. He envisaged MOSOP as the vehicle to challenge those companies to clean up our environment, to compensate our people for the damage done and force them to pay a fairer rent for the land. He observed that Shell was not only flouting Nigeria's environmental laws, but also paying lip service to its own commitment to a clean and safe environment. He accused Shell of hypocrisy and racism, pointing out that while the multinational used its record in Europe or North America to trumpet its commitment to the environment, it was operating to a very different standard in Ogoni.

He was convinced he had a case. He had done his homework, studying Shell's own statements, travelling to Scotland and the north of England to marvel at how Shell worked with local communities to ensure a safe and healthy environment. But in challenging Shell, he was challenging a monolith. Although the oil industry in Nigeria was nationalized in 1977—and Shell operates in a joint venture with the government (Shell Petroleum Development Corporation [SPDC] is 55 per cent owned by the government, with Shell owning 30 per cent)—to all intents and purposes Shell wears the trousers in the relationship. It is the partner making all the day-to-day operational decisions. Moreover, Shell Nigeria's holding company, Shell International Petroleum Company (SIPC), is one of the biggest companies in the world; its annual turnover of $100 billion dwarfs Nigeria's annual budget of $30 billion. Shell's operations in Nigeria alone are worth some $14 billion and the company considers its operations there to be "arguably Shell's largest and most complex exploration and production venture outside North America."

And what is good for Shell is apparently good for Nigeria. In a country that depends on oil for 90 per cent of its foreign-exchange earnings, Shell is in a position to dictate the terms of its operations. Everyone is aware of the close and mutually beneficial relationship between Nigerian governments and Shell—and of the consequences of questioning that cosy arrangement. Everyone including my father.

Before oil was discovered there, Ogoni had a reputation as the food basket of the region, but by the early 1990s that was no longer the case. A once self-sufficient community of subsistence farmers now had to buy and import food. Farm yields were declining, and in an area with a high population density there was increased demand and pressure on land use. Strange strains of palms were starting to replace the mangrove trees whose roots used to provide a habitat for crabs, periwinkles, mudskippers, mussels and shrimps.

It never occurred to me, until my father began to draw my attention to them, that the gas flares in Ogoni might be contributing to the acid rain that destroyed the aluminium roofing of the houses in the area. I had no idea that the incidence of oil spills in

Ogoni was one of the highest recorded in the world. Our people had never stopped to consider that the pipelines that ran through our villages were responsible for polluting our environment. We rarely complained about the discrepancy between the wealth of the oil companies and the poverty of our people. Some of our people were aware of our predicament, and some had even spent their lives fighting the oil companies. There had been periodic riots, protests and letter-writing campaigns since the 1960s, but most of these fizzled out after the leaders were intimidated into silence or bought off. Our people endured their situation silently, suffering the indignity and humiliation of wallowing in poverty in an oil-rich land. Our people had accepted their status as second-class citizens.

I was teased at primary school because I was an Ogoni. I used to flinch whenever my classmates taunted me with shouts of "*Ogoni pior pior.*" I did not know what the words meant, but I knew that they were an insult and that they hurt. I grew up watching grown Ogoni men taunted by children in public. I was so ashamed of being an Ogoni that I used to beg my mother not to speak Khana in public. I didn't know of any Ogoni man or woman who had ever done anything significant in Nigeria. No Ogoni man had ever even played football for Nigeria. People said that we were dirty, that we were cannibals. We were the wretched of the wretched of the earth, suffering under the yoke of our double discrimination as a minority within a minority.

My father had a love-hate relationship with Ogoni. Although he was proud of his roots, he despised the slavish mentality and our poor reputation. When he formed MOSOP, he was determined to change all that, but even he was surprised at how quickly the organization altered our people's psyche.

In many respects, my father was MOSOP. He set up the organization, and he wrote, published and persuaded the Ogoni people to sign the Ogoni bill of rights (which set down a list of our demands from the oil companies and the government). He was tried and tested in the battle against the conspiracy of silence in Nigeria, and he was responsible for wooing the international media and sceptical non-governmental organizations to the struggle.

I remember the depressing responses he got when he took me to the headquarters of environmental groups in London after I had graduated from university. He was trying to enlist them to campaign on our behalf.

"When you say the situation is tantamount to genocide, Mr. Saro-Wiwa, exactly how many of your people have been killed?"

My father's eyes would light up. "Well, it's not genocide in the conventionally understood sense of the word."

The eyes on the other side of the table would glaze over as my father began to explain the United Nations definition of genocide as "the commission of acts with intent to destroy a national, ethnic, racial or religious group." My father would soon be shown the door with a polite but condescending look that suggested he come back when a few more people had been killed.

He never gave up trying to bring our plight to international attention, though. In July 1992, he gave a speech on the dilemma of the Ogoni people to the United Nations Working Group on Indigenous Peoples. That speech paved the way for MOSOP to link up with international organizations like the World Council of Churches and the Unrepresented Nations and Peoples Organisation (UNPO). My father also got some attention from the media, including coverage on CNN and in *Time* magazine, but it took his first detention in 1993 before outsiders really to begin to take more than a passive interest in the Ogoni struggle. The bandwagon began to roll after he was arrested for the final time, in 1994, but it wasn't until he was sentenced in October 1995, ten days before he was hanged, that my father's story and the Ogoni struggle finally became a major international news story.

While he was fighting to put Ogoni on the map abroad, he

was also busy doing his homework. He bullied, cajoled, persuaded and organized MOSOP into an effective movement. He read extensively about grass-roots organizations. He studied how Gandhi's satyagraha had moved the Indian people and how Martin Luther King had used non-violent protest to draw attention to the civil-rights movement in the United States. He copied their example for the Ogoni, organizing MOSOP into an umbrella group with democratic sub-units that reflected the different social classes within the community. There were MOSOP sub-units for traditional rulers, chiefs, students, youths, church groups, professionals and women. The goal was to involve everyone in the decision-making process. MOSOP was designed as a bottom-up organization. At the top of the tree was a steering committee that was originally set up to decide the structure of the movement.

But in addition to taking on the rigours of day-to-day organizing, my father was also MOSOP's driving force. He wrote most of its pamphlets and speeches. When he initially set up the organization, he decided not to stand for election as its president. He didn't want to create the impression that MOSOP was his personal business, so instead he stood for and was elected as its publicity secretary. But as hard as he tried to remain in the background, his energy and commitment meant that he was the face and the voice of MOSOP. He wrote letters and opinion pieces, and filed newspaper reports. He even wrote under assumed names—anything to create the impression that this was a hot story. He was always ready to grant interviews: he had the facts at his fingertips and always made good copy. He had an instinctive rapport with journalists and editors. In a sense, MOSOP was the end product of his life, the distillation of all his careers, the actualization of his Joycean ambition to forge the uncreated conscience of his race in the smithy of his soul.

He was determined to revive Ogoni culture: in 1991 he published a book of folktales, *The Singing Anthill*. Many of them he rewrote from memory, but he also sent out researchers to archive and collect the stories. Folktales are an essential part of Ogoni oral tradition, and he took up the task of writing them down because he saw a need to preserve an essential part of our cultural memory and heritage. He had, even before then, been involved in ad hoc, piecemeal efforts to provide symbols to rally our people. In 1968, he wrote what has become the Ogoni song, "Ake, Ake pia, Ogoni Ake" (Rise up, rise up, Ogoni rise . . .). And five years before he published *The Singing Anthill*, he sponsored an archaeological dig to excavate the original site of the first Ogoni settlement. He was always encouraging Ogoni historians to research and write our history.

Up to 1990, his efforts at keeping our traditions alive had been haphazard, but once he formed MOSOP he was conscious of the need to revive our culture. He began to "rewrite" our history. When he insisted that the Ogoni had lived in harmony with their neighbours and the environment until the Europeans arrived on the scene, he knew it was a myth. It was a romantic notion—like the American dream or the Victorian age—a myth that was supposed to fire the individual imagination and the collective quest for cultural identity and survival. When he railed against the use of the terms "Ogoniland" or "Ogoni people"—insisting that "Ogoni" was the correct term because "the land and the people are one"—you had to marvel at his cheek, at the way he could blithely forget that *he* had ignored that special relationship when he came up with the acronym for MOSOP. And the estimates that put the Ogoni population at 500,000? Ken Saro-Wiwa, the census maker, was responsible for that figure. Ogoni with a landmass of 1,046 square kilometres? Ken Saro-Wiwa's estimate.

Before I slaughter too many sacred cows, I should point out that he did check an ordnance survey map to establish his facts, but you also have to remember that what is and is not Ogoni is not clearly defined. There are five kingdoms in Ogoni—Khana, Ken Khana, Gokhana, Tai and Eleme. Members of each kingdom speak a mutually unintelligible language. A man from

Khana speaks a different language from a Gokhana man although many words are similar. Although I speak Khana, my poor grasp of the language means I have difficulty understanding Gokhana. There are communities that claim to be Ogoni when it suits them and not when it doesn't. Precision is an imprecise science in Nigeria. My father often had to dig up the facts himself, make history on the hoof. When he was invited to address the United Nations in 1992, he realized he had no history, no text to draw from, so he sat down, did his homework and came up with the research material that later formed the basis of the book *Genocide in Nigeria*. He never had the luxury of sitting back to reflect and rewrite, but he knew and understood the power of myth, and he had an acute sense of history and his place in it. Even the pipe was part of his kit: it was meant to leave a lasting image of him in the minds of his people. Ken Saro-Wiwa understood, as André Brink observed, that the invention of a past, whether it "occurs in therapy, in historiography, or in literature, the powerful act of appropriating the past through imaginative understanding—that is, through the devices of metaphor rather than through a 'scientific objectivity' which tries to mask its own uncertainties—is necessary for the sanity of the whole community."

Ken Saro-Wiwa was cranking himself up for a superhuman effort. He was the Wiayor whose task was to arrest, almost single-handedly, the decline and extinction of our people. Like Prometheus, he took control of his environment, shaping his own and his people's destiny until forces beyond his control conspired to end his life prematurely.

5

Hidden Names, Complex Fate

▼

Nobody knows my name.
—JAMES BALDWIN

I would love to know what my father was thinking when he named me. My full name is Kenule Bornale Saro-Wiwa. It means "In troubled times, I am fearless—the first son of Wiwa." Perhaps my father took it as a good omen that, like him, his first son was born during a war. I sometimes imagine, in more cynical moments, that when he looked into my eyes on November 28, 1968, he saw a reflection of himself.

One of my earliest photographs shows me standing on a balcony, looking slightly surprised, a little unsteady on my feet. On the back of the photograph, my father has written, "Kenule Bornale Tsaroti, first steps, aged seven months." Since my father also walked at seven months, I imagine him staring at that photograph, beaming with pride, his pen poised to mark the milestone, excited at the thought that his first son and namesake is already following in his footsteps.

At home I have always been known as Junior, but I was surprised when my father took me aside and told me, as we were preparing to leave for England, that my name was actually Kenule. I had never wondered why I was called Junior, but I loved the name because it made me stand out from all my friends, who had dull Nigerian names like Ibinabo, Nwachuwkwu or Dike. I was distinctly unimpressed by Kenule, and I told my father so. But he was adamant. Kenule was my name, and I was now to answer to it.

I remember staring at the name on my passport before we left Nigeria. Kenule Bornale Tsaro-Wiwa. Although I couldn't envisage myself as Kenule, I had no idea, as I swapped the securities of my childhood for the uncertainties of England, just how much of an identity crisis that "new" name would cause me.

Tsaro-Wiwa was the family name when we left for England, and it did grow on me. I loved it when people wondered if I was Russian—was I in some way related to the tsar? People would also sometimes assume I was Japanese—until they saw me. Eventually the novelty wore off, and I got tired of always having to explain myself and spell out my name.

Even though it has now become a name recognized around the world, Saro-Wiwa still gets horribly misspelled and mispronounced. The correct pronunciation is Saaa-ro-Weee-Wah—you almost have to sing the Saro, with a nasal inflection on the Wiwa. But Sa-ro-We-wah has become the unofficial official pronunciation. This is the Anglicized, plum-in-your-mouth, stiff-upper-lipped, BBC-World-Service-approved pronunciation. And it is hopelessly wrong. But what can you do, since it is the pronunciation that has become indelibly linked with my father and the Ogoni struggle? There is hardly any point in trying to reclaim the name now, especially as our own people, who should know better, often use the Anglicized version as well.

When my father tired of seeing and hearing Tsaro-Wiwa misspelled and mispronounced, he decided to simplify things by changing our surname to Saro-Wiwa! That was in 1982. I was fourteen years old at the time, and I had no choice but to give up my identity once again. This time the change wasn't quite as traumatic as before, however.

Being Ken Saro-Wiwa meant different things depending on which part of the world I was in. In Nigeria, people often did a double take when they saw or heard my name. The name opened doors, but that second look wasn't always welcoming. You would hold your breath once the connection was established, hoping that recognition would evoke the warm and generous response of my father's admirers and not the hostility that he also attracted. But each time a customs officer at Lagos airport hassled me simply for being Ken Saro-Wiwa's son, I would curse the fates that had given me the same name. I was always glad to get back to England, because there my name was not loaded with the same kind of expectations or prejudices.

But while England offered me refuge from the implications of being Ken Saro-Wiwa's son, it couldn't protect me from the complexities of being *my father's* son, especially after I became conscious of the fact that he was trying to mould me in his image. When he insisted that I follow his example and cut my hair, polish my shoes, iron my shirts, take pride and care in my appearance, I did the opposite. I resisted him, cutting off my nose to spite any traces of him in my face. But as long as he was paying my school fees, giving me the best opportunities in life, I couldn't rebel against him like my English friends did their fathers. I misspent my youth cautiously instead, nursing my resentment of my father's ambitions for me.

I retreated into myself. My father could never understand why I was such an introspective, uncommunicative slouch around the house, especially when my school reports suggested I was "outgoing" and "gregarious." He started nosing around my life, invading my privacy, trying to understand what, if anything, was going on in my head.

I once caught him reading my diary. He was standing by my bed, casually flicking through it. He didn't apologize, just carried on reading as if I wasn't there. I was livid, but I didn't protest: in our culture, as he was always quick to remind us, you never argue with your elders. I stopped writing the diary, but that didn't stop him from prying. He started opening every letter that was addressed to Ken Saro-Wiwa, even though it was not that difficult to work out which were his and which were mine. I retreated further into myself, nursing my grudges against my father, slyly resisting the strait-jacket of identity he was trying to impose on me and dreaming of the day when I would take control of my life and change my name.

I was twenty-three years old when I finally did it. I instructed a solicitor to draw up the documents, and in a lavish flourish of my new, shortened signature, I declared my independence from him and became Ken Wiwa. It wasn't the liberating experience I had hoped, though. Ken Wiwa seemed flat, rather unimpressive, especially next to the more colourful and flamboyant Ken Saro-Wiwa.

It took me two years to break the news to my father. He was in detention by then, and when I wrote to him, I deliberately signed myself Ken Wiwa instead of Junior, as I had always done in the past.

He was furious.

He wrote back, complaining that "nobody will ever know that you're my son." At least that's how I used to tell the story. When I re-read the letter after he died, I saw that what he had actually written was a more anguished "there is no way in our culture that Ken Wiwa can be the son of Ken Saro-Wiwa."

Which, linguistically at least, is not true.

I later found out that my father was born Kenule Beeson Inadum Nwiwa—or that was the name he used at school in

Umuahia. Many Ogoni words and names beginning with *W* used to be written as *Nw* to accommodate the nasal tone of the sound. My father dropped the *N* from Nwiwa to help distinguish us from the Igbo people, many of whose names begin with *Nw*. He changed his name again to Tsaro-Wiwa when he went up to university in the 1960s, and thirty years later I came to appreciate, as he must have done, that because our languages are tonal, Ogoni names can be written a number of ways. Ogoni is an oral society, and we do not have a written language. The Roman alphabet does not capture the intonations and inflections of our language. So while our identity, as well as the meaning of our names and how we pronounce them, is perfectly clear to any Ogoni, it is only when we step outside our culture that confusions arise.

▼

Gian and I were the only Africans out of 150 boys at our boarding school in Derbyshire. We were mercilessly teased at first—just as my father had predicted. We were picked on for all sorts of reasons, but our "funny" names attracted most of the attention. Wee-wee was the predictable crowd-pleaser. Sympathetic friends called me Ken-yule, which was almost as bad (I was used to Ke-noo-lay) thankfully Ken-yule never caught on because in English boarding schools people are generally known by their surnames or by nicknames, so I was known as Tsaro-Wiwa or Tiswas.

My transformation from African to English boy began at Stancliffe Hall prep school, and was accelerated by a curriculum that took it for granted that England was the centre of the universe. "Us" was England and "them" meant the rest of the world. Although I was never comfortable with the notion, I never questioned the way the world was being revealed to me; I was more concerned about fitting in. I wanted to be one of "us" and not one of "them." In Africa I had wanted to be different, to stand out from the crowd. In England I wanted to blend into the background.

But as my allegiances shifted, I was stranded from time to time in no-man's land. This son of a proud African sat in agonized silence through the film *Zulu* as my friends cheered the men in the heavy, starched stiff uniforms that seemed so inappropriate for the blistering heat of Africa, fighting off wave after wave of swarming, menacing Zulus who never spoke, never had any character or humanity. The message was clear: the black man was so inferior that it took only a handful of blond, blue-eyed, brave white men to overcome us. As I watched in the darkened silence of a room in northern England, Africa tugged at me, reminding me that no matter how much I wanted to be like my friends, I was more like those Zulu warriors. I hated the film—I wanted to denounce it there and then—but I kept my mouth shut while my friends probably absorbed the message that they were God's chosen race.

The lessons I was learning from my British education were slowly undermining my confidence in my identity as an African. In the cultural battle for my heart and mind, the odds were stacked against me. I felt like a fourteen-year-old Zulu warrior standing before a swarm of red-uniformed officers; I swallowed my pride and meekly surrendered because I just wanted to be one of "us."

Which was what my father had feared most when he sent his children to England. He tried to tell me that I was not like my friends, insisting that it was pointless to aspire to the same things because "everything had been set up for them." I, he suggested, had another agenda, a different purpose and a higher destiny.

He tried his best to ensure that our education did not alienate us from Africa. At first, he imagined that we would attend school in England but spend our holidays in Nigeria. The cost and logistical headache of flying us all back and forth three times a year made it impossible, however. When we left for England, my mother was already pregnant with my youngest brother, and my twin sisters, Zina and Noo, were two years old. She wanted to be close to all her children, so my father bought a small house just outside London where we could stay during the shorter school holidays. We were supposed to return home for the longer, summer holidays, to spend at least three months a year in Nigeria. But the notion of buying eight return tickets made the trip as much a financial consideration as a cultural one. My father still managed to make sure that I returned home at least once a year for the next ten years, keeping the African flag flying, insisting that Africa was home.

But since my father placed himself and Africa between my determination to be one of "us," it was probably inevitable that Africa and my father would become one and the same thing in my mind. When I chose to reject my African identity, I was only rebelling against my father.

The irony was that it was my mother who made sure that I never severed the most potent, and perhaps most important, link to my culture. The fact that I can still speak Khana is entirely due to her. She was the one with whom I always spoke, and still speak, the language. I hardly ever spoke Khana to my father, always English. I particularly remember how awkward it felt when he deliberately spoke Khana to me: he had just formed MOSOP and was becoming conscious of the political importance of language in our struggle for cultural survival. I understood what he was trying to do, but it didn't feel right. It was far too late to change the habit of a lifetime, so I replied, equally deliberately, in English.

English was my father's gift; Khana is my mother tongue.

▼

In the grand plan that my father had mapped out, I was supposed to attend Eton or Harrow before going on to Oxford or

Cambridge to study law. He wanted the very best classical English education for his first son. I never got close to his ambitions for me. At Tonbridge School, a school established in the sixteenth century for the children of wealthy merchants who had made good on the fur trade in Russia, I excelled at sport, coasted through five years of an expensive education and did just enough to get into London University, where I took a first-class degree in beer and drank some history.

After my first year at Tonbridge, my father called me into his study one day and gave me a book—*Nigger at Eton*—to read. He was concerned that all my cultural references were becoming Anglocentric, and he prescribed his favourite remedy—a book. He was always giving us books to read during the holidays. He hated the thought of his children watching television or lazing around when they could be reading a good book instead. "At your age I had read *Anna Karenina*," he once barked at me. I stared at him blankly, wondering who the hell Anna Karenina was and why, if she was so good, I had never heard of her. He decided to put me on a crash diet of literature. I ploughed through the English classics on sufferance. But I read *Nigger at Eton* in one sitting.

It isn't a classic by any stretch of the imagination. It is a memoir of an African's experience at Eton College, and it was a minor *cause célèbre* when it was published in 1972. The author, Dillibe Onyeama, the son of a senior and internationally respected Nigerian judge, was one of the first Africans to attend the school. And the experience destroyed him. *Nigger at Eton* graphically described the racism Onyeama experienced there. Yet much of what he writes about didn't actually shock me—I'd experienced some of the racist incidents he described at schools in Nigeria as well as in England. But I had refused to let racism upset me—not consciously anyway.

Onyeama chose to confront the discrimination he faced, and publicly too. He never stood a chance against the passions he unleashed. If Eton scarred Onyeama, the reaction to his book broke his spirit, leading him to write a ridiculous book—*John Bull's Nigger*—in which he quoted and endorsed Charles Carrol's view that "the Negro is a beast, but created with articulate speech, and hands, that he may be of service to his master—the White man."

Onyeama was, as James Baldwin once described himself, "as isolated from Negroes as I was from whites, which is what happens when a Negro begins at bottom, to believe what white people say about him. . . ." *John Bull's Nigger* and, to a lesser extent, *Nigger at Eton* are classic examples of what happens when someone is trapped in his own skin, unable to make sense of the dilemmas and contradictions of a bicultural upbringing.

My father gave me Onyeama's book to serve as a warning of what could happen to me if I tried to deny my culture. But at fourteen I had already slipped past his cultural gate. I was already living a double life, negotiating between two identities: at school I saw myself as English, but at home I was African. My English friends rarely met or knew my African alter ego, and my parents barely knew about my other life as an English schoolboy. I was so good at keeping my two identities separate, in fact, that when my father was executed, some of my English friends who had "known" me for years were surprised to find that I had grown up in such a political home. They had assumed I was just another child of those wealthy Nigerians who were fond of educating their kids at private schools in England.

It wasn't until much later, when I became a father, that I began to understand why my father had been so anxious about my identity. He tried to encourage me, and when that didn't work, he tried to force the issue. In the end, you can only give your children so much and hope, pray, that they will eventually understand the importance of the values you are trying to sell them because there always comes a time, usually a critical time, when they have to decide which is their true identity.

6

The Shadow of a Saint

▼

The other side of Saro-Wiwa is an epitome of evil.
—NIGERIAN GOVERNMENT PUBLICATION, 1995

Y father liked a good argument. He was always in court, recovering bad debts, chasing his creditors or trying to force someone or some company to honour a contract or an agreement. When he wasn't in court, he was hounding the marketing departments of companies. If he wasn't satisfied with a product, he would fire off a letter of complaint, exercising his statutory rights. He was particularly rough on airlines, especially if he suspected he had been maltreated because of his colour. He had a long-running feud with British immigration after he was once strip-searched at Heathrow. He was incensed that a man of his stature could be subjected to such an indignity, especially as the British Council had invited him to the country in the first place.

He kept his lawyers busy, but he saved his best arguments for his newspaper column in the Lagos *Sunday Times*. He was born to be a satirist. The character of the man shone through in a column that took on sacred cows in a humorous, self-deprecating but polemical style that showed off his literary credentials and classical erudition.

The column was axed after its first year. Although no explanation was given, it was clear that the powers that be were uncomfortable with its controversial and irreverent tone.

They should have known better. Although the editorial board of the government-owned *Sunday Times* knew the cut of his jib, they thought they could control and co-opt Ken Saro-Wiwa into the system. His first column should have warned them that the man had not mellowed.

"Don't get scared," he began ominously, "The title only means 'like cures like'. . . . If you wake up on a Sunday morning feeling groggy after a hard-drinking Saturday night, cure your headache by having more drinks. In other words, to cure drunkenness, get drunk the morning after. Which is what I am doing. Since I decided to be a full-time writer, or something near it, I have come close, many a time, to putting my pen on the table like a tried warrior hanging up his sword. But each time I try to do so, I realize that the only way to cure my weariness of writing is to write. So, here we go again, long after I thought I was done with newspaper columns. . . ."

"Writing 'Similia' has been quite a revelation," he wrote towards the end of its first and only year. "It has taught me many things I did not know about myself. Reacting to this column, and the book *On a Darkling Plain*, readers have called me such names as 'problematic Nigerian', 'coward', 'Igbophobist', 'Igbo-hater', 'Yorubaphobist', 'fool', 'tribal irredentist' and some have condemned my 'misplaced aggression'. On the other hand, there are those who have styled me 'bold', 'patriotic' and 'witty'. Such contradictory views must have a humbling effect on a writer."

After yet another one of his columns had sparked more controversy, my father wrote that he "took stock of all I have written in the past five years or so; the ideas I have challenged, the actions I have castigated, the men and women I have lambasted on television, in the newspapers and in books." He took stock and came to the "unhappy conclusion that if truly the word 'opponent' does not exist in Nigerian languages and the only synonym for it is 'enemy', then certainly I have had it. So, then, I questioned myself, should I stop? Stop what? Creating enemies for myself, of course."

When those enemies finally found a pretext to silence him, they tried to paint my father as an egocentric man who had tried to compensate for his lack of inches with a vaulting, Napoleonic ambition. In *The Ogoni Question in Nigeria: The Reality of the Situation*, an unintentionally entertaining pamphlet that the Abacha propaganda machine circulated to justify my father's execution, he was described as a "tyrant," but even the anonymous author had to concede that in "spite of his midget stature," Ken Saro-Wiwa had an "irresistible" personality.

People are always surprised to discover that he was only five-foot-one. "Oh, but he seems so much bigger on television," they say. Or, "I imagined he was much bigger than that." It is almost incongruous to think that a man with such a big voice, such a large personality, could be so short.

I don't know how much his size affected him, or if it played a role in shaping his character, but I remember his reaction when his friends teased him about it during his fiftieth birthday at a public hall in Lagos. Typically, he had chosen to use the occasion to launch the seven books he had written that year, as well as to make a political speech. Some of his best friends and school chums were in the audience that day, and one of my father's oldest friends, Prof. Theo Vincent, made some introductory remarks. "The thing I remember about Saro," Professor Vincent said, reminiscing about their school days in Umuahia, "was that he was always going round saying, 'What's height got to do with it?'"

My father's friends were rolling in the aisles. I glanced along the front row to where he was sitting. He was grinning sheepishly.

When he mounted the podium he said, "Don't worry if you can't see me, as long as you can hear me."

He could make light of his size by then because what he lacked in inches he had made up for in his achievements, as Vincent went on to point out. But height, or the lack of it, was not what fuelled my father.

In *On a Darkling Plain*, he reveals that his obsession with the Ogoni struggle was born as a schoolboy in Umuahia. In 1957 there were elections to the Eastern region's House of Assembly and the Ogoni, as was the wont of the minorities in the area, voted against the ruling party of the majority Igbos.

> We were playing a match that afternoon and everybody was on the field cheering teams. We repaired to the dining hall as dinner time drew near. . . . As I drew nearer the hall, all the cooks and stewards, who in normal circumstances were quite friendly with me, began to molest me.
>
> "You, Wiwa, you are an Ogoni boy, not so?"
>
> I said I was.
>
> "And your people, they no like NCNC [the ruling party]."
>
> I was not yet sixteen.
>
> "And you be government scholar too."
>
> As I had won my scholarship on merit, I did not see what being an Ogoni and the Ogoni not liking the NCNC had to do with it.
>
> "Na stupid people," one of them said. And someone else advised that I should go and warn the Ogoni people. I? Warn the Ogoni people? At 15? And that thing on stupidity stung me. I was not a taciturn student by any measure, but that day I was tongue-tied.

On his way home at the end of term, he was again abused by Igbo who felt insulted that the Ogoni had refused to toe their party line. When he got home, he went to seek his father's advice.

> In the market [where Papa was in charge], I tried to find out from him how many stalls belonged to the Ogoni people. At the police station where we went to play table tennis every afternoon, I asked how many policemen were from Ogoni. It appeared very odd to me that there were hardly any traders and policemen, clerks, and tax collectors [who] were Ogoni. Perhaps Ogoni people were actually stupid? . . .
>
> The incident in the dining hall at Umuahia made me rather conscious of the problems of the Ogoni people. When I narrated it to my father, he told me to forget it. He counselled that neighbours often had a poor opinion of each other and that words spoken in anger should not be taken to heart.

So my father committed it to his mind instead, and that's how Ken Saro-Wiwa, thirty years later, would have us understand that the seed of rebellion was planted in his fifteen-year-old mind. But his account still begs the question *why*. After all, there were many educated Ogoni like him who hated the injustice of our predicament. What was it in my father's psychological makeup that separated him from the others? What made him determined to dedicate—and eventually give—his life to the prosecution of the Ogoni cause?

Although I did not know it at the time, he actually offered me the answer to that question when I was twenty years old. It was during one of our fireside conversations when I plucked up the courage to raise the issue of his other women. "You know, I once challenged your grandfather about the very same thing," he confessed. His voice trailed off, and he stared into the fire, as if to contemplate the thought that he had visited the sins of his father on his own son. "I didn't think Papa could afford it," he explained.

They eventually patched up their differences. My father's collection of short stories, *A Forest of Flowers*, is dedicated to Papa, and the story "A Legend on the Street" is a prose poem to him.

After my father was killed, my mother told me that Papa's polygamy had so upset him that he once "turned his back when Papa came to visit him at Umuahia."

I suspect that his drive, his desire to be the best student at Umuahia, was fuelled by his desire to best his father. When he went up to the University of Ibadan he decided to call himself Tsaro-Wiwa instead of Wiwa. Since he was the first in the family to attend university, I imagine he was making some kind of statement to himself and to his father.

His struggles with his own father informed and influenced the subtext of our relationship.

One of the few times I ever stood up to him was in Los Angeles in 1982. We were on holiday, travelling around the U.S. My father had decided to take me and Gian on a whirlwind, two-week sightseeing tour of six cities. "I'm training you," he explained one day in Miami, after we protested that we couldn't survive on one meal a day. By the time we got to Los Angeles, we couldn't stand any more of his training regime, and we decided to mutiny. When he gave us some money and packed us off to Disneyland, we spent the whole day sunbathing and comparing fantasies of how we would kill him. We decided that when we returned to the hotel that evening, we would pointedly watch television instead of reading a book as he insisted we do every night.

When the revolutionary moment came, I switched the television on, but Gian got cold feet and carried on reading. I was mortified but kept watching the television. I was wary of the silent, brooding figure lying on the bed behind me, however. "My friend, turn that telly off and read your book," he bellowed. I picked up my book, flung it down in front of him and stormed off. I barricaded myself in the bathroom. And waited. And waited. After a few minutes I heard my father gently encouraging, then praising, Gian for reciting the poem he had made us memorize when we began the holiday:

The heights by great men reached and kept
Were not attained by sudden flight,
But they, while their companions slept,
Were toiling upward in the night

When I couldn't stand the shame any longer, I crept out of the bathroom. "Come here," my father barked at me. "Kneel down," he growled. I knelt at the foot of the bed and he tossed me a copy of the Bible. "Where in the Holy Bible," he said, pointing to the Gideon with his chin, "does it say you should disobey your father?" I thumbed the Bible half-heartedly. He repeated the question. Twice. I burst into tears. "Aw, take it like a man," he griped. That night, I went to sleep convinced I was going to kill him before the holiday ended.

The next day, he was all smiles. I was suspicious at first, but when he treated us to hamburgers for lunch, everything was forgiven. As we walked around the city centre after lunch, Gian and I were following a few steps behind my father, taking it in turns to re-enact and exorcise the previous night's drama. "Where in the Holy Bible does it say you should disobey your father?" we bellowed, mimicking his heavy African accent and repeating the question louder and more boldly as he walked ahead in silence. As we passed a window, I saw his face reflected in the glass. He was grinning.

Although I was relieved, I was also baffled. It was only much later, when I was in Johannesburg two years after his death, that I finally understood why he was smiling that day in Los Angeles.

I was hosting a round table of Nigerian pro-democracy activists in exile. Someone suggested that Ken Saro-Wiwa had been wrong to insist on non-violence as the best way to confront a vicious military regime. Most of the participants were adamant that pacifism was futile in the Nigerian context, that Abacha had given my father an emphatic answer to the efficacy of non-violence.

One of the exiles disagreed. "Ken Saro-Wiwa came to lecture at our university once," he recalled, "and we put this very same question to him. And Ken replied that it was just like challenging your father. Your father is too strong, so you have to outwit him with your brains."

7

Ken Saro-Wiwa's House

▼

We disliked the rigours of existence, the unfulfilled
longings . . . the ignorance of parents . . . in the midst of
the simple beauties of the universe.
—BEN OKRI, *The Famished Road*

My father barges into my room without knocking. I am lying on my bed, reading. He wanders over to my bed with an inane grin on his face. In his hand is a photograph. He offers it to me. Snatching it from him, I find myself staring at a grainy black-and-white picture of a young boy. I have no idea who the boy is, and I hand the picture back with a look that suggests I don't know what I am looking at and I don't really care. My father senses my hostility, takes the picture and leaves. He pauses at the door, smiles lovingly, almost wistfully, at the picture, then looks back at me. He purses his lips, shrugs and walks out, closing the door behind him.

The problem with fathers is that by the time you finally understand them, it is too late. As Mark Twain noted, when you're fourteen your father is the most ignorant man you know.

By the time you're twenty-one you're surprised at how much the old man has learned in seven years.

I was exactly fourteen when my father barged into my room with that picture of himself as a little boy. I would give anything now to hear him tell me the stories behind the picture, but we never established the kind of connections that fathers and sons are supposed to make. If I could live my life again, I would probably start at that moment when my father first invaded my privacy. When he handed me the picture. And I would smile, turn to him and say, "Jeje, tell me everything. Tell me everything I need to know about you so that in about seven years from now I will understand when . . ."

If only. If we could only see forwards while looking back, see the future in our past, then life would be so much simpler.

▼

I would love to know what was on my father's mind when he named my youngest brother Tedum Tambari. Loosely translated it means "the tree of life, the one sent to do God's work." I don't know what sort of expectations my father had of Tedum, but he turned out to be the kind of son he had always wanted.

I didn't take much notice of Tedum at first. He ate. He slept. He cried. But mostly he ate. He had an uncanny knack of knowing when it was time to eat. You would just be settling down for supper, taking advantage of a moment's peace around the house while the baby slept, and he would start crying. The little man, as I later came to call him, loved his food. He especially loved African food, which was unusual for someone who was born and brought up in England. Tedum was proof that Africa is in the blood, because he loved going back to Nigeria. While the rest of his brothers and sisters were barricading themselves in air-conditioned rooms, Tedum was outside, soaking up the sun, feeling right at home.

Everyone, especially my mother, loved my little brother. Nene needed something to hold on to because when we moved to England, she had to raise five kids on her own while adjusting to life in a foreign country and squeezing in a degree in her spare time.

The first time I realized she was unhappy was when I walked into the bathroom one day and almost choked on the pungent mix of tobacco and air freshener in the room. She hardly touched a drink, let alone cigarettes. Although she tried to conceal it from us, we all knew. But it was only when she started complaining about Mrs. Jukwey that I realized why my mother had started smoking.

It wasn't the first time my father had strayed. Years later, Nene would tell me that friends had often warned her. But she was prepared to put up with his infidelities as long as he remained faithful to the family.

I'd always been aware that my parents fought over his "other women." I must have been about four years old when Nene came back from boarding school and I heard my parents arguing. I was listening from my bedroom when my mother suddenly burst in. "Junior," she rasped, her chest heaving with rage, "has someone been in this house while I was away?" He often had women over in the evenings, especially when Nene was away at school, but as she stood in the doorway, I had a feeling my answer might have serious repercussions.

I told her I hadn't seen anyone in the house.

She asked me if I was sure, repeating the question slowly and deliberately. I was gripped by a kind of terror I had never felt before. I didn't want to lie to her, but I also wanted to protect my father. More than anything, I wanted to keep the peace. I imagined that a no would somehow diffuse the tension. My mother stormed out and I lay on my bed, tormented by guilt as my parents carried on fighting.

That was where I would always stand: between my parents, in the middle, mediating, trying to keep the peace. Although I felt it was my job to protect my mother from my father, I never truly offered her much protection from him. I never dared challenge my father, because each time I announced that I was ready to disown him, Nene would beg me to reconsider. "He loves you, you know," she would say, warning me never to turn my back on him.

Tedum was the only one who stood up to him.

My little brother was ten years younger than me, and I only began to take an interest in him when he started pestering me to play football and cricket. We became very close, although he was close to all his brothers and sisters. He was my parents' favourite, especially after he fulfilled my father's ambition to send a son to Eton College.

The little man grew about five inches in his first year at Eton. I am glad my father chose a wife who was taller than him, since no man is shorter than his mother. I am an impressive five-foot-seven. My younger brother Gian outdid me, reaching the giddy heights of five-foot-ten. My sisters showed just enough deference to their oldest brother, but Tedum had no such respect. I remember the cheeky little grin on his face when we met up at my London flat one December morning. I was taking him to his first football match that day, and when I opened the door to my flat, we both immediately realized that he was a couple of inches taller than I was. He was fourteen years old.

The next time I saw him was at Christmas, when I went down to our home outside London. Tedum was in festive spirits, especially after he thrashed me at table football for the first time. I took it on the chin, smiling ruefully. I was proud of him. I sensed that the dynamics of our relationship were changing. On New Year's Eve, I went back to my flat. Tedum saw me out of the house. As he closed the door, I vividly remember the smug grin and knowing look on his face. It was the last time I ever saw the little man.

A month later, I caught a cold that lasted for two months. Nene kept calling to check up on me. I'd been having dizzy spells and occasional blackouts, and she was worried about my health. I assured her that it was only a cold, that there was nothing to worry about. She begged me to come home, but I told her I was happier staying at my flat. What I didn't tell her was that I'd started seeing Olivia Burnett. I'd first set eyes on her six years earlier, in my first year at university, and I wasn't about to let a persistent cold spoil the moment, especially as Olivia was doing such a fine job of looking after me. But then I gave her the bug too. We went to see a doctor, and he diagnosed tonsillitis, which was odd considering Olivia had had her tonsils removed. We shrugged and took the prescribed dose of antibiotics anyway.

I didn't want to worry Nene, because she was preparing to visit Nigeria for the first time since her father died eight years earlier. I promised her I would look in on the house while she was away. After she left, I went to house-sit and nurse myself through an illness that was still defying medical opinion and antibiotics.

On March 15, the ides of March, I woke up feeling much more like my old self. It was a sunny day, the first day of spring, and the daffodils were out. I remember every detail of that day. I rang Olivia in the morning and told her that I felt strong enough to come back up to London. We arranged to meet at my flat later that evening. I still felt a little feverish but I had some catching up to do at college. I was coming to the end of my media course at journalism school. I remember sitting on a lawn at college, laughing and joking with my friends that afternoon. At about 4 p.m. there was a chill in the air. I went inside, pottered around for a couple of hours, then left for my flat. I spent some time catching up with my flatmate, Mike Mullarkey. We talked about the usual things: rugby, girls. After about twenty minutes, the doorbell rang. It was Olivia. A few minutes after she arrived, the phone rang. Mike took the call.

"Someone wants to speak to Mr. Saro-Wiwa," he said, announcing my name with exaggerated formality as he handed the phone to me.

"Hello? Mr. Saro-Wiwa?"

"Yes?" I answered.

"It's Mr. Wright here."

My mind went blank.

"I'm Tedum's housemaster at Eton," the voice explained. "I've, err, got some very bad news, I'm afraid."

What had Tedum done? Has he been expelled? Smoking? Drugs?

"I'm afraid Tedum is dead," he said, interrupting my train of thought.

"What?" I gasped.

"Tedum was playing the field game," Mr. Wright began to explain. "He played really well, as usual." I just kept shaking my head, saying no, no, no. I wanted to drop the phone. "At the end of the game, Tedum said he felt a swelling in his left ankle," Mr. Wright continued, determined to provide me with all the facts. "He went to sit down by a tree. He said he felt dizzy and thirsty. A friend ran to get him some water. By the time his friend came back, Tedum was lying on the ground unconscious. An ambulance arrived on the scene within minutes. The paramedics spent forty-five minutes trying to revive him. I'm sorry."

I hung up and collapsed on the floor. I was absolutely devastated, not just because my little brother was dead but because I knew what the last few seconds of Tedum's life would have been like: the familiar light-headed feeling, the sudden tightness in the chest, the vague sense of falling. Losing consciousness is a terrifying experience—if you're lucky enough to come round again. I had always regained consciousness. Tedum didn't have such luck. He was fourteen years old, with so much potential, so much to live for, and he was dead. I broke down, overcome as much by grief as by an overwhelming sense of guilt. Olivia was trying to comfort me.

"Tedum is dead," I kept repeating to her, as if trying to convince myself. One minute he had been full of life and now he was dead, at fourteen, of a heart attack. It just didn't add up. It was impossible. Olivia never got to meet Tedum, but she knew how much he meant to me. She later said that when she first heard my reaction to the call, she imagined it was Nene.

I was desperately trying to gather my thoughts when the phone rang again. Olivia answered and handed the phone to me. It was Mr. Wright. "I just wanted to give you some more details, Ken. I've spoken to your parents in Nigeria and they are on their way. Tedum's body is in the mortuary but we will wait for your father to arrive before we do anything else. I'm sorry, Ken. Good night."

I grabbed a pack of cigarettes and went for a walk, taking the same route Tedum and I had walked to watch his first football match just three months earlier. I couldn't believe that the strapping, gawky kid who was so looking forward to his first match was now lying in a mortuary. I sat on the pavement on the corner of Fulham Road. All kinds of thoughts were swimming around my mind. Nene . . . I couldn't believe the timing. I felt so desperately sorry for her; I felt impotent, unable to help her once again. She was so far away from the little boy she had pinned so much hope on. My sisters . . . Christ, I thought. I hadn't even spoken to them. I rushed back to my flat and dialled a Brighton number.

Noo was the first to come to the phone. Then Zina. Neither of them had been told. My father had instructed their teachers not to tell them until he arrived in England. He had wanted to break the news to them himself. The next day, Tedum's death was reported in the papers: "The son of a wealthy Nigerian businessman died tragically at Eton College yesterday." I can't imagine how my sisters would have felt it they had found out from the newspaper. My father was just too far away to understand or appreciate some things.

I went home the next day. He had arrived from Nigeria but was alone in the house. "Where's Nene?" I barked at him. He told me she was arriving later. I was incensed that they hadn't flown together. He glared at me as if to suggest that it was none of my business. An uneasy silence fell over the house and it didn't break until three days later, when we were heading home from the mortuary after seeing Tedum's body. My father was driving and I was in the passenger seat; my mother and my sisters were in the back. The atmosphere was unbearable: there was grief, resentment and anger in the air. When my father wondered aloud whether the campaign against Shell might not have had something to do with Tedum's death, my sisters and I exploded in unison. We told him to keep his politics out of Tedum's death. Although his concern was at the forefront of our minds as well, we didn't want him to bring it up. We knew the risks he was taking in Nigeria, but the thought that his political enemies would target his children was too much to take, especially at that particular moment. "I'm just trying to protect the rest of you," he protested, but we ganged up on him again. He was surprised by the strength of feeling in the ranks. He fell silent, stuffed his pipe in his mouth and started puffing away, popping his lips furiously.

Looking back on it, I feel sorry for him. It was as if his children were telling him that he had forfeited his right to be their father. We had willingly given up our father to his political commitment, but we were desperately trying to resist the notion that his politics might invade, jeopardize and compromise our privacy—and even our lives.

After the funeral, we went back to Eton to plant a tree near the spot where Tedum had died. We walked back to the car, my father leading the way, his family trailing behind him. He had completely withdrawn from the process by then, and he was conscious that I disapproved. He was probably desperate to go back to Nigeria; in England, he was a stranger in his own house, and he was being made to feel guilty about his shortcomings as the head of his family. In Nigeria, on the other hand, he was being hailed as the father of his people. He could do no wrong there.

He looked a mess as he trudged back to the car through the muddy field. He was wearing a long, shabby brown fur coat, the hem of which almost touched the wet grass. As he walked along he suddenly kicked the air in frustration. I don't know why but I just had this feeling that he only did it for my benefit, to show me that he did care.

It took me a long time to reconcile myself to the guilt I felt that Tedum had died instead of me. Tests later showed that I had a milder form of the congenital disease that killed him. I had an operation that summer, but I couldn't sleep for months after Tedum died. Nene spooked me when she told me that she had had a vivid dream before she travelled to Nigeria. She dreamt that one of our ancestors came to take me away, but she had pleaded so hard for me that they took Tedum instead. I kept wondering about my bizarre cold that winter. Tedum's autopsy said he died of heart failure, but I knew there was much more to it than that. I became convinced that Tedum died for me.

On the night before Tedum's funeral, Zina, Noo and I had sat in his bedroom talking about our little brother. Noo recalled how Tedum had once made my father cry.

"How did he do that?!" I exclaimed.

"Oh, he just confronted him about Nene, and Jeje broke down."

I was astonished. My little brother had done what I should have been doing all along—protecting Nene from my father. I was proud of the little man—and embarrassed for myself. The next day, as I scattered earth over Tedum's coffin, I paused and made a silent promise to the little man.

In many, many ways, Tedum's death was the turning point in my life. Trying to make sense of it, I began to look into the ways Africans deal with death, and I came to understand that my little brother was a spirit child. A spirit child is born and reborn many times, moving between the spirit world and the real world. When a spirit child is recalled, he has to go, and thus spirit children often die in childbirth or at a young age. Ben Okri's wonderful evocation of childhood, *The Famished Road*, tells the story of Azaro—Lazarus—a spirit child who refuses to return to the spirit world when his time is up.

While I had seen myself as Tedum's substitute father and mentor, I came to appreciate that he had actually been my guiding angel, a spirit child, the son that shone over my father's house. He kept the house warm, comforting my mother until his time was up. Tedum Tambari, the tree of life, the one sent to do God's work, left us just as storm clouds gathered over Ken Saro-Wiwa's house.

8

1993

▼

And we are here as on a darkling plain
Swept with confused alarms of struggle and flight.
—MATTHEW ARNOLD, "Dover Beach"

My father once told me that he didn't like years that ended with an odd number. Which surprised me, because I never imagined that he had a superstitious bone in his body. He was a self-made man who liked to present himself as an intellectual man of action. As far as he was concerned, luck had nothing to do with anything. You made your own luck, and the harder you worked the easier it was to shape your destiny.

He told me about his preferences for even-numbered years in 1990—just as he was starting MOSOP. I think he was trying to bless the ship with luck because he knew that MOSOP would sail some pretty choppy waters. I would love to know how he felt on December 31, 1992, because 1993 turned out to be his worst nightmare of an odd-numbered year.

Ironically, the year began with what he regarded as the greatest achievement of his life: when 300,000 Ogoni came out to demonstrate their support for MOSOP.

The road to the January protest march was a long one for a people who had been cowed by years of discrimination, but the Ogoni made the trek in less than three years.

MOSOP had been informally established during a meeting at the Ogoni home of Chief Edward Kobani in 1990. A year later, on August 26, 1991, my father wrote the Ogoni bill of rights and persuaded the chiefs and elders to sign and adopt it as the sacred text of the struggle.

The document lists, in a twenty-point memorandum, the rights of our people, pointing out, among other things, the Ogoni's enormous financial contribution to the Nigerian nation over thirty years, and that:

> . . . neglectful environmental pollution laws and sub-standard inspection techniques of the Federal authorities have led to the complete degradation of the Ogoni environment, turning our homeland into an ecological disaster.
>
> . . . the Ogoni people wish to manage their own affairs . . . [and] the Ogoni people be granted POLITICAL AUTONOMY to participate in the affairs of the Republic as a distinct and separate unit by whatever name called, provided that this autonomy guarantees the following:
>
> a) Political control of Ogoni affairs by Ogoni people.
> b) The right to the control and use of a fair proportion of Ogoni economic resources for Ogoni development.
> c) Adequate and direct representation as of right in all Nigerian national institutions.

d) The use and development of Ogoni languages in Ogoni territory.
e) The full development of Ogoni culture.
f) The right to religious freedom.
g) The right to protect the Ogoni environment and ecology from further degradation.

The bill of rights concluded by noting, "We demand these rights as equal members of the Nigerian Federation who contribute and have contributed to the growth of the Federation and have a right to expect full returns from that Federation." There were thirty signatories from Babbe, Gokana, Tai, Nyo-Khana and Ken-Khana—five of the six kingdoms of Ogoni. Eleme, the sixth kingdom, did not sign.

The bill of rights was presented to the Nigerian military government, then led by General Ibrahim Babangida, which ignored it. A year later, an appeal to the international community was added to the bill. That eight-point addendum noted that "without the intervention of the international community, the government of the Federal Republic of Nigeria and the ethnic majority will continue these noxious policies until the Ogoni people are obliterated from the face of the earth."

My father, as MOSOP's publicity chief, was tasked with trying to attract the attention of international NGOs and the international media to the struggle. But despite his successes abroad, by the end of 1992 it was clear that the Ogoni people had not quite registered as anything more than a blip on the radar screen of Shell and the Nigerian military. Something dramatic was needed to draw their attention.

Up until then, MOSOP had been the business of community elders and leaders, but in November 1992 my father saw that there were community members who "had nothing to lose" by standing up to the Nigerian military and Shell, and were prepared to prosecute the cause to the bitter end. That month he was touring Ogoni, trying to advance a motion calling upon "Shell, Chevron and the Nigerian National Petroleum Corporation (NNPC), the three oil companies operating in Ogoni, to pay damages of $4 billion for destroying the environment, $6 billion in unpaid rents and royalties, and all within thirty days or it would be assumed that they had decided to quit the land." The resolution was carried in all six kingdoms, but it was on that tour that my father found, as he writes in *A Month and a Day*, "that there was a large number of youth angry with a society that had cheated them and who were therefore eager to hear us, to learn."

Excited by the fervour among the young people, my father spent the week after the tour planning a massive protest march for January 4, 1993. On December 3, 1992, a demand notice was sent to the three oil companies. After submitting the notice, my father travelled to London, where he tried to convince several NGOs and the media to attend the march.

January 4 had been specifically chosen because that day had already been earmarked as the start of the United Nations International Year for the World's Indigenous Populations. It was also the day after General Babangida had promised to hand over power to a civilian government. The protest march was to send a message to the incoming administration, but in the end Babangida reneged on his promise.

My father spent the whole night of January 3 working on his speech and editing the other speeches that were to be read the following day. "The speeches," he recalled, "were ready by four that morning and I retired to bed quite exhausted. But by six o'clock I was up again. I had no appetite for breakfast and tended to be at the very short end of a fuse, being brusque with all those who were unfortunate enough to be around me."

Arriving in Bori, at the playground of the Birabi Memorial School, where the main rally was to take place, my father found that "the cream of Ogoni society was present and the atmosphere was euphoric. . . . Drummers thumped away and dance troupes performed skilfully." The speeches were read out. When it was his turn to speak, my father took the stage.

"From a vantage point above everyone, I saw a new profile of the Ogoni people," he recalled, "a profile I had not identified. I saw eagerness, determination and joy on the young faces that looked up to the men on the rostrum. And I knew that a new seed had germinated and everything would have to be done to water, nurture, grow and harvest it. Ogoni would surely not be the same again. And I also felt that I must not let them down ever, or they would be right to lynch me!"

He read his speech, reminding the assembled crowd of the main points of the bill of rights, and congratulated the Ogoni people for taking "upon themselves the historic responsibility for saving themselves, their land and their environment." Then, departing from the prepared text, he declared Shell *persona non grata*, and vowed that the company would have to kill off all Ogoni men, women and children before it could take any more oil from Ogoni.

"Memories of the march were to linger in my mind for a long time," he later wrote. "Almost two-thirds of the Ogoni population had marched peacefully. Those who could not go to the central venues had marched in their village squares. It was a great dance of the anger of the people. Not a stone was thrown and no one was hurt."

My father and the people had laid down the gauntlet. The scene was set for a confrontation between one man and his people on one side and a brutal military regime and a giant multinational oil company on the other.

The stage was set for a struggle that would claim thousands of lives.

After Shell was declared *persona non grata*, my father travelled to Europe, where he appeared on CNN and in *Time*. Shell executives meeting at The Hague in Holland voiced their concerns that the company's reputation was being tarnished in the media. An internal memo following that meeting in February 1993 ordered "SPDC and SIPC PA [public affairs] department to keep each other more closely informed to ensure that movements of key players—what they say and to whom—[are] more effectively monitored to avoid unpleasant surprises and adversely affect the reputation of the Group as a whole."

The events between January 1993 and May 1994 are the story of an unfurling tragedy as divisions among the Ogoni were deepened by the heavy-handed and naked aggression of the military government. In the stand off, 99 per cent of the victims were Ogoni. Ogoni villages were flattened, Ogoni men were killed and detained, Ogoni women *and* children raped by soldiers who were supposed to be keeping the peace so that Shell could resume its operations in the community. But there is more to the Ogoni story. It is also a saga of remarkable grace under pressure, of devastating betrayals, of cowardice and courage in the face of calculated aggression. Brother was set against brother, community against community, as the authorities and the oil companies exploited the poverty in our region. Until you understand what poverty can do to the soul, it is hard to comprehend what happened in Ogoni between 1993 and 1994. Poverty can, at its best, be the foundation of generosity and a devotion to an idea that is inspiring. But, at its worst, it can corrupt minds, harden hearts and deaden the appetite for the truth.

A Month and a Day: A Detention Diary, published posthumously, is my father's recollection of the events between January 4, 1993, and May 21, 1994, when he was arrested for the final time. In it he reflects that after the protest march of January 4, 1993, he "began to think my life was seriously at risk. I was, however, ready for such a development, and wrote my Will and informed my family that they should prepare for the worst." In fact, he did not warn me in 1993, and his will was signed more than a year later, on May 20, 1994.

Still, he had good reason to be concerned for his safety: security agents had begun to monitor his movements in Nigeria. That was why he wondered whether there was anything suspicious about Tedum's death. He was never convinced that Tedum died of natural causes, and the Nigerian journalist Chuks Illoegbunam, who knew my father and wrote an excellent obituary in *The Guardian*, noted that "something died" in him after Tedum's death, and he became even more determined to stand up to Shell and the Nigerian military.

After Tedum's funeral my father returned to Nigeria, where he was prevented from addressing a student body on April 3. On April 18, 1993, he was arrested at Port Harcourt airport after returning from Lagos. He was taken to the headquarters of the State Security Service (SSS). Documents and tapes were taken from his office and home, but he was released after eighteen hours of detention. Five days later, he was arrested again. He was questioned until he collapsed from exhaustion, when he was released and ordered not to leave Port Harcourt.

On April 30, Shell decided to resume work in Ogoni after consulting what it claimed were Ogoni leaders and representatives of the communities. The company requested security protection from a Nigerian military unit while it buried part of the major pipeline ferrying oil to the terminal at Bonny Island. When our people arrived to demonstrate against the destruction of their farms for the pipeline construction, soldiers opened fire on what Shell later described as "hostile villagers." Protests continued for a number of days, until the first Ogoni was shot in the back and killed.

Meanwhile, the military government promulgated the Treason and Treasonable Felony Decree, which allowed for the death penalty for anyone who "conspires with himself" to "utter" the words "ethnic autonomy" or plans secession or seeks to alter the boundaries of any local government or state previously decreed by the military authorities. By "coincidence,"

Shell also released a briefing note accusing my father of targeting the multinational "in his efforts to raise the international profile of his concerns for the Ogoni people and to meet his objective of their political self-determination."

In June, the country was preparing for elections to return its first civilian government in ten years. The elections were to be the culmination of a long, drawn-out, four-year transition to democracy that eventually cost the country $12 billion. The result of the interminable consultations, electoral commissions and constitutional debates was a two-party political system within a federal structure. The country's military dictator, General Ibrahim Babangida, had chosen the two parties—one a little to the left and another a little to the right—that were to contest power. Everyone was gearing up for the elections. Everyone except my father.

He floated the idea that since MOSOP was a grass-roots, non-aligned movement, it should steer clear of the elections. He also moved that MOSOP should go even further and boycott the elections, since the constitution did not guarantee protection for minority rights. Some members of the organization's steering committee disagreed, arguing that MOSOP would be better served by having a political interest in the new dispensation.

The debate over MOSOP's role in the elections widened the divisions in the organization's leadership and split the movement into two factions: a radical, militant wing and a conservative, pro-government faction. The conservative element was incensed that my father had seemingly unilaterally declared that MOSOP should not be involved in the elections. A meeting of the steering committee was called and the motion put to a vote. MOSOP voted 11–6 in favour of a boycott. The elders on the steering committee were furious. Dr. Garrick Leton and Chief Edward Kobani, president and vice-president, resigned in protest.

Meanwhile, some of the conservative members of MOSOP joined the political parties contesting the elections, and my father argued that they were trying to deliver the Ogoni vote to their respective parties. He dismissed the conservatives as "gerontocrats," accusing them of hijacking the aspirations of the collective community to further their individual political ambitions. They were, he declared, "quite content to take the crumbs of today in preference for the riches of tomorrow. They collaborate with our enemies in return for personal advantages."

In the debate, my father had the firm support of Ogoni youth. "I find myself in alliance with the youths who have chains to lose," he said, "and the old men cannot accommodate that." The conservative elders never forgave my father for undermining their authority in Ogoni, the differences of opinion gave the military an opportunity to exploit the divisions.

During the elections, my father was arrested for "election-day offences" and charged with treason. He was detained for a month and a day. He was alleged to have inspired a gang of youths who had attacked the homes of conservative Ogoni in the lead-up to the elections. He was released following a campaign in the British media, but his detention was a portent of things to come.

When early returns indicated that Chief Moshood Abiola, a billionaire Yoruba businessman, would emerge as Nigeria's new president, General Babangida cracked under pressure from Abiola's opponents and annulled the elections. The Yoruba were incensed. They complained that their man had been denied after what were regarded as the freest and fairest elections in Nigeria's tortured experience of democracy. Under pressure from the international community, Babangida relented and installed an interim government. That government lasted for all of four months before its defence minister, General Sani Abacha, seized power in November 1993.

Nigeria has a reputation for being bigger and brasher than every other country in Africa, and it is in keeping with that billing that the country has had more military coups than any other on the continent. And it is a truism that every military dictator is more vicious, more notorious than the last. A new dictator has to establish his authority and notoriety, and he must do so in the only language that dictators understand—repression. It is the iron law and first rule of dictatorship, and no one understood this better than Abacha. When he seized power, Abacha declared war against his opponents, against the people, against civil society. Against everyone. Insecure, paranoid and deeply secretive, Abacha was a Kanuri, a minority ethnic group in northern Nigeria. When he joined the army he was patronized by his peers, who felt that the dim, taciturn and uncharismatic officer did not have the right qualities to progress through the ranks. Abacha narrowly escaped being court-martialled in the early 1970s, when he was stationed in Port Harcourt after the civil war. The story I heard was that he executed a civilian in cold blood at the airport. Army top brass only decided to spare Abacha because they needed to maintain their quota of Kanuri officers in the army.

For much of his early military career, Abacha was a peripheral figure who carried out his duties quietly and efficiently. He acquired a reputation as a ruthless officer who was feared as much for his secrecy as his cunning. All of this made him a valuable officer to have on your side when it came to the machiavellian business of coup plotting. Abacha was involved in every successful coup in Nigeria from 1976. His was the voice that announced the coup that ended the country's second experiment with democracy in 1983, and he was defence minister in the subsequent regime. He sat out his role as trusted and able deputy for ten years, nursing a chip on his shoulder, coveting his leader's job, waiting like Macbeth for his chance. When Babangida decided to annul the 1993 elections, Abacha sensed his time was at hand. He went along with the contraption of the interim government until he couldn't resist the lure of power any longer.

Once Abacha had achieved his ambition, he set about terminating all his rivals, real and imagined. He retired or eliminated all the officers who had underestimated and humiliated him during his silent ascent up the ranks. He drove a coach and horse through the law to eliminate his opponents; serving and retired generals were arrested, tried and sentenced to death for alleged coup plotting. He cast his net wide, trapping newspaper editors and opposition leaders in a phantom coup plot. Chief Abiola, an obvious threat to Abacha as the presumed winner of the 1993 election, was arrested. Abiola's senior wife and most outspoken defender, Kudirat, was gunned down by hired assassins in broad daylight. So was Pa Alfred Rewane, the leader of NADECO, a coalition of democratic groups opposed to military rule. Newspapers were shut down, and scores of journalists detained and harassed; many of Nigeria's leading figures fled into exile. Nobody was safe from Abacha's paranoia. Wole Soyinka escaped only after he was tipped off that Abacha had sent his death squads for him. He was a cliché of a dictator who was even thought to have killed his own son (the rumour was that he was behind the plane crash that killed Ibrahim in 1996). There are also rumours that when the heat was on his regime, he resorted to a Rasputin-like figure, a marabout who encouraged him to perform human sacrifices to ward off the evil spirits trying to remove him from power. I was informed by a very sober civil servant who worked inside Abacha's Cabinet that bodies were found on the grounds of Aso Rock, the presidential residence, a year after Abacha's death.

While Abacha was plotting his *coup d'état* in the summer and autumn of 1993, MOSOP and the Ogoni experienced unprecedented levels of repression. In July, 132 Ogoni men, women and children were attacked as they returned from a fishing expedition in neighbouring Cameroon. Only two Ogoni women survived. Their assailants had used sophisticated weapons and heavy mortar. The authorities blamed the massacre on "ethnic clashes" over access rights to fishing grounds. Over the next five months, hundreds of Ogoni were killed and villages flattened in similar "ethnic clashes." These clashes have never been fully and properly investigated and MOSOP remains adamant that Shell and the Nigerian government were behind the massacres.

As tension escalated in Ogoni, friends begged my father to take time off, travel to Europe and recuperate with his family. He took some persuading, but he eventually came over to England in October.

His passion for his people's struggle was now foremost in his mind, however. When he came to London, we immediately locked horns when I pointedly refused to talk about the struggle. I reminded him that the bills for Tedum's funeral still hadn't been paid, and that his son's grave did not have a headstone. "Why didn't you tell me?" he asked. I shook my head in disbelief.

He stayed long enough to honour our commitment to plant a tree at the spot where Tedum had died. When he got back to Nigeria, he paid a visit to General Abacha to complain about the military's involvement in "ethnic clashes" against our people. Abacha lied that the security forces in Ogoni had fed him exaggerated and misleading reports that MOSOP was plotting armed insurrection. My father briefed him about the struggle and Abacha assured him that he would look into the situation. Before my father left, Abacha asked whether he was interested in becoming oil minister. My father told the general that the Ogoni struggle was about justice for the community, not political appointments for individuals.

My father, the eternal optimist, came away from the meeting in a buoyant mood. Friends warned him about Abacha, but he genuinely felt, or maybe he just hoped, that he had won over the taciturn little general; he declared that Abacha was sympathetic to the Ogoni cause. But the two men might as well have been speaking different languages: what my father didn't know was that Abacha was already planning his coup. While my father left with a positive impression of Abacha, the general quietly marked his cards.

▼

He came over to London again at Christmas. I'd moved in with Olivia Burnett by then, and I invited the family to our place for Christmas Day. It was our first Christmas since Tedum's death, and I hoped it would help to get out of the usual routine at my parents' home. My father turned down my invitation, explaining that he would rather fast for our people, that we had no right to enjoy a meal while our people were suffering. I took the snub as it was intended—as a protest against my apolitical stance—but I felt the family needed to come first.

The next time I saw him was in the New Year. By then my brother Gian, who had suffered a breakdown in Nigeria two years earlier, had returned to England to get treatment after having a relapse and contracting malaria. Gian was in a terrible state. He was wasted from the malaria, and he was severely agitated by his experiences in Nigeria. Arrangements were made for my father to visit Gian's doctor so they could establish the cause of my brother's relapse. I saw Gian on the day of the scheduled appointment. When I asked his doctor how the meeting with my father had gone, the doctor shook his head.

"He never turned up."

"What? What do you mean?" I snapped.

"He didn't make the appointment. We waited for him, but your father never showed up."

When I left the hospital, I was determined to give him a piece of my mind. But when I arrived at home, he wasn't there. My mother was in the kitchen, and when I told her what had happened at the hospital she sighed. A few minutes later, he shuffled wearily into the house. His tie was hanging loosely around his neck, the old brown coat looked shabbier than ever, and he was struggling with a pile of documents. He paused in the doorway when he saw me, smiled nervously, and walked into the sitting room.

"Have you been to see Gian?" I barked at his back, following him into the lounge. He hauled his briefcase onto the dining table, took off his coat and glared at me. I stared him down and he backed off. He sat down and started rifling through the papers on the table. He looked broken, almost pitiful, as he absent-mindedly patted the documents strewn on the table. After a few moments, he glanced up at me plaintively. That look is frozen in my mind. It still haunts me, because I suddenly saw through my father. His hair was matted, there were flecks of grey stubble on his chin, and his eyes looked tired and bloodshot. In that moment, I saw my father for what he was: an old man struggling to meet the incredible personal and political demands on him.

My anger began to dissolve. A little voice was urging me to confront him, but another voice insisted I leave him alone. I hovered between anger and guilt for a few seconds. Then, cursing under my breath, I walked away. He was staring at the wreckage of his life scattered across the dining table as I left. It was the last time I ever saw my father.

That we parted on such a bad note is one of my greatest regrets. But when I stormed out of my house that afternoon in January 1994, we were poles apart. I didn't understand him; I just couldn't see how he could be leading a struggle that he said was for the future, for us, his children, while he neglected those children's immediate needs and well being. That afternoon, I only understood that his youngest son was dead and another was fighting for his life in hospital, and that all he seemed to care about was his political campaign. I saw a pattern developing, and I didn't want to sacrifice my life for his political conscience. So I turned my back on him.

A week later, he went back to Nigeria, leaving the battle on his homefront for another war.

9

The Trials of
Ken Saro-Wiwa

▼

A year has gone by since I was rudely roused from my bed and clamped into detention. Sixty-five days in chains, weeks of starvation, months of mental torture and recently, the rides in a steaming, airless Black Maria to appear before a kangaroo court, dubbed a special military tribunal, where the proceedings leave no doubt that the judgement has been written in advance . . . The men who ordain and supervise this show of shame, this tragic charade, are frightened by the word, the power of ideas, the power of the pen; by the demands of social justice and the rights of man. Nor do they have a sense of history. They are so scared of the power of the word, that they do not read. And that is their funeral.

—KEN SARO-WIWA

When General Abacha came to power in November 1993, he moved quickly to assert his authority. High on his list of priorities was the resolution of the Ogoni crisis. He wanted to send a signal to investors that he was a man with whom they could do business, a man who would protect their investments. Abacha softened up our people by sending a high-powered delegation into the community in early 1994. Once he had assessed the situation, he set up the Rivers State Internal Security (RSIS) task force, which had orders to "re-establish government presence in the area so as to bring to the knowledge of the citizenry that they are still a part and parcel of Nigeria." In April, the RSIS, a combined force of police, army, air force and navy personnel, invaded Ogoni, massacring more than eight hundred men, women and children and destroying six villages. A Catholic nun living in the area wrote that "the military are busy flattening anything left standing in the six villages and are taking up residence there to eat the goats and crops."

Abacha, thinking that Ogoni had been pacified, invited Shell to return. My father pointed out that "if Shell [goes] in, it would further confirm to the world that [it is] stealing the oil with guns, like armed robbers." Shell saw the logic and declined Abacha's invitation.

Enraged by his soldiers' inability to establish authority in Ogoni, Abacha ordered an intensification of repression. In a televised conference the leader of the RSIS, Lieutenant-Colonel Paul Okuntimo, a hard-drinking, Bible-loving psychopath, boasted that he had perfected 221 ways to kill Ogoni, and vowed to "pacify" them and rid the area of the "MOSOP virus." On the twelfth of May, he fired off a memo to Lieutenant Colonel Komo. "Wasting operations during MOSOP and other gatherings making constant military presence justifiable . . . Wasting targets cutting across communities and leadership cadres especially vocal individuals of various groups." He appealed for "regular inputs" to continue his campaign.

While Ogoni villages were being flattened to facilitate Shell's return to the community, the country was gearing up to elect delegates to a National Constitutional Conference (NCC) that was supposed to draft yet another constitution ahead of yet another election. Despite my father's reservations about the process,

MOSOP's steering committee put his name forward to contest the elections to the NCC. On May 19–21, he toured Ogoni, addressing rallies, trying to convince the people of the need to come out and vote for Ogoni representation at the NCC.

On May 21, RSIS troops prevented him from addressing a scheduled rally in the village of Sogho. He turned around without protest and headed for Bori to attend a seminar for delegates and polling officers. The following is my father's recollection of the next few hours:

> On arrival at Bori, I found that the seminar had started when Lieutenant P. C. Nwatu gruffly told me that if the Seminar turned into a rally (how could it?) he would disperse it. I knew my presence at Bori was not welcome and decided to return to Port Harcourt. It was at that point that Ledum Mitee, Deputy President of MOSOP, whom I met at Bori, invited me to drinks at his home in K. Dere. I again solicited the permission of the security agents to go there and, when they gave me their consent, set off in that direction. . . . We drove in a convoy of three cars and had gone past Giokoo when the security agents overtook my car and stopped it. An army car went past our three cars and blocked the road. Troops jumped out of the car and cocked their rifles. The security agents told me they had decided against my going to K. Dere. When I asked why, they explained that it was in my own interest. I only had time to wave goodbye to Ledum Mitee, who had alighted from his car and stood beside my car window. I immediately ordered my chauffeur to turn back and drive off. I drove non-stop to Port Harcourt to the offices of *Sunray* [newspaper],

where I reported all that had happened and did an interview. Thereafter, I tried to contact the Military Administrator, Lieutenant Colonel Dauda Komo, but he was not available. I left the telephone numbers to my residence and office and requested that he please contact me whenever he became available. I did not hear from him even though I waited in my office until 6:00 p.m. that day. At about 5:30 p.m. I received a telephone call from *Sunray* newspaper informing me that there had been trouble at Giokoo and that some prominent Ogoni men may have been murdered. I was shocked, traumatised. I did not even remember to ask for the name of the caller. We decided to go to *Sunray* to get more details of what had happened. The *Sunray* editor said the news had been brought by Mr. Justice Peter Akere, himself an Ogoni. We went to Justice Akere's, but he was not in. Thence we proceeded to the Commissioner of Police's residence. He told us that he did not have detailed information, but was expecting it. We then went to Government House in an effort to see the Military Administrator. He was said to be attending a command performance of a play and was not available. . . . We met a distressed Mrs. Badey [the wife of one of the murdered men] there. We returned to my office, and at about 10 p.m. I repaired home.

Shortly after midnight, armed men broke into my residence and I was taken away at gunpoint. I was driven to the Bori Camp headquarters of the 2nd Amphibious Brigade, beaten, kicked and brutalised and locked up in the mili-

tary guardroom. The next morning, I was put
in legcuffs and driven to Afam [HQ of the
RSIS]. On Monday morning, Lieutenant
Colonel Okuntimo, Commander of the Rivers
State Internal Security Task Force, before
whom I had been led the night of the 21st of
May, arrived, took video and still photographs
of me in leg and handcuffs and returned me to
Bori Camp, where I was asked to make a state-
ment to the Police about the murder of Chief
Edward Kobani, Albert Badey, Chief S.N.
Orage and Chief T.B. Orage.

What happened at Giokoo on the afternoon of May 21,
1994 is lost, probably forever, in the mists of perjured eyewitness
accounts and the failure or unwillingness of the authorities to
carry out a proper and thorough investigation. What is known is
that the Gokhana Council of Chiefs was holding a reception at
Gbenemene Palace for two local men who had been appointed
commissioners with the Rivers State government. Suddenly, an
angry mob descended on the reception. The assembled chiefs
were denounced as "vultures" and sell-outs as the mob invaded
the palace. During a riot that lasted for several hours, Albert
Badey, Edward Kobani, Samuel Orage and Theophilus Orage
were clubbed, hacked and stoned to death. At least one of their
bodies (the prosecution did not clarify how many) was alleged
to have been stuffed into a Volkswagen Beetle and set alight.

The following day, Lieutenant Colonel Komo called the
press conference at which he blamed MOSOP for the murders.
The baby-faced, soft-spoken officer described my father as a
"dictator" and paraded a bag that he claimed contained the
bones and remains of the murdered men. Komo declared that he
was satisfied that the perpetrators of the crime had been appre-
hended, and he warned that "Ogoni was bleeding not because

of the genocidal federal troops, but by irresponsible thuggery of the MOSOP element, which must stop immediately."

In February 1995, my father was charged—nine months after he was arrested. He was brought before a military tribunal that was raised under the Civil Disturbances Decree of 1987. In the summary of charges, Ken Saro-Wiwa and four other defendants were accused of "procuring and inciting" ten co-defendants to murder. The state prosecution charged that when my father was prevented by troops from proceeding to K. Dere on May 21, he got out of his car and addressed some of his followers. He was alleged to have told his supporters that the men meeting at Giokoo were responsible for preventing him from speaking, and that they were to "go and deal with" the chiefs.

The trial was a farce, a political proceeding clearly designed with one purpose: to eliminate Ken Saro-Wiwa from the scene in Ogoni. The catalogue of judicial irregularities and inconsistencies would be laughed out of any reasonable court. The defendants were held without charge for nine months and denied access to legal representation during that period; two prosecution witnesses who swore that my father had told the crowd to go and "deal with the vultures" later retracted their signed statements and revealed that they had been offered government contracts to testify against my father.

The British Lawyer Michael Birnbaum QC, who spent a month observing the proceedings of the trial, compiled a comprehensive document for the pressure group Article 19. His concerns about the legality and fairness of the trial are outlined in a nine-point summary, in which he observed that "the tribunal is not independent of the government. There is no sensible, pragmatic reason for the appointment of a Civil Disturbances Special Tribunal in this case other than the desire of the Federal Military Government that any trial relating to the Giokoo killings should take place before a tribunal which it hopes will favour the prosecution and a desire to avoid the scrutiny of its case by the ordinary courts."

Lawyers from all over Nigeria, including Gani Fawehinmi and Femi Falana, two of Nigeria's most celebrated and fearless legal minds, volunteered to represent the defendants. Although he was sceptical from the outset that he would get a fair hearing, my father co-operated with proceedings until June 22, when Auta refused to allow the defence to present the affidavits of the former prosecution witnesses or the video footage of Komo pronouncing my father guilty twenty-four hours after the May 21 murders. It was clear by then that my father was being framed, and he instructed his lawyers to stop acting for his defence. He argued that putting up a defence gave the trial a veneer of legitimacy.

The regime inadvertently revealed its intentions three months later, when Abacha's legal affairs adviser, Professor Yadudu, declared before the United Nations Committee for the Eradication of Racism and Discrimination that he was responsible for the murders. The verdict was still pending, but Yadudu's slip merely confirmed what my father and everyone already knew—that he was being framed. My father went on hunger strike in protest, but it was one of his last acts of defiance.

The trial itself was held in a court in downtown Port Harcourt. During the proceedings my father was taken from his cell in Bori military camp and driven to court in a Black Maria, an imposing nine-ton, reinforced-steel truck that he memorably described as a coffin. He would sit in the front row of the dock, his co-defendants beside and behind him, as he listened to the proceedings with the air of a bored, precocious student at an uninspiring lecture. As the tribunal stuttered to its predetermined conclusion, he would often be seen reading, which irritated the three wise men sitting in judgement on the dais at the front of the court.

Justice Ibrahim Auta had been persuaded out of retirement to preside over the case, and he was particularly offended by my father's attitude to the trial. Auta tried to impose a semblance of judicial protocol and authority over the courtroom but his interventions were comical and rebounded on him. Some scenes were even filmed and distributed around the world by the junta as evidence that my father had received a fair trial! In one sequence, Femi Falana, a flamboyantly articulate speaker with an extravagant goatee, is seen denouncing the tribunal. Falana seems to be enjoying himself, but Auta, a heavy-jawed, sour-faced man who looks like an undertaker, is outraged at Falana's antics. "The tribunal," he thunders in his black suit and bowler hat, "is not surprised at the action of this bunch of defence counsels [sic]. They have err . . . they have, right from the beginning of this case, had no intention of carrying out this case to its *logical conclusion* [my italics]."

Auta says this while appearing to read from a prepared script.

"Do you," he asks, looking up from his crib notes to direct the question at my father, "have anything to say pertaining to this issue?"

My father shakes his head.

"Do you want a counsel of your own choice?"

My father shrugs.

"Mr Saro-Wiwa we want you to answer 'yes or no'," Auta bellows impatiently.

My father looks up and replies, "Yes or no."

One of the defendants sitting behind him starts giggling.

"We are not joking here," Auta warns. "Can you get up?" he orders, trying to re-establish his authority.

My father stands up. He looks thoroughly fed up at even having to go through the motions. He clearly has no time for "the pompous buffoon in the bowler hat," and as he stares at Auta, I imagine he was probably thinking of the lines he wrote in his poem "The True Prison":

The magistrate writing in her book
Punishment she knows is undeserved
The moral decrepitude

Mental ineptitude
Lending dictatorship spurious legitimacy
Cowardice masked as obedience

He just wanted the whole tortured process to end. He was waiting for the moment when he would read from a final statement he had prepared. Auta refused to allow him to make the statement, and when he was sentenced, my father replied that it was a "black day for the black man."

In his "logical conclusion," Auta suggested that though the prosecution had not being able to prove that my father had incited a mob to murder the four chiefs, Ken Saro-Wiwa "must have known" of a plan to eliminate them. And with that, he sentenced my father and eight of the fifteen defendants to death.

As crude and transparently unjust as the prosecution's case was, there are many who still maintain that my father had a case to answer. Those critics point to the activities of vigilante groups in Ogoni. These groups, they say, raised doubts about the non-violent nature of the Ogoni struggle. The following passage is taken from the defence my father was prevented from making. It is his response to the issue of the vigilantes.

> At the time of the attacks on various Ogoni villages [in 1993 and 1994], all Ogoni people were nervous and there was considerable fear. Each village called out its youth and ordered them to organise the defence of the village. The youths called themselves "vigilantes." It was a desperate measure, since the youths were not armed, but it was important psychologically. However, when the armed attacks on the villages stopped, the vigilantes became a social problem. Instances of "witch-hunting," in which Ogoni youth were encouraged to go into villages to

search for and either extort money from or actually kill suspected "wizards," were reported. We [MOSOP members] were terribly appalled by this barbarism and fought the development with our usual vigour, issuing letters of warning to all village heads and holding rallies to educate the people as to the legal consequences of lawlessness and murder. Dr. Leton [the former president of MOSOP] and his group did not condemn the "witch-hunt" at any time, which made us believe that they either initiated it or gave it their tacit support as a means of discrediting a MOSOP which they had abandoned. We succeeded in the end in stopping the barbaric practice.

But not according to the Ibrahim Auta tribunal, which alleged that the vigilantes were responsible for a breakdown in law and order in Ogoni and for the mayhem at Giokoo. The Alice-in-Wonderland logic of the prosecution and how it arrived at the verdicts is contained in an eighty-page summary of the tribunal. It basically accuses my father of setting up the National Youth Council of Ogoni People (NYCOP) as his personal army and armed wing of MOSOP, and using it to eliminate any rivals to his political ambitions for Ogoni.

The Ibrahim Auta tribunal cannot be taken seriously. It was a political exercise that patently failed to address a serious case of homicide. It failed to provide answers to at least two crucial questions: Why did policemen refuse, despite several entreaties by concerned individuals, including my uncle Owens, to proceed to the scene of the riot at Giokoo? And who was responsible for the riots and the murders that day?

The verdicts of October 30 and 31 were a crude attempt to pin the violence in Ogoni on MOSOP, and the charge is ludicrous. Non-violence was the basis on which my father pursued the

Ogoni struggle. In his detention diary, he wrote, "It is also very important that we have chosen the path of non-violent struggle. Our opponents are given to violence and we cannot meet them on their turf, even if we wanted to. Non-violent struggle offers weak people the strength which they otherwise would not have. The spirit becomes important, and no gun can silence that."

MOSOP lays the blame for the escalation of violence in Ogoni firmly and squarely on the shoulders of the unholy alliance between the military and Shell. The movement has always called for independent investigations into *all* murders, rapes, extrajudicial killings and lynchings that occurred at the height of the struggle. Ogoni has been traumatized and may never recover. The truth was the first and most important casualty, and without it the road to reconstruction and reconciliation will be a long and painful one. There is a need for full disclosure by all parties involved, including Shell. I don't expect that will ever be forthcoming, though. Too many hands have been soaked in Ogoni blood, and there are uneasy consciences who would prefer that the whole saga was forgotten.

But it is for every individual to examine his or her conscience. I know who killed my father, and that is enough. I set out to understand why and how, and along the way I ran into a truth that has enabled me to rise above the injustice of it all. The way I see it, the dead cannot be brought back, and all that is left for us—the living—is to honour the dead by building a better future from the despair of the past, because those who forget the mistakes of the past, are condemned to repeat them.

10

Rumours of Rain

▼

*I was struggling with a monstrous resentment against the claim . . .
of blood, shared genes, the semen from which I had issued and
the body in which I had grown.*
—NADINE GORDIMER, *Burger's Daughter*

It was past midnight when I heard the news. The phone rang
at my flat in West London. My mother was on the other
end. I knew it was bad news.

"Junior!" she whispered. "*Tanga le be-e!*"

There is trouble at home. My heart sank.

"*Orage le Kobani a ua. Waa fea Badey, eh le dorna wuga Orage.*"

I had a numb, sickening feeling that life wouldn't be the same
again. Four Ogoni Chiefs—Albert Badey, Tom Orage, Sam
Orage and Edward Kobani—were dead, and my father had been
arrested in connection with their murders. One of the murdered
men, Sam Orage, was my uncle. He was the husband of my aunt
Elizabeth, my mother's oldest sister. Images of my cousins
Barine, Tom, Desmond and Tuma flashed up in my mind's eye.
What kind of sick twist of fate could have brought this on my

family? I wondered. I couldn't imagine why or how my father could be implicated in the murder of his friend Edward Kobani, the father of my childhood friends Tombari and Edward. I hadn't seen the Kobanis since my Nzimiro Street days, but they were a part of me, we had shared history. Now that shared past suddenly, in the space of one telephone call, meant nothing and everything.

I paced around in a daze, trying to understand the news. But it just didn't make sense. I hadn't been following events in Ogoni, and I had no idea of what had been going on down there. To my apolitical and distanced mind the violence seemed so out of place, out of character, for the Ogoni I knew. It seemed like the kind of senseless butchering that you read about in places like Rwanda. The Ogoni I knew was a docile, peaceful place.

The most distressing part of it was that the murders split my family right down the middle. On one side was my father's family and on the other was my mother's. Family ties and loyalties were suddenly stretched. Childhood friends, favourite cousins, would now be separated by a blood feud. As I paced, I tried to figure out what to do. Make the wrong move, say the wrong thing, and it would have far-reaching, emotionally wrenching consequences.

In such circumstances all you can do is trust your instincts. I picked up the phone and dialled a number in Los Angeles. My cousin Desmond Orage answered. He could barely speak.

"I'm sorry. I'm so sorry," was all I managed to say. There we were, two cousins who had been making plans to meet up in Los Angeles in a few months time, but now his father had been hacked to death by a mob and my father was alleged to have ordered the killing. "You have to be strong now—for yourself and your family. If there is anything I can do, please let me know." I said, speaking for myself as well as for my cousin.

Desmond accepted my condolences. But I could barely make out what he was saying, let alone imagine what was going through his mind. We spoke only for a few minutes, but I was exhausted when I hung up. I sat on the floor, cursing my fate to have been born my father's son. I was living in London and he was thousands of kilometres away in Africa, and yet his life was still affecting mine. I was facing the mother and father of all dilemmas: my parents were on opposing sides in a deadly family feud. I was torn between the two people who loved me most in this world, and I would be forced, once again, to make a choice between them. I pounded the ground in frustration, despairing of ever finding a clear line through my loyalties.

Two weeks after he was arrested, I received a letter from my father.

In detention 4/7/94
Port Harcourt, Nigeria

Dear Junior,

I'm pretty disturbed that I've not heard from you since all the hulla-baloo down here started. Are you well? Your health and that of Gian have been a source of additional anxiety for me. I pray all the time for you all, especially in these most troubled times.

To get rid of the very bad news. There is absolutely no truth in the statement being bandied about by some that I had a hand, directly or indirectly, in the gruesome murder of Kobani, Badey and the two Orages. Neither in thought nor deed have I ever wished any harm to them or to anyone. The Ogoni struggle is for justice, it is not for power and the enemy was always Shell & the rulers of Nigeria. I felt secure in the following of over ninety-eight per cent of the Ogoni people and the opposition of a few of the elders was not making any difference to the struggle. But both Shell & the Nigerian authorities were always after me and Mosop and the attempt now is to break both. Whether they will succeed is left to providence. It is a terrible period for the Ogoni people as they are leaderless, all the Steering Committee members of Mosop hav-ing either been held or gone underground. . . .

There is not much more to say. I'm currently in a cruel detention. The conditions were initially hard, but they are getting better. I expect to be charged to court for murder or conspiracy. I will not get justice in the lower court. But will do so at the court of Appeal. This means I may be away for two or three years, if no one bumps me off before I can be taken to court.

If you wish to write, please use the Lagos address, PO Box 696, Surulere, Lagos. I'll receive it in time. My health is deteriorating, which is another cause for worry.

With best wishes,
your father,
Jeje

P.S. Regards to your girlfriend.

It is hard to recall what I felt when I first read that letter, but the way he signed off—*your father*—seems, even at this distance, almost desperate.

I have never been a good or conscientious letter-writer. My father, in contrast, was an inveterate letter-writer, always firing off missives in his beautiful, slanted handwriting. I later found out that his handwriting helped launch him as a writer: when he was at college in Umuahia, the boys with the best handwriting got to rewrite articles for the school newspaper, and that's how Ken Saro-Wiwa the writer was born. Later, he wrote his novels and essays in longhand and had the work typed up by his secretary. He could type but he never looked very elegant on a typewriter; he would hunch over the keyboard, using three fingers— the second and third of his right hand and the second of his left hand—to peck at the keys. Which is also exactly how I type.

I replied to his letter, commiserating with him but explaining that I was busy settling into my first job since leaving journalism school. I told him about the difficulties I was having trying to place the story of his arrest in the British media. It was a small lie, because all I had done was send out a press release. I knew, deep down, that he was innocent, but acknowldging his innocence would mean I would have to abandon my life to help him. And not only would I be pulled into the struggle, but I would have to take a position against my cousins who had already publicly sworn to avenge their father's death.

I told him that my cousins and other Ogoni in London and in Nigeria had been trying to persuade my mother to turn against him. I wanted him to realize that his fate was in my mother's hands, to pay him back for all the times he had hurt her. I wanted him to sit in his cell and contemplate the fact that she would be justified in taking her family's side against him. It was a cruel thing to do, but our emotional attachment had been almost severed by the years of mutual suspicion and misunderstanding.

I didn't hear from him for two months. In a way, his silence was a relief because it shielded me from having to make a decision I would have been happy to put off for the rest of my life. I buried my head in the sand, hoping the situation would somehow resolve itself.

But the silence was unbearable. His silence and my own. My silence gnawed at my conscience, especially as my mother's relatives were trying to exploit his shortcomings as a husband. I was getting conflicting messages from people I used to trust; it was their word against my father's, and against the background of my ignorance of the situation at home.

Then a package from Nigeria dropped through my letterbox. In it was a bunch of clippings from Nigerian newspapers and a letter from my father.

11/8/94 Still in detention
Dear Junior,

Thanks a lot for your letter of 29 July. I felt a lot better after reading it. I had been extremely anxious not having heard from any of you in London. Thanks for doing all I asked for in my letter. The purpose of my letter was to prepare you for any eventuality. And to ensure that I had tidied up all my affairs on earth, and that you know about it. A good business practice, you might say. You must expect the worst and prepare your mind for that. What you will always remember is that I did my best to fight the injustices I found in my society. I am happy that in the event of death, which will surely come, I can only pass into Ogoni folklore if nothing else. Now, I could not demand more than that. And there are the books too. So, there's everything to be thankful to God for. I am in good spirits and you must all be the same. Do not fear, and do not be distressed. I imagine you can be proud of your progeny.

You do not let me know the precise nature of the problems you are having in your encounters with the British public on my behalf. But I would think that what you need to do is to keep them informed of all events. I do not know what material you have, but I'm asking Apollos to send you all the newspaper cuttings so far so you can keep abreast of the latest information. The best thing to do is to cultivate the media—BBC African Service, Voice of America, Radio France International & the print media in the UK. Also the environmental & human rights groups and of course International Pen so that news of the Ogoni struggle is not blanked out. It is going to be a long struggle whether I am there or not and heroes will be born of it. So getting involved is not bad at all for anyone.

After Birabi [where the murders took place] I am not surprised at anything that happens. The young Orage's reaction would have shocked me otherwise. What it shows is that we have to choose our friends carefully & that those closest to us may be the ones who hurt us most.

As of today, my situation has not changed much. Since I have not had access to a lawyer, I cannot challenge my detention properly in court. I need medical attention, but cannot get it. Where I am held is tolerable, but the food is atrocious and I do not have access to the family or anyone. I am denied access to radio, newspapers and books. Two armed guards are stationed outside my door twenty-four hours a day. My sense of justice is outraged but I'm in good spirits and in fighting mood. Express my gratitude to International Pen and Amnesty International. The state is yet to charge us to court if they have any evidence whatsoever. I gather *they are now trying to establish a remote link between the leadership of MOSOP and the murders. But that is an exercise in futility. There was nothing to gain by the murder of any Ogoni man—all of us are victims of the State & Shell. The Ogoni cause is a quest for justice and not for power. So there is nothing to kill for.*

I have had considerable support from Professor Ake (whom you've met), Apollos Onwuoasoaku, Iheme and a Miss Elfrida Jumbo (whom you have not met). You must express my thanks to them. My parents have also given me wonderful support and encouragement (their age notwithstanding) and the Nigerian press have been very supportive.

You will have to keep some money aside to enable you fly at short notice to Nigeria should it become necessary in the near future.

I look forward to hearing from all of you, when I hope you can let me have intimate information of your health, your careers and your hopes for the future.

I am writing even here. I smuggled in my computer, but that has now being seized after I published an indictment of my captors in the dailies here. The materials I referred to as needing to be published in future are in that computer (and now in the computer in the PH office).

I believe that my mail is being censored, my letter-boxes as well, and I've not devised an alternative means of getting the mail. When I do, I'll let you know.

The political situation here is most uncertain. In its resolution will lie what happens to me. But being out of detention is the least of my problems I have to face. Extricating the Ogoni people out of their death bond is going to be a much more gargantuan task. A lifetime's work. The exhilarating thing is the near total support of the Ogoni people & the support I find in the national and international community. It makes my suffering worthwhile. I doubt that's much comfort to young children who need the attention and care of their father or wives who require the same. But then, to everyone his fate. How I wish we could choose our parents! Keep smiling. God bless you.

Jeje

My father's letter is a courageous, generous letter, full of good, sound advice, but in 1994 it had to filter through my dense fog of resentment. Although I tried to ignore him, he kept nibbling away at my conscience. How, a little voice insisted, could I abandon him, especially when he really needed me? Wouldn't my silence be eating him up? I flinch now at how cold I was. It seems obvious, especially with the benefit of hindsight, that anything, however banal, would have kept his spirits up. But I was paralyzed by an awareness that if I wrote to him, I would have to answer the issue dangling like a large question mark between his hot, filthy prison cell in Port Harcourt and my comfortable misery in London: What was I going to do?

I proposed to Olivia. It wasn't premeditated, but it felt like the right thing and the right time. Although we'd been together for only two years, we had lived through so much in that time—Tedum's death, my operation after Tedum's death and my father's detentions.

You learn about yourself and the qualities of those around you in times of crisis. Olivia is resourceful, tough and intelligent, with a positive outlook that complements my introspective, gloomy perspective. She likes to solve problems, while I tend to avoid them. The night Tedum died, I told her it would be best if we went our separate ways. I wanted to protect her from the implications of getting too involved with my family. I patronizingly imagined that my political life would be too much for her. But she's as stubborn and wilful as I am, and she refused to take up my "offer." I came to be very grateful for her determination. She met my father only once—at Tedum's funeral. As we buried my little friend, she stepped in to take Tedum's place—someone to watch over me and protect me from my father and myself. She is the calm centre of the political storms that have raged around my life.

"What day is it today?" Olivia asked after she surprisingly agreed to my proposal.

"I don't know," I shrugged.

"It's October 10," she said as a slow smile lit up her beautiful face.
"What?"

"It's your father's birthday today," she said.

"So what?" I growled, trying to cover up my embarrassment. "We never celebrated his birthdays anyway."

A few weeks later, another letter arrived from Nigeria.

Dear Junior,
 I have not heard from you in months.
 Your father

Only three lines, but three lines that spoke volumes. In that anguished letter, I felt his pain, his anger. He must have thought that I had abandoned him. I threw it in the bin. I felt my anger was justified, but the letter sat in the bin, insisting that I stand up for my father. I received another letter shortly thereafter. MOSOP had been awarded the Right Livelihood Award, a prize that is also known as the alternative Nobel Prize. Someone had to go to Sweden to represent him, but I had just taken a holiday with Olivia, celebrating our engagement.

"I hear you've been on a holiday. How did it go?" my father wrote, hitting the right nerves, since I was already feeling guilty for taking a holiday while he was fighting for his life. "Go to Stockholm," he pleaded, suggesting that I "sit at the back" of the hall. It was the excuse I was looking for: I fired off a letter protesting his suggestion that I should take a back seat. I informed him that what I did or didn't do with my life was my choice, and not for him to decide.

I got an immediate response from him by courier.

3/12/94
Dear Son,
 This is going to be a longish letter—an epistle sort of—written in a hurry because I live by the minute, unsure what my captors will do next.

The intention is to destroy me. I am presently in what should be called a "hothouse," a filthy, rat- and cockroach-infested longish room where I'm held in solitary confinement. The last time I was here was in the early days of my arrest. Then I was in chains. But there were 34 other Ogoni young men. Most of these have now been freed or are in the hands of the police. I remain in Army hands, under constant surveillance, able to get out thrice a day to perform my ablutions. I was brought here on 25th November. Before then, from about the 29th of May, I was in more "comfortable" surroundings, in terms of physical discomfort, but again I was alone, three armed guards outside my door. Had I not been a writer and given to solitary life, it would have been hell. For a start, I had no books and no paper and borrowed a Bible from one of my guards— which I read from cover to cover.

Along the way, I found divine intervention, in the shape of the sol-diers who guarded me, and a man whom you must not forget—God-win Okoli—an engineer and officially in charge of the Afam Power station in which area I was held. He got me beddings, some books (including Papillon, which I enjoyed very much). As time progressed, I began to smuggle books and even my laptop computer into the place (there was uninterrupted electricity) and I wrote my heart out, so to speak. Poems, short stories, novels, and completed the diary of my first detention. Challenging my captors, I had an article published on the 31st of July, "Sanitising Ogoniland," and I lost my laptop com-puter. It was thought I was using it to send messages out! Believe it or not. I was pleased that the article rattled the goons that much. The computer confiscated, writing rate dwindled, but I kept at it until writer's block came in, I stopped writing, but was reading until some-time in early November, when things went sour again and I "lost" everything including my pen.

To cut a long story short, my attempt has been to stay psychologically superior to my captors. It has worked so far. I am in good spirits, remain quite convinced of my cause, have been buoyed by the unflagging spirit of the Ogoni people (I get letters from the faithful) and the support of the family. . . .

I don't know if I succeeded in giving you a sense of the barbaric system sitting on top of a people, dehumanising them, turning them to the lowest of beasts. It's a shame that a man of my mind, my education, my cultivation should be under the thumb of such barbarians. Pity too that in spite of the struggles of the few, this situation will persist for the next hundred years if all the people have not been ground to dust by then. Terrible vision, isn't it? My joy (and yet it is not such joy, come to face it) is that I gave you, my children, a choice to escape this horror. But then can you be happy in the West? Are the adulation and respect I enjoy here not preferable to the discrimination and dim prospects which the West offers you, in spite of all your education? I don't know, oh my dear son, but I would have wished that Ogoni (if nowhere else), small, extremely rich, and with an industrious and humorous population, could be allowed to develop at its own pace, using its resources, human and material, for its progress. It would be a wonderful home to all its people. . . .

I've been rambling, but it is a sign of my mind. I was thrilled to bits to receive your note and Zina's undated letter (trust her not to date her letter). That is because I thought you had all abandoned me since I had not heard from you after your first letter. And given the emotional investment I have in you all, you can understand the way I felt. I feared very much that the propaganda against me might have influenced you. A detainee tends to fear the worst since he is no position to receive proper information or cross-check what information he receives . . .

My plans for Stockholm were changed on pressure from Prof Ake, who has done so much for me. He thought that you accepting the prize on my behalf would personalise the struggle whereas so many other Ogonis have suffered & died for it. He therefore thought my family should be there but in a back seat. I had to reluctantly accept that. So it was nothing to do with devaluing your work or person. Not at all. I'm happy that Zina and Noo will be there although you cannot make it. I'd have wanted you to be there since the Nobel awards proper are to be made the next day. Would not have been bad rubbing shoulders with the great of the earth.

The award itself came as a great surprise and a palm to the hands of the Ogoni people & of myself. It earned us, the Ogoni, the envy of our neighbours too while firing others with ambitions to follow in our foot-steps. The government responded with their military tribunal which is supposed to send me to the gallows even though there is no shred of evidence, and there could never be, that I've done anything wrong. In the skewed way they think here, it is also possible that the Tribunal will never sit but is an excuse for their holding me without trial. The point is to shut me away for some time. That is what Shell would want most. They are likely to get it. But that will not be the end of the story. I doubt that Shell can resume oil activities in Ogoni whether I'm alive or dead, in or out of prison. The vast majority of the Ogoni have accepted the MOSOP idea and adversity has taught them to be courageous. It's wonderful that they have withstood all the brutality for so long and are still holding out.

The Orages have, unfortunately, decided to aid government propaganda and Lera has gone over the top displaying his ignorance and immaturity. Some of what he has written is incredible and will surely create bad blood between you and him in future. It will also destroy him before the Ogoni people. He is badly advised! He has not realised that a reputation I built over twenty five or thirty years worldwide cannot be destroyed by his immature rantings. And that I am a protector of the Ogoni. I wish him luck. The other families have been more decorous although the unemployed and unemployable Alhaji Patrick Mohammed Kobani has now found occupation. It's a pity really. The security agencies did their dirty work and are, as usual, looking for a way to blame it on the Ogoni and to use it to destroy more Ogoni.

The only thing that can save the situation is overseas assistance. That is why I'm earnestly hoping that the lobbies in Europe & America will be able to do something about it all. I am, as I told you earlier, prepared for the worst. So neither death nor imprisonment scares me. It is the solution to the Ogoni problem that is my overriding concern. There has to be an equitable and just solution. . . .

My love to you, Olivia, the rest of the family. God bless you all.

Jeje

The first thing I noticed about the letter was the *Dear Son*. Although the letter was written to me, I knew it was also clearly meant for public consumption. Much of what that letter contained eventually found its way into my campaigning articles and speeches, but when I first received it, I went to see my mother to try to resolve my dilemma.

My mother and I had not consciously sat down to talk about the crisis—we had discussed it only in a roundabout fashion. She was always more concerned about my personal well-being than that I get sucked into my father's politics. This time, we talked about her family. She revealed that Sam Orage had been like a surrogate father to her, that she had met my father at his house. I listened patiently. I had never asked her before about her side of the family because the focus had always been on my father's side. As I listened to my mother calmly speaking, I felt her pain. She had been through so much with my father, always putting him first, sacrificing her life to his causes and choices. I was determined to stand by my mother, make good the promise I made to Tedum the day I scattered earth over his coffin that I would protect her from Jeje. When it was clear that I needed an answer from her, she looked me squarely in the eye and, in her gentle but insistent manner, said the words that saved me a lifetime of anguish: "Junior, no matter what anyone says about Kenule, he never killed anyone."

I shudder to think what would have happened to me if my mother had not insisted that I defend my father, if I had stood by and watched my father executed for a crime he did not commit. I was fortunate with my parents, because in addition to having a courageous father, I was blessed with the most gentle, loving and forgiving mother.

Although she had decided to stand by my father—and by the truth—I knew it couldn't have been an easy decision. She was effectively putting her husband before her oldest sister. I appreciated the fact that she had decided to forgive my father for all the difficulties and heartache he had caused her down the years.

And she understood that I needed her blessing. At the time I imagined she made that choice for me; it was only after my father died that I realized she was still in love with him.

My parents' marriage was not a conventional one. Although she was one of the most beautiful women in the village, she was not the most socially attractive match. My mother came from a relatively poor family, and I imagine my father took a perverse pleasure in marrying for romantic love rather than accepting the traditional arranged wedding. One of his early poems, written on the eve of the civil war, shows how much she meant to him.

Voices

They speak of taxes
of oil and power
They speak of honour
and pride of tribe
They speak of war
of bows and arrows
They speak of tanks
and putrid human flesh
I sing my love
For Maria

Like much of his writing, "Voices" eventually took on a dramatic irony that probably wasn't originally intended. I never imagined my father as a romantic, but there he is seeking refuge from politics in love. How things changed.

The most significant line in the poem is the last. I used to misread the last two lines as one, but the capital *F* on the last line clearly shows that my father intended it to be read separately. *I sing my love . . . For Maria.* The dedication is subtle but clever, and thirty years later, it's a poignant reminder of the demands he was to make on that love.

Love is nothing until it has been tested by its own defeat. And love is what enables us to transcend that defeat. Her love for him had stood the test of time, survived so many defeats, but when it spoke to me in December 1994, I didn't appreciate that it was love that had compelled her to stand up for him and ask me to do the same. I was grateful for her backing anyway, and I went off to make good on my promise to Tedum.

I wrote a long letter to my father.

I have kept almost all the letters my father ever wrote to me, but I wish I had been as careful and conscientious with my own. I wish I could retrieve that particular letter I wrote, because it changed the dynamics of our relationship. I used to have it, and all the others I wrote to him while he was in detention. They were stored on my laptop, but the computer was stolen from my flat weeks after my father was executed. (It was practically the only thing that was taken, which, when added to the fact that there was a concurrent robbery at the family home—the first and only one in twenty years of living in that house—is a strange coincidence.) Anyway, all I have left is my unreliable memory of what I wrote.

What I do remember clearly is that I finally found the courage to confront my father about his relationship with my mother. I told him he was lucky to have a wife like her, and I explained that she had always been responsible for keeping his children, especially me, loyal to him, that she had never once tried to turn me against him. He had done that all by himself. I told him that she had always advised me to stand by him, no matter how rough their marriage was for her. I reminded him that he hadn't always been as faithful, and that he had often tried to blame her for his difficulties with his children.

I also told him I was going to marry Olivia; I went about it in a cautious, circumspect way. I had read somewhere that Ogoni were forbidden to marry outside their race, and I somehow imagined that since he had become such an Ogoni nationalist, he would disapprove of my choosing to marry outside.

His reply came back to me in less than a week. Nigeria's notorious postal system had never been so efficient.

24/12/94
Dear Junior,
Your letter of 15/12 got to me this morning, and thanks a million for a very encouraging and cheering Xmas gift. I remember how I failed to honour your Xmas dinner invitation last year and think now the dreary Xmas I'm going to have in this terrible prison cell tomorrow. . . .

Your mum. She is truly a wonderful person, and I mean it. I did write her once I was held, but she did not reply. She's been through a lot. In my best moments, I do realise that I must be one of the most difficult persons for any woman to cope with. Yes, I'm okay when I'm there, but how often is that? And to live the six or seven lives I live and all the contrariness (is it contrariousness?) that involves, demands of all my acquaintances a forgiving, understanding, "admiring" spirit which few people can offer. It has not helped that she was married so young, that her background was so different; but she did her very best. She gave me every support, although she had to develop herself to meet my exacting standards. And then my desires for you, my children—the best education that money can buy—and the usual intrusion of public life/peripatetic business & the writer's madness all came in and blew everything apart. To my eternal chagrin. And I, who was ever so proud of my family, found myself explaining off events etc etc. Just too bad. You may be surprised to hear that I'm still in love with her, but I fear that she finds it difficult to forgive me. She was always a good "catholic" girl with dreams of a loving, tightly-knit family. I don't think she can bear all the many women in my life and then my problems keep driving me into more women! It's criminal, but there, I promise I'll try to keep her not so sad. It's been hard on her. She did not, and I hardly knew myself, what waves were going to afflict me in life. I don't know how much more time I have, but I'll do my best now that you have urged me to it.

About Olivia. I wonder who ever told you I'd have liked you to marry from home. You should have known now that I never prescribe for my children. My belief is that I owe my children a good education and that that is enough to make them discriminate for themselves and make their choices. I do not even make suggestions in fields of study. And as to marriage, you know what Shakespeare says: "Hanging and wiving goes by destiny." I'm not trying to build a dynasty. I'm happy that you all had an excellent education. I expect you to make your choices. I'm on hand to offer advice, if requested, but no more than that. I met Olivia at Eton, and I can assure you I would not recognise her on the street. Your choice is okay by me. All I know is that you have both to work at it— I'm impressed that you have kept up a friendship for 7 years. You should not delay a union much longer. Long courtships are not normally good. But then, there can be exceptions. You have my best wishes & blessing.

I feel sorry that you are having to scratch around, and that I'm in no position to assist you in England. Nigeria would have been a different matter. I have resources here. But I've expended a lot on the Ogoni struggle. And your experience is so different from mine. I became a cabinet member the year after I left University and the world was always at my feet. I did not even have to plan a future. Things happened to me. God was always on hand to ease me into new careers and help me make a success of everything (or nearly everything) I touched. All I contributed was damned HARD WORK. And that is all I can recommend to you. Three jobs at a time? No sweat. The steps by which great men reached and kept . . . you must be awake when others are asleep, if you are to get to the top. And if I were your age and in England, that's precisely what I'd be doing. Secondly, SAVE. If Jesus saves, so must you. I'm happy that the prospect of marriage is now impelling you to hard work, thrift and creative use of the imagination. Because if I had a criticism of you, it would be that you were not hard-working enough, failed to save money and were generally idle. For all your writing ability, your education (including travel) and other experience there is no reason why you should not have produced a book by now. Finally, you have to be able to sell yourself. You must believe in you, before others can believe in you. You have a name now in three lobbies—the environment, human rights, literature—and there are also those in business & private life who will remember the name. If you have a plan, and you let members of the lobby know, they will introduce you to others and before you know a thing, you should be able to get what you want. Knowing what you want out of life is the real thing. Once you are clear, you can work towards it and make alterations where necessary. You must have ambitions, goals. I don't see you, with your education, scratching around on the fringes of British society. You should use the advantages which your British experience has offered you to promote your African/Ogoniness. And don't feel intimidated by my "success." I do not demand, will never demand, the same of you. I repeat: I'm not trying to build a dynasty. Be yourself. You can . . . [unclear] a success in even a little way, in one little field, you will have satisfied me. I cannot recommend the sort of life I've lived to any of my children. It's been too dizzying, too controversial. But it was my destiny. I hope you relax, build a good family and help our people when you can. But always write. You have a good style.

As to the Ogoni struggle, I'm quite content with what is happening. I don't even mind a term of imprisonment. And should I die in it, I would end up a martyr. I think you put your finger on the correct button when you discerned that each mistake the government made has advanced my cause. It's amazing to think what we we've achieved on a slim budget and with such few men on the ground. We have to thank my prolific writing maybe. But there is the finger of God in it. And I remain as convinced as ever that the Ogoni people will win in the denouement. And that should be a signal for other oppressed and exploited people in Africa. If I can pull this off, I should have started a revolutionary trend in Africa which may in fact be what the continent has needed. We have to destroy Berlin of 1884, and remake Africa according to our traditional lines, smashing the native oppression of the past & the present in the process.

The need is for Africans of good education and cosmopolitan outlook—self-confident, well bred and honest and hard-working. This is where people like you and your children come in. I'll be quite content with you growing your children in the UK, unless of course we smash the Nigerian jinx over Ogoni and are able to set up a first-class system in Ogoni as I hope to do, since the area is very rich. So to end, you can rest assured that I am in good spirits, quite clear as to what I want and convinced that neither torture nor jail, nor death, can fail my cause. . . . I am, indeed, expecting the bum Nigerian government to fall into more Ogoni ditches and so hand us a victory which would have cost much more to win had they been more intelligent. . . .

I wish you and Olivia all the very best, if you do see Bobby Reid, say I wish him well and will rely on his advice as to what to do about our difficulties with Shell, and that there is now need for some people with the requisite knowledge, such as him, to help resolve the conflict. . . .

Jeje

I was glad he had reverted to the more personal *Dear Junior*, and I was relieved and touched that he had the grace to acknowledge his debt to my mother. As for the rest, that letter remains the most important one my father ever wrote to me. But as was my wont in those days, I zeroed in on his criticisms of me: I was ashamed that he felt I was "lazy." He could have said I was lacking in direction, but my father never minced his words, especially when he was trying to motivate me. It did the trick, however, because I handed in my notice at work the very next day. I decided it was time to show him what I could do.

At the time, I rationalized my decision as giving up my life to try to save his. But when I look back on it, it is probably fairer to say that I had decided to make something of my life by trying to save his.

11

Darkness at Noon

▼

Things fall apart; the centre cannot hold ...
The ceremony of innocence is drowned.
—W. B. YEATS, "The Second Coming"

I was standing in a newsroom of the BBC World Service in London when I heard that he had been sentenced to death. I was leaning against a desk when a disembodied voice suddenly bounced out of a nearby speaker, announcing that Janet Anderson, the BBC correspondent in Nigeria, was standing by to file a report from Port Harcourt. The volume on the speakers seemed to rise a couple of notches as a voice boomed out like an announcer at a train station:

"KEN SARO-WIWA HAS BEEN SENTENCED TO DEATH..."

I had gone to the Bush House to give a reaction to the news that five of the fifteen on trial had been sentenced to death. In the parallel universe that was Nigeria under General Abacha, my father and his co-defendants were tried in two separate cases, sometimes using the same evidence in both trials. The verdicts in the first trial were announced on Monday the thirtieth of October, and twenty-four hours later, the verdicts in the second, including my father's case, were announced.

The news filtered in and out of my head. It didn't register at first, because by then Ken Saro-Wiwa was someone I had been writing and talking about for a year, someone I prefaced as a minority-rights activist, as an environmentalist, a poet, a writer, an Amnesty International prisoner of conscience or a Nobel Peace Prize nominee. The name Ken Saro-Wiwa had lost some of its personal meaning to me. He was already a symbol in my mind, and it took a few moments before it registered that my father had just been sentenced to death. But as soon as I absorbed the thought, I quickly blocked it out and concentrated on my response.

"Ken Saro-Wiwa is a pawn in a political game. The rules of this game are clear; the Nigerian regime and Shell feel threatened by the successes of the Movement for the Survival of the Ogoni People and by my father's growing international profile. This so-called trial and sentencing is a pretext to send him to jail for a long time, and thereby suppress the vitality and energy of the movement by emasculating MOSOP's leadership."

My reaction was on the tip of my tongue. I barely had to think about it because by then I was a fluent activist. I was playing the role my father had always hoped I could play; I was his witness, his mouthpiece. Ken Saro-Wiwa and Ken Wiwa flowed seamlessly from one to the other.

I had come to accept my role. I actually enjoyed being his "spokesman." I travelled around the world, meeting the good and the great as he had predicted, basking in the spotlight of his name, seduced by the prospect that he was becoming a *cause célèbre*.

I shouldn't have been concerned when they sentenced him to death—everything was going according to plan. He would be sentenced, then the verdicts would go to the court of appeal, and though he might be in jail for a while, he would become a focus of resistance, like Mandela or Gandhi or Martin Luther King. It was in the book of saints. Abacha and Shell were playing right into our hands, helping us to write my father's chapter in that book.

But I had already found out that my father had been keeping the truth from me. I had stumbled across it two weeks before he was sentenced, and something I had heard the night before confirmed it.

That night, a group of supporters had met up at the Groucho Club in London to discuss the trial. The club was filled with the good, the noble, the rich and the famous—Ken Saro-Wiwa the *cause célèbre* drew a good crowd. The verdicts in the first trial had been announced, and there was speculation about what would happen to my father. My friend Chidi Odinkalu, a Nigerian human-rights lawyer with good instincts about the country's politics, cut through the analysis and insisted that all the press attention my father was receiving was useless unless the international community leaned on General Abacha. Chidi went on to predict that not only would my father be found guilty, but Abacha would defy any calls for clemency and execute him.

I tried to reassure myself that General Abacha would not dare execute my father. International observers had already exposed the tribunal as a politically motivated kangaroo court. Everyone knew that the charges were trumped up, and that it was a show trial designed to prove who was in charge of Nigeria. My father—the man who knew everything, the man who had always been in control of his destiny—had told me so himself. But as hard as I tried to convince myself that night, Chidi's comment confirmed what my father had been trying to hide from me.

I had stumbled on the truth a couple of weeks earlier, in a letter he had written to his nephew Barika Idamkue. I was meant to pass the letter to Barika, but when I received it, I decided, for some reason, to read it.

The truth was a sentence casually tossed in among all the usual words of advice and encouragement: "You know what is going to happen to me. I know too and have known all along."

I was stunned. My whole understanding of what was at stake in the tribunal was suddenly turned upside down. I felt betrayed, and was annoyed that he had kept it from me. He had known he would be killed all along. When he wrote telling me to "expect the worst," the worst, he said, would be a long spell in jail. I had assumed that those words were meant to whip up public sympathy for the cause. I had used them in my articles and speeches, but I never believed them. I thought I knew and understood his mind. In what turned out to be his last letter to me, he had even advised me to prepare for his being "put away for a long time," and he told me that I was to start making preparations for a "free Ken Saro-Wiwa campaign."

On my way to the World Service, I had wondered about that letter to Barika. What if that had been a lie too? Had he written it so that Barika would use it to drum up sympathy? Could I use it too? I had chewed it around in my mind, but it was an unpalatable thought. As I waited in the newsroom, I found myself hoping that they would somehow find him innocent.

Once the sentence was confirmed, something went off inside me. There was an upsurge in media interest, and I rushed around London trying to satisfy all the requests for interviews. I put the active in "activist." He would have been proud of me that day.

Three days later, I was on a plane, heading to Auckland, New Zealand.

My father had written to Anita and Gordon Roddick of the Body Shop, urging them to send me to New Zealand to make a last-ditch plea to the Commonwealth Heads of Government Meeting (CHOGM), which was to convene in Auckland in the first week of November. The Body Shop had been actively supporting the Ogoni struggle since July 1993, when Anita

Roddick had met Ogoni delegates in Vienna, at a UN conference on indigenous people. She had thrown her company's
considerable campaign experience behind the Ogoni struggle,
funding trips for activists, giving us an office in London and
helping to raise awareness of the Ogoni story through her net-
work of franchises and contacts around the world. My father
felt that my presence in Auckland would give us another
opportunity to raise the profile of the cause.

When I was asked to pack my bags for Auckland, I didn't
pause to consider that it might be too late to save my father. I
saw it as a chance to save his life and finally prove myself to him.

▼

Before the summit began, I got an opportunity to lobby Jim
Bolger, who was the prime minister of New Zealand at the
time. I was sitting in the canteen at the media centre having
lunch with Richard Boele, an Australian activist who had been
detailed to look after me in Auckland. Richard had been working on the Ogoni issue since 1993, when he was a researcher at
the Unrepresented Nations and Peoples Organisation. He had
actually spent some time in Ogoni in 1995, when he posed as a
tourist and slipped under the security blanket to document the
human-rights abuses taking place there. Now, in Auckland, he
had gathered together a team of six volunteers to help me co-
ordinate our media and lobbying strategy.

We were discussing our plan of action when Richard spotted
the prime minister and his aides walking by. He leapt up and ran
after them. A few minutes later he was back, announcing that he
had secured an audience with the prime minister. I almost
choked on my sandwich.

He took me through the procedure. "You've got three minutes with Bolger," he said in his clipped Australian accent.
Richard is a Buddhist but behind the studious appearance is a

sharp mind honed by years of campaigning as a human-rights activist. "You have to put your case clearly in that time, matey," he emphasized. "Leave him no doubt how serious the situation is."

I was still eating when two men in suits came by and sat down on either side of me. One of the suits did all the talking. He was a large man with a friendly face and a gentle voice. "G'day mate, how you doing?" he said curtly.

"The prime minister will see you only on two conditions," the other suit said. "You can make an appeal for clemency for your father, but you can't tell the media about the meeting."

I glanced at Richard. He shrugged and I nodded, agreeing to the conditions. The suits stood up to leave. One of them announced that someone would be along shortly to escort me to the meeting. When they'd marched off, I asked Richard about the conditions. He told me that the media embargo was diplomatic protocol—the Nigerians could otherwise protest about the Commonwealth host government meeting a member of the Nigerian opposition. I was thrilled to be listed as a member of the Nigerian "opposition" but more concerned about the clemency appeal; surely the whole point of my trip to Auckland was to try to persuade the Commonwealth to put out a stronger warning to the Nigerian regime?

"You've got three minutes with the PM," Richard grinned conspiratorially.

A few moments later, a security official came to escort me to the conference hall where the government delegations would meet when the summit began. The conference hall was as luxurious as the media centre was functional. Plain-clothes security officers patrolled the entrance, and I was ushered into an inner sanctum with soft carpets. Waiters and waitresses scurried back and forth, carrying trays of sparkling empty glasses and bottles of wine. Armed policemen swaggered around nonchalantly. Farther inside, we came across the prime minister standing behind a glass partition, surrounded by his aides. Bolger shook my hand

and ushered me to a corner with three chairs arranged around a low, round coffee table. I was invited to sign the register on the table. The prime minister sat with his back to the French windows overlooking the courtyard below. I could see across the courtyard to the entrance of the media centre. I glanced over Bolger's shoulder, half hoping to catch a glimpse of Richard for reassurance.

When I had signed the register, a sour-faced aide wandered over and sat in the spare chair. He took out a notepad and pen and started making notes.

"When did you get to Auckland?" Bolger asked. He had a large, craggy, weather-worn face and thin lips.

"Er, yesterday," I ventured timidly.

"What is the latest with your father's situation? Is his health bearing up?"

I took my cue, sketching out a brief outline of the facts, with which he was probably already familiar. Everyone in the room looked bored as I trotted out the approved script. As I droned on about how I hoped the prime minister would appeal to General Abacha for clemency, I found myself thinking that I was letting my father down. When I came to the end of the approved script, I added that unless the Commonwealth made a strong appeal to Abacha, they would have my father's blood on their hands. I had barely finished speaking when Bolger stood up, shook my hand, smiled tersely and thanked me for my time. I was led away and dumped outside the conference hall.

Back in the real world, Richard asked me how it had gone. I told him. At least, he said, the prime minister was now aware of my feelings.

Watching the news that evening, I was startled when an item on the summit was introduced with the headline "Bolger meets imprisoned Nigerian writer's son."

"How the hell did that get out?" I cried.

"Nothing to do with me, mate," Richard protested.

We shrugged it off. We actually laughed about it. But we weren't laughing three days later when, on the morning of the execution, Jim Bolger insisted that I had simply asked the Commonwealth to plead for clemency on my father's behalf.

I always imagined I had no illusions about politics and politicians. I grew up in a political house, and it had turned me off politics. When many of my friends were looking for a political cause because they were tired of living uncomplicated lives, I just wanted an uncomplicated life because I was tired of living a political cause. I thought I had found every reason to loathe politics and politicians, but I found some new ones during the last week of my father's life.

Our strategy in Auckland was simple: I tried to drum up as much media interest and public sympathy for my father's cause as possible, hoping the politicians would respond to the weight of public opinion. Within twenty-four hours of my arrival in Auckland, my father's case became the lead item on the agenda at the Commonwealth summit. But for all the interest we generated, for all their professed sympathy, I couldn't help feeling that the politicians had another agenda. Although I implored the Commonwealth members, in interview after interview, to take collective, decisive action against Nigeria, they seemed bent on adopting a softly-softly approach, working behind closed doors. To my astonishment, when he was pressed about my father's case, Nelson Mandela insisted that "quiet diplomacy" would save the day, leading Shell to smugly suggest that "those who knew Africa best, like Nelson Mandela, were advocating quiet diplomacy."

So despite all the media attention, and despite our repeated warnings that Abacha was going to kill my father, it quickly became clear that the politicians would weigh their interests behind closed doors, in smoke-filled rooms, and come up with a strategy to handle this Ken Saro-Wiwa business.

The day after I met Jim Bolger, I was sitting in a taxi, heading for a meeting with Lady Lynda Chalker, Britain's overseas development minister, when I spotted Wole Soyinka strolling solemnly down a street in downtown Auckland. Soyinka had gone to Auckland to add his eloquent and powerful testimony to the demand that the Commonwealth take the firmest action against Nigeria and address human-rights abuses of the Abacha regime. Soyinka was fired up that week. He was in a foul mood because Abacha's thugs had not only run him out of Nigeria, but also tried to assault him in New York.

You didn't need a doctorate in political science or an impassioned testimony from an exiled Nobel laureate to realize that the only language Abacha understood was violence. And yet the Commonwealth kept blabbing on about constructive engagement, quiet diplomacy and all the other lily-livered cop-outs that served only to pamper Abacha's ego and inflate his sense of his own importance. A few people, such as Desmond Tutu, had seen the signs and had already spoken out, urging the Commonwealth to take a firm, principled and unequivocal stand against Abacha. I had heard Tutu's comments as I was preparing for my meeting with Lady Chalker, and when I saw Soyinka, I jumped out of my taxi and ran to relay Tutu's statement to him.

"Alleluia!" Soyinka said wryly.

I told him I had a meeting with Lady Chalker and then with the Australian foreign minister. I wondered if he would like to come along.

"I'm not going to talk to *that* woman," Soyinka said, sneering, "but I will see you at the other meeting."

I was intrigued by his reaction to Lady Chalker, but when I got back to the taxi, Richard announced that he'd just received a call from John Major's people. They were offering me a chance to pose a pre-assigned question at Major's press conference— they imaginatively suggested something along the lines of asking for clemency for my father—or I could go ahead with the scheduled meeting with Lady Chalker.

"Let me get this straight," I said. "They want to tell me what I should ask *them* on *my* father's behalf?"

"Yep," Richard replied curtly.

It was obviously too good an offer to refuse, but I was curious to find out why Soyinka was such a fan of the honourable minister for overseas development.

▼

The British delegation had commandeered a couple of floors of the Sheraton Hotel in downtown Auckland. The corridors were full of policemen and security people, and we even had to be escorted the thirty metres from the elevators to the rooms where we were scheduled to meet Lady Chalker. A news crew started filming as we emerged from the elevator.

"What are they doing here?" I asked Richard.

One of Lady Chalker's aides stepped forward and asked, rubbing his hands obsequiously, whether we objected to having the meeting filmed. I shook my head in disbelief but agreed.

Lady Chalker liked to call herself Mama Africa. I was curious about that, since Mama Africa is an honour, an affectionate nickname, given to Miriam Makeba, the internationally renowned singer, in recognition of her lifelong struggle against apartheid. Chalker had appropriated the name for herself and I soon found out why.

She must have modelled herself on Margaret Thatcher, because when we sat down to talk she hectored me, with her head at an angle, as she peered at me over the top of her glasses. The effect was more tea lady than iron lady, however, as she lectured me about how much her government was doing to keep my father alive and how she was thrilled to meet me. I sat there wondering what the woman was talking about. My father was about to be executed, and she was telling me how thrilled she was to meet me. I can't remember what I said when she finished, but it was something along the lines of Britain stepping off its high horse and confronting its hypocrisy. Whatever I said obviously upset Mama Africa because she looked mortified.

She wasn't about to give up without a fight, though. As I was getting ready to leave, she had another go at painting a little vignette with nice sound bites for her viewers back in the mother country. But the mandarin started flapping around like a harassed chicken. She was apparently late for her next appointment, and the aide was desperately trying to catch her attention. As we waited outside the room to be escorted the thirty metres back to the elevators, Richard overheard one of the film crew complaining that the footage couldn't be used because there was too much background noise. We could hear Chalker, back in the room, bawling out her aide for ruining her *pièce de camera*.

When our escort showed up, we were led to the elevators, where we bumped into Wole Soyinka.

"Ahhh, young man," he said, grinning. "How was Mama Africa?"

At about the same time, halfway around the world, the preparations for my father's execution were starting with a security search and a head count of all the Ogoni inmates at Port Harcourt prison.

▼

It all began to fall apart twenty-four hours later. I received a telephone call from my father's cousin in Chicago. Dr. Vincent Idemyor is the son of my father's cousin, and is normally an easy-going and phlegmatic character.

"Junior," he was shouting, "you have to move fast. I have just heard that executioners arrived at Jeje's cell but were turned back. They didn't have the right paperwork, but they will be back tomorrow."

I was standing in the grand ballroom of an Auckland hotel, where members of the media were having a buffet lunch with some politicians and heads of state. I'd almost run into the Nigerian foreign minister, Chief Tom Ikimi, a few moments before Vincent's phone call. I was standing on one side of the ballroom, watching the scrum of journalists around Ikimi on the other side. The lunch was meant to be an informal get-together with the media, but journalists were not about to miss an opportunity to pin down Nigeria's foreign minister on a developing story. As soon as Ikimi entered the ballroom, he was surrounded by news-hungry hacks wanting to know whether Ken Saro-Wiwa would be executed. When one of the journalists was thrown out for trying to take a picture of the generously proportioned minister, Ikimi took advantage of the respite to go foraging for some grub. He came charging across to my side of the room, looking like a wounded bull elephant on the rampage, the wings of his lavish agbada billowing behind him. When he spotted me he stopped suddenly, did a U-turn and headed for the drinks.

I was feeling pleased with my little triumph when Richard came running over and handed me his mobile phone. "It's Vincent in Chicago," he said, looking agitated.

"I have tried to call Clinton's people," Vincent was saying. "You have to get in touch with Mandela and Major. *Now*. Tell them what is happening. They must each make a personal call to Abacha right now, because Abacha works between 2 a.m. and 6 a.m."

I couldn't believe they would actually execute him in the middle of the Commonwealth conference. But there was no doubting the edge in Vincent's voice. He had contacts in Abuja and was communicating regularly with Port Harcourt. I suddenly had a feeling that it was all over. I glanced at my watch, it was just past 2 p.m. in Auckland. In Abuja it was 2 a.m. All the people I wanted and needed to speak to seemed so far away now. We'd tried everything, but no one, *no one*, was listening, or wanted to listen, or seemed to understand just how desperate the situation was. I wanted to stand in the middle of that ball-room and yell so loudly and with such blood-curdling venom that everyone from Auckland to Abuja would hear my despera-tion and see sense. But it was useless. I barely had enough energy to speak. In a few hours my father would be executed unless something dramatic happened. I glanced at Richard. He already knew.

We rushed back to the media centre to issue a press release and call a press conference. We called our team of volunteers at the makeshift office in the hostel where we were staying. We told them to drop everything and try to get me a private audi-ence with Mandela or Major. When we arrived at the media centre, Richard went to reserve a room for the press conference and I sat down at a computer to type out a statement. I was just finishing when he came back and announced that a room had been booked for 4 p.m. I typed the time of the conference onto the press release and printed it out. Richard ripped it off the printer and rushed off to fax, photocopy and distribute it around the media centre.

I spent the next hour pacing around the building. Everyone was going about their business, seemingly oblivious to the unfolding tragedy. At 4 p.m. I went down to the conference room. It was barely half full. I read out my statement wearily and took some questions. I tried to make an impassioned plea, but I was flat. When the press conference finished, I wandered out of the room in a daze. A man in a suit collared me and dragged me into a corner of the hall. I looked at his identification tag. It was turned into his chest. He told me he was part of the Nigerian delegation. I froze.

"Ken, you're going to have to be brave over the next few days. Your father is a good man. He supported me when I was starting out."

That was all he said before he vanished. I barely had time to reflect on his words when Richard came by to remind me that we had a scheduled meeting with the Canadian prime minister, Jean Chrétien.

I had been looking forward to the meeting with Chrétien because he had been the only head of state to take a public stand against General Abacha, explicitly criticizing him in his opening address to the Commonwealth and specifically referring to my father's predicament. Here at least was a political leader who understood the urgency of the situation.

We hurried across to the meeting, and after we had exchanged formalities, I updated Chrétien on the latest news from Port Harcourt and begged him to convey the urgency of the situation to the rest of his colleagues. When I came out of the meeting, I was asked to brief the press about my meeting with Chrétien. We gathered on a grass verge outside the hotel, and a journalist asked me if I knew how my father would be executed. I rolled my eyes—and spotted an African man standing a few metres away, taking notes and speaking into a mobile phone. As I walked away, I glanced over my shoulder at the man. His security tag was turned into his body. I guessed he too was a member of the Nigerian delegation, but I could tell from the look on his face, he wasn't a friend of my father's.

On the way back to our hotel, I told Richard that I wanted to get out of Auckland. I wanted to be with my family when the news came. He tried to persuade me to stay, insisting that we still had work to do, but I knew it was all over. I had done everything I could do. It was in God's hands.

There was an eerie silence around the media centre as Richard and I strolled across the courtyard on our way to a farewell dinner with the team. The atmosphere in the city that evening reminded me of the brooding silence before a thunderstorm in Nigeria. I particularly remember the sunset. As we climbed to the top of one of Auckland's hilly streets, I looked back over the harbour, where a fiery orange sun was setting. I stopped to watch as it slowly dipped into the ocean. The sea shimmered for a few minutes as the sun hovered over the water before darkness fell over the city.

At dinner that night there was good-natured banter around the table and I joined in, trying to keep my mind from the events back in Nigeria. Just before midnight I felt a short, violent, tugging sensation in my chest.

That was the longest night of my life. Although I was shattered, my nerves rubbed raw, and I hadn't had a full night's sleep since my father had been sentenced to death, I couldn't let go. I knew my father was probably dead, but I clung to a forlorn hope that everything would be okay in the morning. I fretted, tossing and turning in a state of suspended anxiety, drifting in and out of a fitful sleep. At one point I became conscious of movements outside my room, doors opening and closing, people whispering and shuffling around in the corridors. I wanted to get up and find out what all the noise was about, to confront the news head on, but I couldn't move. I lay there, paralyzed by fear. Waiting. Waiting for the morning and God knows what. After a while, I noticed that there was an ominous silence in the corridor. The only noises I could hear were the sporadic sounds of early morning traffic drifting in and out of my room from the streets outside.

When I heard a timid knock on my door, I jumped out of bed and threw on some clothes. My hands were shaking as Richard slipped into the room. He was as pale as a ghost. He had spent the night trying to confirm the sketchy reports coming out of Nigeria. It was written on his face. I stood in front of him, searching for a sign that everything was still okay. He looked at me, then pursed his lips.

"Your dad's dead."

12

The Singing Anthill

▼

Memory of me will be a process of conscious and unconscious exorcism.
—DENNIS BRUTUS, *For My Sons and Daughters*

My father is reclining on a bank of grass by a stream in the forest. He stares at the ground, propping up his head with one hand. His hair is matted, his body covered in cuts and bruises and his skin dry and cracking. I imagine, for some reason, that he has been involved in a bad car accident. When he sees me approaching, he kicks the ground in frustration and gets up. He glares at me, then turns around, folds his hands behind his back and wanders off into the forest, shaking his head sadly.

It took two years, two months and thirteen days before I finally came to terms with my father's death.

I don't know which was harder to stomach—the fact that he was hanged or the rumour that acid was poured on his corpse. There were all kinds of other grim rumours flying around, including the one that Abacha had filmed the execution for his personal viewing pleasure. Although Abacha was capable of anything, I suspect, or at least hope, that he encouraged some of the rumours to serve as a warning of the consequences of challenging his authority.

The thought that there might be film footage of my father's execution lying around filled me with all sorts of savage anxieties. What if it suddenly became available? Would I want to see it? I imagined I wouldn't be able to resist—since I had never seen his body, the film would be the only evidence that he really was dead. I recoiled at the thought. How could I live with watching pictures of my father being hanged? What would that do for my sanity?

I'm not sure where or how the rumours that acid was poured on his body came about, but if it is true (and at the time of writing, this still hasn't been confirmed or denied) I imagine that Abacha wanted to wipe him off the face of the earth, obliterate him from memory. His paranoia about my father was so intense that Abacha was determined to prevent any kind of memorial being erected to him. Anyone in Ogoni caught wearing black, anyone suspected of mourning or even carrying a picture of him, was liable to arrest. After the executions, the Internal Security Task Force continued its campaign to pacify Ogoni, raping women and setting up roadblocks to extort money from our people. The aim was to crush our spirit. Abacha wanted to teach us a lesson, stamp his authority on the nation's psyche.

In an echo of the civil war my family was targeted and victimized. On the first anniversary of the executions, my cousin Charles was arrested, tortured and savagely beaten. He was in a bus, heading to Bori, when a soldier overheard him talking about Ken Saro-Wiwa. He was released only after Papa intervened. Charles eventually fled the country, joining the exodus of Ogoni refugees who left Nigeria after 1995. So as long as Abacha was in power, there was no question of my returning home to fulfil my duty as the first son and bury my father.

Unable to give my father his last rites, I had no choice but to try to handle his legacy from England. Many people assumed I would take on his political mantle and lead the struggle from abroad. I was his first son, namesake and heir; I was the public face of the campaign. One Ken Saro-Wiwa was dead and another was primed and ready to fill the vacuum. But that was the last thing I wanted to do. I was tired of politics and politicking. The disillusionment that had set in in Auckland was completed when I had a meeting with the then secretary-general of the UN, Boutros Boutros-Ghali ten days after the execution.

When a large ship stops, the motion carries on in the sea. This is called the solitoon wave. Everyone kept telling me that my father's "death must not be in vain," and I was swept forward in the groundswell of opinion and anger to Strasbourg, where I lobbied the European Union to isolate the Abacha regime. After I addressed the European Parliament, word reached our delegation that the UN secretary-general was in town and available for a meeting.

I was leaning against a corridor in the parliament building when a hunched, dapper-suited, tanned old man emerged from the Gents. There was a space in his schedule for him to relieve himself, and he agreed to cut himself short to meet me.

Bobo, as he was known, wandered out of the Gents and instinctively turned to shake hands with the members of our delegation who were lined up against the wall. He moved along the line with the assurance of a seasoned diplomat, pressing flesh and making small talk. When he reached me, he took my hand, paused and beamed for the photographers, who leaned in and started snapping away furiously. I blinked as a volley of flashbulbs exploded in my face.

Once the all-important photo op was out of the way, Bobo ushered me into a spacious office with panoramic views of the Strasbourg skyline. He sat on the edge of a soft leather sofa, still grinning inanely, and I leaned forward and blazed away.

I basically told him that the world was looking to the UN for moral leadership. The smile that was frozen across his face slowly melted. When I finished, he offered his condolences and assured me that he would do everything in his power to ensure that my father was not forgotten. Then he stood up, shook my hand limply and wandered over to the window. He stood with his back to the room, staring across the skyline. His aides looked embarrassed, unsure of what to do. The photographers hung around, waiting for another photo op, but Bobo was preoccupied with the view over Strasbourg.

That was the final straw for me. I realized that the politicians didn't care that my father was dead. All the moral indignation in the world wasn't going to change the fact that Ken Saro-Wiwa was, to them, a minor detail in the bigger picture. He was expendable as long as the oil continued to flow in the right direction and at the right price, as long as the system worked to the advantage of the multinationals oil companies and their hired thugs in vicious military regimes. If rich and influential nations continued to enjoy cheap fuel and a good standard of living, and their people slept soundly in their beds, then what did it matter that the human rights of millions of nameless and voiceless people were being trampled on? What did it matter that one man had been hanged after a dubious trial? Why rock the boat or change the system for that?

I had lost my father and the world was outraged, but all these politicians seemed to care about was that they were *seen* to be doing something. As long as there were photographs or news footage showing them meeting or talking to me, that, as far as they were concerned, was all they needed to do to show that they were in step with public opinion.

I was tired of their hypocrisy. I was tired of the rhetoric, the manipulations, the lies and the deceptions. I was tired of playing a role. Although the world was outraged, I knew that the attention would only last until the next crisis, when the politicians would crank out more excuses for doing nothing and move on. The few people who really cared would continue the struggle, but most would forget who Ken Saro-Wiwa was, why they were so angry when he was killed and what he had died for. It was an unpalatable truth, and I was sick of having it repeatedly shoved down my throat. I just wanted to go home. I wanted my innocence back.

I went back to London and tried to pick up the pieces of my life. I went back to work. Olivia and I fixed a date to get married. We hoped our wedding would lift the family, give us something to look forward to and help us to move on. We bought a house together; our first child, Felix, was born in February 1997. We were rebuilding, moving on, trying to forget. I almost convinced myself that I had come to terms with my father's death.

But you can't easily forget a man like Ken Saro-Wiwa.

▼

As hard as I tried to forget, his hanging haunted me. The strange thing is that I can't actually remember when I discovered *how* he was executed. I have no recollection of where I was or what I was doing or how I felt. Which is strange since one of the reasons his death so shocked the world was its almost medieval brutality. There is something primitive about a hanging that stirs our deepest, most visceral fears. For me, a hanging conjures images of Klan lynchings. That is what springs to mind when I see a headline like "A Fine Day for a Hanging," which is how one newspaper described the execution.

I don't know why, but people kept sending me newspaper clippings and magazine articles describing the events leading up to his execution. I couldn't bring myself to read them. I even had a detailed eyewitness account of my father's last moments on the gallows. It was written by an Ogoni in the prison and smuggled out. I had actually asked to see the letter. It was on the first anniversary of my father's execution, and I thought I was ready to face it. But when the letter was e-mailed to me, I couldn't read it. I renamed it "The End" and filed it away. It sat on my computer for two years, daring me to read it. I couldn't even bring myself to say the word "hang." I would flinch whenever I heard it. You'd be surprised how often it comes up in conversation—hang on, hang up, hang around, hang the consequences. Even words like "execution," "death row," "gallows" and "condemned prisoner" made me jumpy. Why is it that when you try to avoid something, you always end up bumping into it everywhere? Why had my father suggested in that letter that "hanging and wiving" go together? And was there any significance to the fact that the narrator in his short story "A Message for Mr. Adamu" had described Waida West as having a short neck, which meant "that he could not be hanged easily"? How did he know, when he wrote "On the Death of Ken Saro-Wiwa," that they would "cheat Ken Saro-Wiwa of six feet of earth"? Did he know he would die a violent death?

While I was desperately trying to forget, everyone else was trying to keep my father's memory alive. In death Ken Saro-Wiwa was reborn, larger than life, and I kept bumping into him. His name kept cropping up in the press. How could you ignore your father when he had suddenly become a global symbol of the struggle for human rights, social justice, the environment and just about everything else under the sun? He would have loved all the attention too. He would have laughed off the irony that NGOs that had politely turned him away two years before were now falling over themselves to write proposals and get funding for projects to ensure that "Ken Saro-Wiwa's death was not in vain." Streets were renamed, scholarships announced and public holidays declared. His name was used and abused. Refugees would apply for asylum, claiming to be related to Ken Saro-Wiwa. I received calls from countries all over Europe asking me to verify that so-and-so was a relative. Bogus foundations were launched, such as the one set up in the Ivory Coast by Stephen Wiwa and Janet Wiwa, who claimed to be the son and wife of someone called Dr. Kenneth Saro-Wiwa. They even received a donation from a lawyer in Pakistan! And while these people were dining out on my father's name, his critics were chipping away at his reputation and character.

▼

One of the toughest things about death is finding a balance between forgetting and remembering. Writing about Salvador Allende's suicide in Chile in 1973, Ariel Dorfmann commented: "His death [Allende's] will also, in the years to come, make terrible demands on those who survive him, cast a shadow on our lives, burden us impossibly. There are some among us who will not be able to carry the sacred weight of Allende's death."

If the cause for which a martyr has died hasn't been achieved, his survivors are condemned to question their commitment to the cause and their motivation to carry on living. That fact alone tested my resolve to retire from the struggle. Initially, I was lucky that my uncle Owens, a passionate and committed member of MOSOP's steering committee, had escaped from Nigeria after the executions and was around to help. He offered himself as the focus of the struggle abroad while I took a step back from the campaign. But while he relieved me of some of the burdens of prosecuting my father's political legacy, I was still overwhelmed by my father's personal legacy.

Undeservedly, you will atone for the sins of your fathers, said Horace. Ken Saro-Wiwa's private life was almost as complicated and controversial as his political one. In all, he had eight children from three women. And as the successful head of a polygamous, extended family he had an onerous set of responsibilities.

Because I was his first son, I inherited his sins, his children and all his other duties and headaches.

I remember the moment it dawned on me that being my father's son was not only about being Ken Saro-Wiwa's son. It was the day I was reunited with my family after I left Auckland. I was in a room with my sisters, Zina and Noo, and my mother, watching the news. It was two days after the execution, and the story was still headline news. When I had arrived at Heathrow, I had a press conference. It was my first public statement on my father's death, and the briefing was on the hourly bulletins. The news never seems quite so authoritative when you are on it, and I remember watching with my mother and sisters and thinking that I was now head of the family. And I remember wondering who that guy on television was, because he looked just like Ken Wiwa but sounded so composed and philosophical. The real Ken Wiwa was tired, apprehensive and feeling very, very lonely.

I used to wonder why people said they felt "lonely" or alone when their fathers died. But that was exactly how I felt on November 12, 1995. Lonely.

Whether he is there or not, your father is the man who defines you. He presents you with a challenge, a set of questions. And the paradox is that he also has the answers to those questions. If you haven't answered your father's questions by the time he dies, then that day is the day you will suddenly realize that you are alone in the world. You now have to work out the questions *and* the answers all by yourself.

I spent two years struggling to find and answer my father's questions, struggling with the paradox of trying to forget but needing to remember, wondering whether I should be following in his footsteps or finding my own way in life. The questions haunted me until I almost fell apart in the summer of 1997; I started having vivid nightmares about my father. After about a month of sleepless nights and hallucinations, I conceded it was time to do something about my father, time to find him and get some answers to all the questions he had left me.

▼

There is an old African saying that when a man dies, it is as if a library has burned down. Fathers are like libraries—they are books that hold the questions and the answers to their sons' futures. When I started writing this memoir, I had no idea how or where to start looking for my father—until I realized that his questions and answers were written and preserved in the books he had left behind, in the hundreds of photographs that he took, in the letters and documents that he had kept and meticulously filed throughout his life. Somewhere in the mountain of words and images that he had left behind were the stories, the clues, the answers to the enigma that was my father.

I started with the books. Apart from the published works, there are unpublished plays, poems, short stories and novels. I'd read some but not all of his published works. I found them rather didactic, stuffed with the politics I had heard a thousand times before. With Ken Saro-Wiwa, you barely get a personal introduction to the writer before he starts dragging you all over his political territory, pointing out the landmarks and signposts on his road to Damascus. He rarely dwelt on the personal. It was politics, politics, politics. He lived a political life.

But the more I read of his books, plays, pamphlets, letters and unpublished manuscripts, the more autobiographical clues I found. I waded through them, trying to reconstruct a picture of my father, but it was slow going. I had brief, tantalizing glimpses of him, but it was like trying to draw a picture of the invisible man. I needed a shortcut; I was starting to lose hope when I heard a little voice urging me to read *Lemona's Tale*.

It is his last published book, and it was the manuscript he lost at Lagos airport, the love story that was meant to introduce his name and writing to the literary salons of Europe and North America. When he was arrested in 1994, he had rewritten the story.

When complimentary copies of the posthumous novella arrived in the post, I had stacked them away on my bookshelf, along with all the other complimentary copies and translations of his work. *Lemona's Tale* sat on the shelf for a year, until I gave in to the voice urging me to read it.

I finished it in an hour. I put it down, and I rushed to the pile of letters he had written to me from detention. I went straight to the letter of August 11, 1994, where I found the words I was looking for. They are the last line of *Lemona's Tale*: "As I mounted the steps of the plane, I thought how unfair it is that children do not choose their parents."

From the first line of the book—"Lemona. Lemona. Beautiful woman. Exquisite. She'll be hanged tomorrow"—to the last, it was clear that my father had written it as an apologia to his children. *Lemona's Tale* is the story of a woman on death row who is visited by a girl who may or may not be the daughter she abandoned at birth. There are so many transparently autobiographical incidents in that novella that I recommended it to my sisters, who read it in one sitting.

After I read the book, some of the anger and resentment I was feeling seemed misplaced. A few weeks after reading *Lemona's Tale*, I went to have dinner with my uncle Jim and his English wife, Linda. It was early evening when I arrived at their home outside London. We talked about the family, its complexities, the rivalries, the jealousies and the enormous vacuum that my father's death had created. We went over all the old slights—real and imagined. Jim and Linda knew and understood many of the passions that divided and ruled my family. They had spent a few years in Nigeria when they were first married, and Linda had heard a lot of my family's history from my grandmother. I wondered how she could have gathered so much information from

Mama when she did not speak much Khana. "Oh," they both said together, "Mama speaks good English."

I was on a steep learning curve that night. Later, Uncle Jim was shaken after I told him how divided I felt about my father.

"Junior, you will die if you carry on like this," he replied. "There is so much pain and anger in your voice. You need to calm down. You need to take care of yourself and your family. Stop worrying about things you can't do anything about."

When I left that night, I decided it was time to call a truce with my father. As I drove home I reached—as I always do when I need to calm down—for U2's album *Achtung Baby*. It was Tedum's favourite. I'd never really paid much attention to the lyrics, but when I heard the song "One" I suddenly found myself listening to the words.

Will it make it easier on you now
You got someone to blame . . .
You gave me nothing
Now it's all I got.

I rewound the song and played it again.

Did I disappoint you?
Well, it's . . . Too late
Tonight to drag the past out into the light . . .
Have you come here for forgiveness?
Have you come to raise the dead?
Have you come here to play Jesus
To the lepers in your head?

Did I ask too much
More than a lot?
You gave me nothing
Now it's all I got

We're one
But we're not the same
We'll hurt each other
Then we do it again . . .

You ask me to enter
But then you make me crawl
And I can't be holding on
To what you got
When all you got is hurt

One love
One blood
One life
You got to do what you should

One life
But we're not the same
We get to carry each other . . .

The song struck a chord in me. And suddenly all the emotion that had been bottled up for so long came pouring out. It dawned on me as I sat crying in my car that I had lost a friend, a wise old man to confide in. I cried like a little boy that night. After two years, two months and thirteen days, it had finally sunk in that my father was dead.

The next day, I sat down at my computer. I clicked on the file called "The End," took a deep breath and started reading:

To Whom It May Concern,
Our experience on the 10th day of November 1995, when Ken Saro Wiwa and 8 of his compatriots were executed in the Port Harcourt Prisons . . .

I read every word of the letter to the end.

. . . The above narration is a near-comprehensive account of our expe-
rience here in the Port Harcourt prisons on the day Ken Saro-Wiwa and
8 of his countrymen were judicially murdered. Attached herewith is a
sketch of the Port Harcourt prisons showing the various wards, cells, the
gallows and the cell of the writer as at the day of execution.

Nyieda Nasikpo
For and on behalf of the OGONI 19, Port Harcourt prisons.

Drained but calm, I closed the document. I slid a compact
disc, *The Indestructible Beat of Soweto*, into the computer. A
sparkling guitar solo danced out of the speakers. I looked out of
the window and up to the sky, where I imagined my father was
watching me, and smiled. I started jumping around the study,
dancing and laughing hysterically. As I leapt around, I remembered a poem my father had written from detention:

Dance your anger and your joys.
Dance the guns to silence.
Dance. Dance. Dance . . .

13

On the Death of Ken Saro-Wiwa

▼

I shall record it as I heard and memorised it. The tone of voice may be hers and it may be mine; it does not matter. As she narrated the story, increasingly I felt it to be mine, and I adopted it as such. But is not that the point of every story . . . that it strikes a chord in us . . . and goes into lore and becomes common property?

—KEN SARO-WIWA, *Lemona's Tale*

Our experience on the 10th day of November 1995, when Ken Saro Wiwa and 8 of his compatriots were executed in the Port Harcourt Prisons . . .

On the morning of his execution, my father would have felt conflicting emotions. He probably had no specific idea that he would be executed that day, but perhaps he might have had an inkling that it would be his last day alive. He woke up before dawn—as he had done for most of his life. It was still dark outside as he began to prepare for whatever the day would bring. Perhaps he was relieved that his life would soon be over, because he was exhausted. He was tired of all the speculation, tired of trying to piece together the conflicting reports, of trying to second-guess what the authorities were going to do with him. He was tired of clinging on for a last-minute reprieve, especially as he had already convinced himself that death would absolve him from his labours, would be a merciful release from the aggravations of trying to square the dizzying circles of his life.

If anything he was grateful for the last eighteen months he had spent in detention. He welcomed the solitude, the time to reflect and the chance to put his mind at rest. He had found solace in religion. He had read the Bible and studied the Koran. He had been a dedicated agnostic for most, if not all, of his adult life, but now he was at peace with himself, a state of mind he had not enjoyed for a while. He smiled at the irony of finding peace of mind in a filthy, hot, mosquito-infested cell that he had once described as a living death. He remembered how he had resolved, when he was first sent there, to endure its deprivations with the cussed determination of a man who had spent his whole life battling to save a cruel, brutish, brutalizing society from itself. He even came to enjoy the hardships of his detention, deriving a perverse pleasure from the squalor around him. As he sat on the damp, cold, concrete floor of his cell that morning, he reassured himself that he had played his part. Destiny was at hand. His job was almost done, and his time had come. He had lived a full life, and he was ready to face death.

Something would have been nibbling away at him that morning, though, a knot of anxiety worming away inside him. He probably turned to his Bible and offered some prayers for all the people he would soon be leaving behind: his parents, his family and his people. He might have offered a special prayer for my mother, then for his children, hoping we would find it in us to forgive and understand him. He felt pain at how his life had compromised ours, at how his execution would haunt us. He reflected on how his controversial life, the choices he had made, had hurt his family, and how his death would surely pursue his children to their own graves. He thought about all the others who had died in the struggle; the Ogoni who had been imprisoned or killed; the men who had been subject to torture, detention, harassment; the women, many of them young girls, who had been raped by soldiers. All this had been visited on his family and his people largely because *he* had encouraged them to rise up and speak out against injustice. He turned to the Koran, and there, in sura 42, verse 41, was the sentence that offered him reassurance: "All those who fight when oppressed incur no guilt, but Allah shall punish the oppressor." It would have been his final statement to the Auta tribunal.

As he finished his prayers and drew himself up from the floor, he took further consolation from the thought that his execution, the sheer injustice of it, would at least draw the world's attention to the discrimination that his people had suffered for so long. He was determined and ready to die a martyr's death. He felt it was a necessary part of the struggle, and as he contemplated the power and symbolism of such a death, he felt at ease again.

Later, as the first shafts of daylight crept into his cell, he realized that his mind had been wandering. He had been thinking about all the efforts being made to save his life. He scolded himself for losing his focus, for clinging to that lifeline when he knew it was over. He reminded himself that he no longer had any control over his life. I imagine that my father allowed himself a smile at that. He had always prided himself on being in charge of his destiny. But as he waited for someone else to decide his fate, he realized that circumstances beyond his control had always been conspiring against him, dictating his choices, shepherding him towards his destiny, which was to die for his people.

He had reached that conclusion a few months before, and had even had his narrator muse on it in *Lemona's Tale*: "Her story . . . fell into neat little episodes . . . as though it had been carefully laid out by some designer, with one waiting to take the baton from the other. Yes, I was the mere baton. And that was my problem, wasn't it? Everything was happening to me. I did not happen to anything or to anyone. Each time I tried to happen, disaster resulted."

Events beyond his control, like the civil war, had changed the shape of his life. Things had happened to him, and not the other way round. But today, he resolved to concentrate on what would be his final act of defiance.

He wanted to leave the world with a few words that would not only haunt his oppressors but also inspire future generations to continue the struggle. He rehearsed his last words, trying to imagine the most dramatic and appropriate moment to deliver them. As he considered the various scenarios, he was conscious of the need to guard against the numbing terror of that moment when he heard the clank of the key as the warder opened his cell to allow the soldiers stationed outside to lead him away to be executed. He didn't want to be surprised. He didn't want to react in a way that would betray any anxiety he might be feeling about dying. He realized that the way he reacted at that particular moment would set the tone for the rest of what remained of his life. He would stiffen his resolve, hold his head up high. He wanted history to record that he did not flinch when they came to take him away.

They came for him at 11:30 that morning. He absentmindedly and instinctively reached for his wallet as the warder handcuffed him and chained his legs. He was escorted from his cell in the Bori military cantonment, on the outskirts of Port Harcourt, and placed in a Black Maria, where he was joined by three men, John Kpuinen, Dr. Barine Kiobel and Baribor Bera. There was a heavy silence as the four men exchanged brief, nervous glances, trying to avoid eye contact in case they betrayed their fears.

My father was still fighting the temptation to speculate about his fate. They'd been in the Black Maria many times before, and he had come to appreciate the ride, since it was his only chance to see the world outside his cell. Along the route, people turned to watch with dread as the truck thundered past, escorted by a convoy of cars, motorcycles and a chorus of wailing sirens.

At Port Harcourt prison, the convoy turned into the arched entrance of a crumbling building with an incongruously elegant Edwardian façade. The men were led out into the prison that inmates called Alabama. They were taken to Block C, a row of one-storey brick buildings where condemned prisoners are held. As my father approached Block C, he would have seen the other five men who had also been sentenced to death. They were huddled together, handcuffed and kneeling in front of an outhouse. When they saw my father approaching, some of them began to cry.

As he joined them, Nordu Eawo turned to my father and sobbed: "Terrh, so we are going to die like this?" My father advised him to be brave, and speaking to all of them, he encouraged them to take comfort in dying for their people, assuring them that they would live forever in the minds of those they were leaving behind. As the condemned men tried to come to terms with the fact that they would soon be dead, some of the prison warders could be heard singing, "Glory, glory be to God, amen, alleluia"—the traditional anthem sung before an execution.

At 11:55 a.m. another blazing siren signalled the arrival of the military governor, Lt. Col. Dauda Komo, accompanied by the state commissioner for justice and Adokiye Amesimaka, the state attorney general. The official entourage proceeded to the office of the deputy controller of prisons, where they were offered and drank a toast. The governor and his aides chose to remain behind in the office. They couldn't bring themselves to watch as the condemned men were called onto the gallows.

Still conscious of his status as the leader of his people and of the verdict of history, my father offered to go first. He straightened his back and shuffled defiantly into the hut that housed the gallows. A priest followed him in with a viaticum, then came out again. There was a short delay, then my father's voice echoed around the courtyard: "What sort of country is this that delights in the killing of its illustrious citizens? What have I done that I deserve death, than that I spoke the truth, demanding justice for my poor people of Ogoni? I have always been a man of good ideas, and whether I be killed, my ideas will live forever, and Ogoni, for which I am dying, will one day be emancipated from the shackles of oppression."

There was a terrible silence around the yard. Then my father emerged from the hut. It later transpired that there had been an electrical failure in the gallows. The executioners consulted among themselves for a few minutes before ordering John Kpuinen onto the gallows. When the executioners activated the gallows equipment, a trapdoor opened under Kpuinen's feet and he was hanged.

Nobody had been able to fathom why Dr. Barine Kiobel was tried along with the others. He was a thirty-six-year-old mature student turned politician, and he had never, as far as anyone could establish, played any sort of role in MOSOP or in the Ogoni struggle. As the noose and hood were placed around his neck, he cried out in anguish: "What have I done to be killed this way? I have served this country well, and God knows I am never violent. God I am innocent, God I am innocent."

There was a haunting silence on the gallows. The prison's medical officer was summoned. He entered the hut and lowered himself into the shallow pit where Kiobel's limp body lay. He removed the hood from Kiobel's head and confirmed that he was dead.

After Kiobel's body was dragged out and dumped against a wall next to Kpuinen's corpse, one of the executioners tried to frogmarch my father onto the gallows. He was incensed and resisted. There are rumours that the authorities couldn't find local hangmen to do the job and had to summon a team of executioners from a prison a thousand kilometres away. The executioners would not have had any idea who my father was, and he probably saw them as victims, inmates of *The True Prison*, "executing callous calamitous orders in exchange for a wretched meal a day." But as empathetic as he might have felt, my father did not appreciate being manhandled crudely. He was too proud to submit to the kind of treatment meted out to common criminals. They were going to have to treat him with respect. His defiance, his bearing, must have unsettled hangmen who were used to dealing with armed robbers and other dregs of society. I imagine that was why it took them five attempts to hang my father.

After his last words echoed around the prison, the gallows equipment was activated. A puff of smoke was seen billowing out of the hut. The prison doctor was summoned. After a few minutes, my father's body was dragged out and placed next to the others.

At 12:45 p.m. on November 10, 1995, the corpses of nine Ogoni—John Kpuinen, Barine Kiobel, Kenule Saro-Wiwa, Baribor Bera, Nordu Eawo, Paul Levura, Daniel Gbookoo, Saturday Doobee and Felix Nuate—were loaded onto the back of a truck, covered by a tarpaulin and taken to a nearby cemetery, where their remains were buried.

I don't think my father would have been surprised that his execution was botched. As he liked to say, "To live a day in Nigeria is to die many times in one day." He had predicted that they would bungle the job in "On the Death of Ken Saro-Wiwa." But even with the incredible drama, tension and trauma of it, he was remarkably prescient and remained focused to the end. It is impossible to imagine what went through his mind in those circumstances, but my father, as was his wont, was determined to have the final say.

His last words were delivered in Khana, and were, in the end, far more powerful than the ones he had scripted in advance. The five attempts to execute him had forced him to extemporize. It meant that his last words came from the heart.

"Lord take my soul, but the struggle continues."

14

The Shadow of a Saint

▼

The world would be a poorer place if it was peopled by children
whose parents risked nothing in the cause of social justice,
for fear of personal loss.
—JOE SLOVO, IN A LETTER TO GILLIAN SLOVO

What is it that compels a man to risk everything—his life, his family, the lives of people around him—to make a stand for human rights?

Martyrs present us with troubling questions. Are they motivated by a desire to make the world a better place? Or are they merely assuaging guilt, or even massaging their own egos? Is there such a thing as a truly selfless act? Can we believe them when they insist that they are driven by altruistic motives, especially when their success requires blatant self-promotion and a sense of self-importance? At what point does a martyr become convinced that he speaks for the people, that he is the conscience of a nation?

One of the things that troubled me most about my father was the fanatical zeal with which he prosecuted the struggle after the protest march on January 4, 1993. The only thing that seemed to arouse him after that day was the struggle. He became so obsessed that he seemed to lose his perspective on life. And death.

His aloofness at Tedum's funeral was disturbing. He treated his son's death as if it was an intrusion, an interruption of his work. He created the impression that he just wanted to get the burial formalities over and done with so that he could return where he was needed. The way he writes about it in *A Month and a Day* is revealing. He devotes one paragraph to it: "On the ides of March, the sad news came of the sudden death of my youngest son, Tedum, on the playing fields of Britain's Eton College. I had to go to England to complete the funeral obsequies of my lovely, fourteen-year-old boy, whose soul, please God, may find eternal, peaceful rest . . ."

Although the book is a chronology of the political events of 1993, it reads as if he felt compelled to mention the death of his son. Did his son's death affect his appetite for or influence his attitude to the struggle? Guilt stalks the relatives of martyrs, and I used to wonder whether it was my hostility to him during Tedum's funeral that pushed him into a suicidal confrontation with the military and Shell, but people who were around my father in 1993 say he seemed to be daring, almost goading, the military into killing him. They say that by refusing to compromise his position, he gave the military no choice.

There is a fine line between martyrdom and suicide, and this is one of the most troubling aspects about martyrs—especially for the people closest to them.

According to the biblical origins of the word, a martyr is a witness, someone chosen to bear witness for his people. But does bearing witness justify the sacrifices that martyrs often have to make? What makes martyrs seemingly indifferent to the pain they cause those closest to them? Is this why they often resort to a mystical calling to justify what they do?

My father used to say that he was writing in his study one night in 1989 when he saw an Ogoni star in the sky, telling him to go and lead his people. I think he was exercising a little poetic licence there, because the die was really cast four years later, when he saw all those people streaming out of their villages in January 1993, and the majority of our people anointed him as some kind of messiah and the conscience of Ogoni. And for Ken Saro-Wiwa, his obligations to his children and to his people were one and the same thing. The line between the personal and the political was blurred, virtually non-existent. But that line cuts right through to the heart of why we are here. Are we here to make the world safe for our children, or do we live to make our children safe in the world?

And the troubled heart of the matter is this: to make the world safe for their children, martyrs must *sacrifice* their children. And unless you are an unquestioning and devoted supporter, the sacrifice may seem harsh, even cruel. In order to understand it, you have to have a certain emotional detachment

In March 1998, I flew to South Africa hoping that Nelson Mandela would help me understand why someone whould sacrifice his family for social justice. I'd been trying to track Mandela down for a few months, but he proved to be as elusive as my father. When I flew out to South Africa, I didn't have an appointment to see him. There is an expression in Nigeria—"man know man"—which means you have to know someone who knows someone to get what you want. I think the expression, or at least the idea, is pan-African, because when I telephoned the South African writer and journalist Donald Woods and told him that I was having problems securing an interview with Mandela, he laughed.

"Ach, Ken," he said from his home in Johannesburg. "Just come down here and we will fix you up. This is Africa. Just imagine you're in Lagos," he advised.

I've always been an admirer of South African writers like Don Mattera, Alan Paton, J. M. Coetzee and, of course, Nadine

Gordimer, whose book *Burger's Daughter* I carried around with me while I was campaigning to save my father. The themes these writers explore, the conflict between the personal and the political, attracted me to them. But there was another, more compelling reason why I wanted to go to South Africa: I hadn't been to Africa in six years, and I was yearning to go back.

I felt Mandela was the only man who could explain my father to me. The two had a few things in common—not least that each had refused to compromise his conscience, preferring to remain in detention regardless of the cost to his family.

I also wanted, or needed, to know why Mandela and the world's leaders had failed my father. I naïvely expected that Mandela could shed light on what had gone on behind the scenes in Auckland. I hoped he would assure me that everything humanly possible had been done to save my father's life.

When Mandela was released in 1990, my father paid him a tribute in his column in the Lagos *Sunday Times*: "Twenty-seven years in jail and the man Mandela emerges looking elegant, presidential, even majestic. If he had died in jail, he would have been a martyr. . . . Out of jail, he is a symbol of the undying spirit of committed man in search of political freedom. He seems destined to lead Africa. . . ."

That "symbol of the undying spirit of committed man in search of political freedom" was what moved my father to suggest that I fly to Auckland to make a personal plea to Mandela. It's a moot point whether a strong statement from him would have saved my father's life—Abacha was probably bent on executing him anyway. But in retrospect, from the moment Mandela stepped off the plane in Auckland, waving and smiling, casually dressed in one of his Hawaiian shirts, it was clear that he didn't want to get too embroiled in any political controversy. He looked like a man who was determined to enjoy his first Commonwealth conference, and he wanted to mark his presence at the summit by thanking the organization that had played such a prominent role in leading the global campaign against apartheid.

Whenever I tried to get an audience with Mandela in Auckland, I was left with no doubt that the president's men did not want me anywhere near him. When I put in a request for a meeting, I was told that Mandela's press secretary was unavailable. When I wondered if I could send a fax, I was informed that Mandela's press secretary didn't have a fax machine. His insistence on "quiet diplomacy" and "constructive engagement" mystified human-rights campaigners and infuriated Nigerian pro-democracy activists. One Nigerian activist even went as far as publicly suggesting that if the rest of the world had been as soft on apartheid, Mandela would not be enjoying his freedom.

Although I was bitterly disappointed by Mandela's position, I felt it was his advisers who had misread the urgency of the situation. When I asked Wole Soyinka about Mandela's soft stance, Soyinka suggested that his hands were tied by South Africa's official policy on Nigeria. Many of the top brass in the Nigerian military had been allies of the Afican National Congress during apartheid. I suspect there was another reason too—in politics, particularly in Africa, business is rarely done in an open, public forum. There were suggestions that Mandela's people had been assured behind the scenes by Abacha's people that my father's life would be spared. I suspect that when Mandela came out fighting after my father was executed, he was mad at the humiliation and at the sullying of his hard-earned reputation. He suggested that Abacha was sitting on a "time bomb" that he (Mandela) was going to personally detonate. Strong, unequivocal and unusual language for a statesman.

Mandela shouldered most of the blame for the failure of the international community to act on my father's behalf. *The Washington Post* reflected the general consensus when it suggested that his strong stance "represented an 11th-hour conversion to the hard line that some critics—including Saro-Wiwa's son—said could have saved the condemned men had Mandela rallied an international campaign."

Pricked by his conscience and the strength of criticism he received both at home and abroad for his handling of the affair, Mandela did at least try to translate his tough words into concrete action. He was instrumental in getting Nigeria suspended from the Commonwealth, and his comments and actions were welcome and reassuring at a time when I'd lost faith in politics and politicians.

But then Mandela spoiled it by sending a letter of condolence to my mother.

Archbishop Desmond Tutu delivered the letter when he came to London as the special guest of honour at an evening in remembrance of Ken Saro-Wiwa. The family had lunch with Tutu before the event, and he handed my mother the letter at the table. All eyes were on her as she read the letter. When she finished, she sighed and folded it away. She asked Tutu to thank Mandela on behalf of the family, but I could tell she was upset. There were nervous glances around the table. I discreetly asked my mother to let me read the letter. She refused. I insisted until she relented. I opened the letter and scanned it quickly, flashing past the embossed president's seal at the top, the Cape Town address, and the short message of condolence. I couldn't see what had offended my mother until it suddenly leapt out at me. It was addressed to a Mrs. Hauwa Saro-Wiwa.

Hauwa Maidugu, to give her proper name, was one of my father's girlfriends. She is the mother of my father's youngest son, my half-brother Kwame. When my father was in detention, his sisters and girlfriends had often had to sign in as his wife in order to see him. Most of the Nigerian newspapers were none the wiser and erroneously reported that Hauwa was my father's wife. Many of his obituaries had also credited Hauwa as his wife.

My mother was distraught. It seemed at the time that the humiliations would never end.

Mandela's handlers hadn't done enough research on who Ken Saro-Wiwa was. But the mistake underlined my point that he had been badly advised, that even their policy was perhaps based on bad information.

I actually saw Mandela in Edinburgh during the Commonwealth conference in October 1997. I went up there to see whether the Commonwealth would make good on its promise from the summit in Auckland to expel Nigeria "within two years if no concrete steps" had been taken to restore democracy. By the time the Edinburgh summit rolled around, Abacha was churning his way through yet another transition-to-democracy exercise, but Nigerians were not impressed. Everyone knew Abacha had no intention of ever handing over power. But that flimsy evidence of Abacha's sincerity was enough for the Commonwealth's members to grant him a stay of execution. Abacha revealed his hoary hand when all the political parties nominated him as their candidate for the presidential elections.

While the Commonwealth was finding new ways of dressing up a U-turn, I was busy trying to get to Mandela, not for political reasons but for personal ones—I wanted to get that interview with him. As had happened in Auckland, however, his handlers kept everyone at arm's length.

Six months after the summit in Edinburgh, I found myself standing opposite Mandela's retirement villa in his home village. It was a hot afternoon at the end of the Easter weekend, and I was on an assignment to write a travel piece—it was the best excuse I could find for turning up at Mandela's home uninvited.

Qunu is where he grew up, and Qunu is where he intends to retire. I slept during the two-hour drive from Umtata to Qunu, and when I woke up there was a horse and cart shuffling along on the road in front of my Eastern Cape tourist-board vehicle. As the driver slowed to pass the cart, a military helicopter floated up out of the valley in front of us and buzzed across the skyline like a giant dragonfly. A few minutes later, we parked in the garden of a bungalow by the side of the N2, the road that runs through Qunu. Little black pigs snuffled around while a couple of stray chickens strutted about, pecking at the bare grass. Mandela's villa—a sprawling, one-storey, red-brick building—was on the other side of the road. The house is based on the floor plan of his quarters at Victor Verster prison, where he spent the last two years of his sentence. In his autobiography, Mandela explains that Victor Verster was the first spacious, comfortable home he ever lived in. He modelled his retirement home on it because he was "familiar with its dimension" and would not "have to wander at night looking for the kitchen."

The villa sticks out from the traditional pink, limestone green and white-coloured rondavels dotted around the rolling hills in Qunu. The only sign of security was a man wearing the familiar light blue shirt and dark blue slacks of the South African police force and he was dozing under a tree at the entrance to the house.

There is a wonderful serenity to the hills around Qunu. But as quiet and peaceful as they look, those hills have also been soaked in blood. They have witnessed, over the centuries, some of the fiercest battles between the Zulus, the Xhosa and the Boers. These days, in the middle of a hot afternoon, there is a haunting silence about them. The only sounds that puntuate the silence are the bells on the necks of goats, which echo around the hills like wind chimes.

I spoke to an old man, a Louis Armstrong look-alike with bulging eyes and leathery voice. Baba Sidlele was Mandela's gardener.

I asked him about the bees.

When I arrived in Johannesburg, I heard an amusing story that Mandela had been attacked by a swarm of bees while he was having a bath at his home in Qunu. A swarm of bees, according to Xhosa legend, is a sign of bad luck, and there was speculation whether Mandela would have to make a traditional sacrifice to ward off the omens. A rather humourless presidential spokesman had declined to enter into the spirit of the story, refusing to either confirm or deny that Mandela would be making sacrifices.

"Did you hear about that in London?" Sidlele wondered incredulously. He grimaced and doubled up, wheezing as he laughed. Many of the villagers in Qunu still can't quite come to grips with Mandela's fame. To them, he is just Madiba, the man whom the Boers locked up for a few years. Apart from the house—the grounds were donated to Mandela—there was nothing to indicate that this was the president's home village, which is unusual among Africa's leaders, who have commissioned everything from international airports to huge replicas of St. Paul's Basilica in their villages.

"Is he around?" I asked Sidlele.

Sidlele exchanged nervous glances with his clansmen. "No, he's just left," he replied unconvincingly.

Another old man wandered over to join the Qunu welcoming committee that had formed around me. Tall, with a goofy, boyish grin, he was wearing a baseball cap and a long-sleeved Hawaiian shirt with a migraine-inducing psychedelic print.

"Do you know who this is?" Sidlele said pointing to the old man. "Do you recognize the shirt?" he said, tugging at the old man's cuffs.

I looked at the shirt and shrugged.

"That's one of Madiba's shirts," Sidlele said with a smile in his eyes. I realized that it did look like one of Mandela's famously bad shirts.

"This is Manlenkosi Ngcebtshana," my tourist-board guide interjected. "He's Mandela's cousin."

There were smiles all around and vigorous nods of appreciation. Mandela's cousin grinned proudly.

And that was the closest I came to meeting Nelson Rohilala Mandela.

When I returned to Johannesburg a few days later, I tried to reassure Mandela's office that I was sympathetic to his predicament, that I hadn't come to embarrass him politically—that my mission was personal, and all I wanted was for him to help give me a better understanding of my father. But no one from the president's office returned my calls or replied to the request I had made through the High Commission in London.

So I gave up. I felt he would be freer to talk as a civilian, as Nelson Rohilala Mandela, than as President Nelson Mandela. After he retired in May 1999, I tried again, this time with Archbishop Tutu's blessing. That did the trick, because I got a response from Mandela's private secretary within a month.

The letter stated that Mandela was too busy and "unfortunately not able to grant you an interview. Since his retirement, Mr. Mandela has been inundated with requests of this nature. . . ." He would be "fully booked for the rest of this year".

Although I was disappointed, I didn't mind too much. I'd worked out some of the questions I had about my father by then, and the irony was that Mandela had helped me find the answers.

Early in *A Long Walk to Freedom*, Mandela describes his feelings on his return to Qunu on political business after having been away for fifteen years. He discovers that his mother has been "living alone in such poor circumstances," and is moved to wonder "whether one was ever justified in neglecting the welfare of one's own family in order to fight for the welfare of others." It's a question that follows him through the memoir, especially when he describes his sadness at missing out on his daughter Zindzi's childhood.

One of the many poignant and moving sections of the book is Mandela's recollection of a recurring nightmare that haunted him in Robben Island in 1976. He would dream that he had been released from prison, but when he arrived at his home in Soweto, "it turned out to be empty, a ghost house, with all the doors and windows open but no one there at all."

When I returned to South Africa in July 2000, I met Mandela's youngest daughter, Zindzi, at the family home in Soweto.

Zinzdiswa Mandela has had an eventful life in her father's house. When Mandela was dispatched to Robben Island in 1962, she was just eighteen months old. The first time she "met" her father, she was fifteen years old.

"It was traumatic, quite emotional," she told me, about meeting her father for the first time. "As much as I had been warned about the conditions, it was still a shock to see him behind the glass, with the warders around us, listening to our communication. I was staring at this man, trying to look for aspects of myself, trying to memorize the voice, looking at his gestures. I knew who he was, but he was a total stranger."

I asked Zindzi what she thought her father saw. "He was conscious of what I was going through, and he tried to make me feel like I was sitting on his lap at home. He is quite a compelling character, charming even to his daughters. The surroundings just receded, and I could focus on him."

And here is Mandela's recollection of seeing his daughter for the first time: "Zindzi was shy and hesitant at first. I am sure it was not easy for her finally to see a father she had never really known, a father who could love her only from a distance, who seemed to belong not to her but to the people. Somewhere deep inside she must have harboured resentment and anger for a father who was absent during her childhood and adolescence. I could see right away that she was a strong and fiery young woman like her own mother . . ."

Like her mother, Zindzi Mandela is a compelling, stunningly attractive woman. She has a powerful, gravelly voice, and large, fiery eyes. Photographs of Zindzi Mandela were treasured items among the detainees at Robben Island.

When I met her, she was cool, a little offhand at first, but she warmed up to me—especially after I told her that my mother was a fan of her mother's. Nene sees a little bit of herself and her life in Winnie Mandela's story. When I told Zinzdi that my mother was barely sixteen years old when she was swept up by the whirlwind of Ken Saro-Wiwa's life, Zinzdi sat up and said, "Oh, yes, that's what happened to my mother too. Mum was so young and not political at all, but then she was forced to fill in for my father. She has sacrificed so much of herself for us, and she used to say to Zeni and I, 'You should never feel sorry for yourself. You have this name.' People will always say, 'Oh, whatever happened to Madiba's kids?' There are so many other children like us who are worse off."

Zindzi Mandela's story is symbolic of what happened to a generation of children in South Africa. That she was Nelson Mandela's daughter was both a blessing and a curse. "I don't know if I was resentful of his not being there. I've known nothing else, so there was nothing to miss. He was always there but never there."

I could understand what Zindzi meant by not missing something you have never had—when at the same time you still know that something is missing. But perhaps this is a rationalization for not having a father around. She was closer to the truth of the matter when she said, "When I first began to understand who he was, I could only relate to what he stood for." And what he stood for had an enormous impact on her life. One night in May 1977, policemen turned up at their house in Soweto and started loading furniture and clothing onto the back of a truck. Zindzi, her sister, Zenani, and their mother were banished to a three-room, tin-roofed shack in Brandfort, a remote town where the people were under the thumb of local white farmers. "We didn't know where we were, and nobody knows to this day why they sent us to the Free State," Zindzi recalled, smiling wryly at the memory. "They just dumped us in this place. We didn't speak the language, and we didn't know anyone."

If Zindzi was ever privately bitter about how her father's life had compromised hers, she has played the faithful daughter in public. Politically apathetic as I was at the time, I remember her famous "My father says" speech in 1985. On January 31, 1985, the then prime minister, P. W. Botha, offered Mandela his freedom if he "unconditionally rejected violence as a political instrument." Zinzdi read Mandela's response at an anti-apartheid rally two months later.

"My father says, 'I am a member of the African National Congress. I have always been a member of the African National Congress and I will remain a member of the African National Congress until the day I die . . . Only free men can negotiate. Prisoners cannot enter into contracts . . . I cannot and will not give any undertaking at a time when I and you, the people, are not free. Your freedom and mine cannot be separated. I will return.'"

Until he returned, freed unconditionally five years later, in 1990, Zinzdi, along with her mother, became the focus of anti-apartheid resistance, carrying the Nelson Mandela name and speaking on his behalf. "Zindzi was a dynamic speaker, like her mother," Mandela thrilled approvingly in his autobiography.

My father once wrote to me from Nigeria, citing Zinzdi Mandela as an example to follow. Interestingly, when I first read *A Long Walk to Freedom* in 1998, the story seemed strangely familiar, as if I had read elements of it before. So much of Mandela's life mirrored aspects of my father's, even down to the premature death of a loved son (Mandela's first son, Madiba, died in a car crash in 1969). But more than that, it was the language of *A Long Walk to Freedom*; its style and tone were similar to my father's detention diary.

Zindzi blushed when I revealed that my father had held her up as a role model for me. Although I found her coquettish and a very likeable character, I was aware that she has had an interesting, colourful and often controversial private life, and opinions about her in South Africa are mixed. One close family friend had warned me that her sister, Zenani, was "more coherent." Zenani is considered the quieter one of the two—she married a Swazi prince and is rarely in the limelight. Zindzi, on the other hand, has always been the more publicly political. But I found her more than coherent. She knew and understood the passions that ruled her life and her family. But knowing is one thing; how to deal with those passions is often the hard part. She did contradict herself once, however, and tellingly.

When I remarked that I wasn't sure what my authentic identity was because I had always pitched myself in opposition to my father, her pupils dilated. "From a very early age," she averred, "I was always conscious of wanting to be myself. I was active politically, but when he was released I wanted to be myself." Wanting to be herself meant going into the "entertainment business." She is involved in music and owns a restaurant, Kofifi, in the centre of Johannesburg. She has swapped her identity as Nelson Mandela's daughter for one that reflects the concerns of the post-apartheid generation. But despite her metamorphosis, the pull of history, her legacy still influences her. "Nothing," she later confessed to me, "will ever divorce me from the movement. I've learned to prioritize my life, but everything comes second to the movement."

When I mentioned to a white South African journalist (whom I shall call Kathryn Visser) that I was going to interview Zindzi, Visser warned me that "she is full of shit." This was in Europe, about eighteen months before I met Zindzi. I was curious, because Visser appeared to have good instincts for the nuances and paradoxes of people caught up in the fight for social justice. Later, in South Africa, I met many people who had strong views of the struggle and the people involved in it. Always at the back of my mind, when I talk to South Africans, especially the whites, is one question: What were you doing during apartheid? When I told a journalist what one of his colleagues had told me about Zindzi Mandela, "*Visser,*" he said—stressing the name—"is full of shit."

God only knows how we would deal with what Zindzi Mandela had to go through. That is not to make excuses for them, but only to try to understand. "It was hard, Ken," Zindzi said, recalling her experiences at Brandfort. It was the first time she really let her guard down during our conversation. "We were intimidated. If you can survive that, you can survive anything."

"But you survived," I told her. I could see tears in her eyes. "Me, I'm tired of arguing with people who have no idea what it is like to live through something such as you lived through," I said. "The best you can really do, Zindzi, is to be able to say, 'I survived.'"

Mandela himself readily admits that his family has paid a heavy price for his principles. "It seems," he has written, "to be the destiny of freedom fighters to have unstable personal lives. When your life is the struggle, as mine was, there is little room left for family. That has always been my greatest regret, and the most painful aspect of the choice I made."

Zindzi told me something that I had heard before, which poignantly illustrates what her family sacrificed. "When he first came out, he wasn't used to physical contact. You would hold his hands, but he wouldn't even know you were touching him. He is better now, and of course he loves children."

Mandela takes an active interest in his grandchildren, and regularly picks them up from school. "People often wonder why I am so proud of him doing that," Zindzi said. "Well, he never went ot my school concerts, never interacted with my schools, so I am proud of him." It seems that Zindzi and her father are reliving their relationship vicariously through Zindzi's children. She has five, one daughter and four sons, ranging in age from three to twenty-one. "One human being and five beasts," she told me with a laugh. "I try to give them the things I never had."

One of the saddest aspects of the Mandela story is the failure of his marriage. But despite their separation and later divorce, the Mandela's still care about each other. On my last trip to Johannesburg, I saw a wonderful documentary that offered an illuminating insight into the man behind the politics. In one scene, Winnie Mandela was red-eyed and tearful as she recalled their early years together. Their love was the first and greatest casualty of the struggle. I remember reading somewhere that on the eve of their wedding, Winnie Mandela's father warned her that she was marrying the cause and not the man.

As the most popular member of the ANC executive, Winnie Mandela is still married to the struggle. But there is a telling photograph at the home in Soweto, a home that is filled with memorabilia of Nelson Mandela: It is of a photograph of Gracha Machel, the current Mrs. Nelson Mandela. When I asked Zindzi about the photograph, she grinned and said, "Oh, yes. I am glad he has found Gracha. She is good for him."

From time to time in *A Long Walk to Freedom*, Mandela stops to wonder whether "politics is merely a pretext for shirking one's responsibilities, an excuse for not being able to provide in the way one wanted?" He never really answers the question, but it is the same question I often wondered about my father. He loved his children, as Mandela clearly enjoys his grandchildren, but I could never understand or believe my father when he confessed that he had always wanted to build a good family. Now, however, when I look at those old photographs of him with his children, I can clearly see a man who is proud of his children. The saddest part about his death is that he never got to see his grandchildren—but most haunting for me is the thought that he might have felt his death was some kind of penance, and that he hoped his children would come to see his sacrifice as a price worth paying, an excuse for his never being there for us at home.

Mandela and Saro-Wiwa: their legends are built on their refusal to compromise. Yet it is obvious that both men had to compromise so much for their principles. The true and full price of freedom is rarely documented. These stories rarely get told, because the innocence of the struggle has to be protected if the end is to justify the means.

Unlike my father, Mandela has the misfortune of being a living martyr. If he had died in jail, he would have been spared the impossible burden of living up to his legend. And my father obviously foresaw some of the problems Mandela would face as a free man. It is a shame and a bitter irony that Mandela couldn't, in the end, save my father. But he did allow me to gain a greater understanding of my father. And for that, I am grateful to him.

15

Unfinished Business

▼

*When we used to go to Anaka, elephants would dance, we were young,
we were young. Erenayo is no more, no more. Mother don't weep . . .
the pillar lies cold.*

—GEOFFREY ORYEMA, "Solitude"

After I lost the scent of Mandela's trail in Qunu in 1998, I drove to a sleepy place called King William's Town. Deep in the heart of the Eastern Cape, King William's Town is a bookmark in the pages of South Africa's bloody history. The Victorian buildings and monuments tell their own story, and as you drive through the town you can't help feeling that there is something incongruous about a place that looks like a slice of middle England in remotest Africa. At the southern end, Africa begins to reclaim the town as you enter the coloured township. If you drive on along the main road, you eventually turn down Cathcart Street to a railway bridge.

I followed the road as it ran alongside the railway line, then turned off it and drove under the bridge into what at first looked like an empty field. In the midday heat, with the sun so fierce it felt like time had stood still, the Steve Biko Memorial Gardens looked a fitting resting place for one of Africa's greatest martyrs.

Twenty years earlier, an open coffin carried Steve Biko, with his bloated and badly beaten face, to his grave in an ox cart. Twenty thousand mourners, including diplomatic representatives from thirteen Western states, crowded around the hillside, their faces full of grief and defiance. Those scenes seemed light years away. Apart from a couple of municipal workers dozing under a tree, the cemetery was empty. I had the place to myself, and I strolled through it until I came to an unremarkable, medium-sized, black marble headstone bearing a simple inscription:

Steve Bantu Biko,
1946—1977
One Azania, One Nation

I stood at the graveside for a few minutes, feeling a mix of emotions: anger, sadness, as well as a curious optimism. My thoughts drifted back to the conversation I had had with Nkosinathi Biko in Johannesburg a few days before.

I hadn't planned to meet the Biko family, but when I arrived in Johannesburg, I rang the writer Donald Woods to tell him I was in town. When I told him why I was trying to meet Mandela, Woods wondered if I had considered talking to the Biko family. I confessed that I hadn't—I told him that I didn't know anything about Steve Biko's family.

"Well, he has a son," Woods hinted.

"Oh, really," I said, excited at the thought of meeting a kindred spirit.

"Would you like to speak to him?" Woods offered. "He's right here. Hold on."

I waited anxiously as he went to fetch Steve Biko's son. I heard two men talking, then footsteps, this time coming towards the phone.

"Hello?" the voice was soft but with a clipped, black South African accent. "Nkosinathi Biko here."

"My name is Ken Wiwa," I said awkwardly. "It's a pleasure to talk to you."

"It's my pleasure too," Nkosinathi replied.

The introduction was a little stiff, but I felt a mutual connection. We spoke briefly and arranged to meet later in the week.

When I hung up, I decided to educate myself about Steve Biko. I only knew the basic details of his life and death, so I found a copy of Donald Woods's book in my host's library and caught up with Nkosinathi Biko's history.

Minutes after speaking to Nathi Biko, I eased myself into a chair, lay back in the shade of the patio that looked out over the swimming pool and started reading *Biko*. I read the opening paragraphs, and sat bolt upright:

"On Tuesday, September 6, 1977, a friend of mine named Stephen Biko was taken by South African political police to Room 619 of the Sanlam Building in Strand Street, Port Elizabeth, Cape Province, where he was handcuffed, put into leg irons, chained to a grille, and subjected to twenty-two hours of interrogation in the course of which he was tortured and beaten, sustaining several blows to the head that damaged his brain fatally, causing him to lapse into a coma and die six days later."

▼

Stephen Biko was the son of a police clerk and a domestic worker. He was born in King William's Town in 1946. His father died when he was four, but he overcame that handicap, and desperate poverty, to emerge as a leading light in the struggle against apartheid. As an activist in black community programs—from his platform as president of the all-black South African Students Organisation (SASO), the Black Consciousness Movement (BCM) and the Black Peoples Convention

(BPC)—Biko became the most important name in the anti-apartheid movement.

After the massacre in Sharpeville in 1960, and the arrest and banning of black political leaders like Nelson Mandela and Robert Sobukwe—the leader of the radical Pan Africanist Congress (PAC)—the BCM and Steve Biko emerged to fill the vacuum in black leadership. Unlike the ANC or the PAC, the BCM was a movement and not a political party. Black consciousness was a state of mind. The idea behind it, as Donald Woods observed, "was to break away almost entirely from past black attitudes to the liberation struggle and to set a new style of self-reliance and dignity for blacks as a psychological attitude leading to new initiatives." Black consciousness was a cousin of the black power movement in the United States and the pan-African movements that influenced my father at university in Nigeria.

When he first met Biko, Donald Woods was editor of the *Daily Despatch*, a newspaper based in East London. Although Woods was a liberal and fervently anti–apartheid, he was wary of Biko. "I didn't want to meet him because I had an idea of what he stood for and I didn't like it," Woods wrote. "After doing my best to oppose white racism I did not feel disposed to tolerate any suggestion of black racism. There seemed no point in replacing one type of racism with another, and all that I had heard and read about the Biko movement led me to regard it as racial exclusivism in reverse."

But when Woods was eventually persuaded to meet Biko, he fell under his spell. "I am slightly under six feet tall, but he stood at least a couple of inches over me and had the bulky build of a heavyweight boxer carrying more weight than when in peak condition," he recalls of his first impression of Steve Biko.

That afternoon, the two men sat around thrashing out their differences, discussing and comparing their strategies to combat apartheid. Woods's hostility to Biko was based on an article Biko had written calling on blacks to dissociate themselves from white liberals because liberal ideology "makes people believe that something is being achieved when in reality the artificially integrated circles are a soporific to the blacks while salving the consciences of the few guilt-stricken whites."

What struck me about Woods's account of their early skirmishes was the way Biko coolly judged that the journalist could be a useful ally in championing his ideals. When Woods asked him why he had requested a meeting, Biko switched on the charm: "Most of the blacks think you're a terrific guy and you've got a big following among blacks because of your editorials—but I wanted to find out if you're a terrific enough guy to start giving some decent coverage to the Black Consciousness Movement . . ."

Almost everything I read about Steve Biko reminded me of my father—the pointed posturing of his writing, the easy charm that was at its most engaging when he was trying to win over someone who could help the cause. At the end of their meeting, Woods was hooked. He was convinced that he had "met an unusually gifted man." He wrote that Biko's "quick brain, superb articulation of ideas and sheer mental force were highly impressive. He had the aura and stature of a leader, and on my way home I concluded that in a journalistic career in which I had met and interviewed some of the great figures in British, Canadian, American, and German politics, this man Biko might conceivably be the most impressive of them all . . . I later came to realise [Steve Biko] was the greatest man I ever had the privilege to know."

What stuck in my mind was Woods's observation that though Biko "had an uncompromising contempt for the Afrikaner nationalist mentality, he had at no time any ounce of hatred or bitterness toward his prosecutors. In fact, he spoke at times almost affectionately about his jailers and interrogators. . . . He simply wasn't a hater of people. . . . Steve understood them and their hang-ups too well to hate them. It was only their racist ideas that he hated. And he hated these to such effect, and opposed them to such effect, and rallied opposition to them to such effect, that because of their merciless rigidity his final collision with the System was inevitable." That passage could, to the last word, have been describing my father's feelings about his own critics.

As MOSOP would do for Ogoni youths in the early 1990s, black consciousness struck a chord among the increasingly disenchanted youth of South Africa in the late 1960s and early 1970s. The movement's message of self-reliance galvanized students and activists as the apartheid government became more and more intransigent. Although the BCM, and its offspring, the BCP, had no leaders, it was obvious who its leading light was; Biko was a magnet to diplomats, journalists and observers. It was only a matter of time before he attracted the attention of the security police.

Biko was detained twenty-nine times between 1973 and 1976. After the Soweto uprising in 1976, the government declared a state of emergency, and he was detained for 101 days in East London under Section 6 of the Terrorism Act. The apartheid government tried to portray him as a man of violence, spreading rumours that he was a CIA spy. All the usual suspects were employed in an effort to smear his image and tarnish his reputation. But it wasn't just the crusty old crocodiles in the apartheid government who regarded Biko and black consciousness as a threat: the anti-apartheid vanguard was also concerned about the militancy of the BCM-inspired youth. In *A Long Walk to Freedom*, Mandela notes that in September 1976, "the isolation section [at Robben Island] was filled with young men who had been arrested in the aftermath of the uprising at Soweto . . . The new prisoners were appalled by what they considered the barbaric conditions of the island, and they said they could not understand how we could live in such a way. We told them they should have seen the island in 1964. But they were almost as skeptical of us as they were of the authorities. They chose to ignore our calls for discipline and thought our advice feeble and unassertive. . . ."

Like Sharpeville in 1960, the Soweto uprising in 1976 was a turning point in the anti-apartheid struggle. It was the start of a resurgence of black resistance, and the authorities responded the only way they knew: by arresting and detaining the man who had put such bold thoughts in the mind of South Africa's youth.

But Biko wasn't the kind of man to be deterred by detention. On his release, he continued campaigning. On August 18, 1977, however, he was arrested for the final time.

He was returning from a meeting in Cape Town with his close friend Peter Jones when they were stopped at a roadblock. The two men were taken to the headquarters of the security police in Port Elizabeth, where Biko was stripped naked and chained for twenty days. On September 6, he was taken to room 619 of the Sanlam building for interrogation. He was beaten so badly that he suffered brain damage and soiled his clothes. On September 8, he was moved to hospital for a lumbar puncture that revealed traces of blood in his spinal fluid. The doctors declared that there was no evidence of brain damage. He was returned to prison, where a guard later found him lying in a bathtub of water fully clothed. On September 11, a warder found him lying naked on a mat in his cell, foaming at the mouth. The authorities decided to transport him to Pretoria. He was bundled naked into the back of a police van, covered in a prison blanket and given a bottle of water. After an eleven-hour journey, he was dumped in a Pretoria prison hospital, where he died on September 12, 1977. Steve Biko was thirty-one.

Biko's death was the forty-sixth in police detention that year, according to official figures, but it was the one that grabbed the world's attention and left such a large and indelible stain on the conscience of white South Africa. The authorities were quick to wash their hands of his blood. On September 14, Justice Minister James Kruger announced that Biko had died after a hunger strike. A private post-mortem showed that Biko had in fact died of extensive brain damage. After a two-week inquest attended by journalists and observers from all over the world, Pretoria's chief magistrate, H.J. Prins, declared that no one was responsible for Biko's death. There were outraged protests around the world. The apartheid government was widely condemned.

"The world," Prime Minister John Vorster thundered, "can do its damnedest."

"Biko's death leaves me cold," said Kruger.

▼

"Hello, Ken? It's Nathi."

I pressed the security lock to the gate and went out to meet Steve Biko's son. I had a mental picture of what Nathi would look like. There is a photograph of him aged six in *Biko*. He has a big gummy grin, and his arm is raised and his fist clenched in a black power salute. The picture was taken just after the inquest into his father's death. Nathi is sitting on a fence next to his mother. Ntsiki Biko is carrying her youngest son, Samorra, and smiling. Although she is trying to put a brave face on her predicament, her smile can't hide the anxiety of a recently widowed mother left to raise two young sons alone. When I examined Nathi's face in the picture and compared it to photographs of his parents, I decided that he was the spitting image of his father. That was why I was expecting to see a tall man that morning. I, of all people, should have known better.

Nathi Biko is about my height, five-foot-seven, maybe an inch shorter. He was casually but neatly dressed in a dark blue shirt, blue jeans and brown suede shoes. His head was shaved and he wore a pumped-fist wooden medallion. He had his father's features: the bright eyes, high cheekbones and small, neat moustache. Although he is a year younger than I am, he looked older, wiser.

We hugged and shook hands South African style, and decided to have a chat on the patio. As we took our seats, I remarked that our fathers had died so that their children could have the kind of luxuries we were about to enjoy.

I explained that I was in the process of writing a memoir, and he revealed that he had just made a film about his father. "Man, I shot twenty-eight hours of interviews and footage for the film, and I had to reduce it to one hour for SABC," Nathi explained, grimacing at the memory of having to condense complicated thoughts and images into one hour of film. "But you know," he said, "it was a great feeling when I stood up at the end of the press conference to launch the film."

I could imagine his relief and was pleased for him. "You'll get the same feeling when you've finished your book," he assured me.

I asked why he had decided to make the film. "Well, it's twenty years since my father died, and I wanted to make the film to mark the anniversary of his death and to tell his story for the kids who were born that year and who will be twenty-one this year [1998]."

I asked him if he had felt any anxiety about making the film. "Yes, I know what you mean," he mused. "There are lots of other families who suffered in the struggle too." He reeled off the names of children whose parents had been killed in the struggle against apartheid, and his voice trailed off.

"But you had to make the film," I reassured him. "If you don't tell your story, no one will ever know how apartheid affected your generation. Your story will be a snapshot, a record of what happened here."

He peered at me. "Are you worried about telling your story?"

"I have my doubts from time to time," I confessed.

"You have to tell your story too, you know. We have to tell our stories," he added in solidarity. "You know, I thought about bringing my camera along—because we have to record these things," he said.

"Well, I've got a Dictaphone in the house, but I want our conversation to be natural. I don't want to be too self-conscious of what I am doing."

He looked pensive for a moment, nodding slowly as he contemplated one of the dilemmas of living a public, political life. I decided that he did not look like his father at all—he had the same impish smile, but he was quietly spoken, slightly reserved, with the same concerned expression that his mother had just after her husband was murdered.

I told him that I was humbled after reading his father's story, that I felt his father's pain.

"You know, when I was coming down here, I didn't know much about your father's story," he said. "But I was feeling bad because, you know, man, I got a scholarship from Shell to go to school."

I laughed and told him not to worry. "We have a saying in Ogoni that if the devil gives you a scholarship, you take it."

He laughed, rolling his shoulders in his shirt.

"How did you find out about your father's death?" I asked.

He paused, looked at me, then looked away. "Well, I was in school and one of my father's friends came to pick me up." He stared into the gardens. "He started joking with me and clowning around like we always did. Then he suddenly stopped and looked me in the eye and said, 'Those Amabulu. Those Amabulu have killed your father.'" He turned to me. "Amabulu is like a bull—that's what we used to call the Boers. He took me to see my mother. She was crying. I had never seen her cry, so I knew something was wrong."

"I saw a picture of your brother crying at your father's funeral," I said. "Do you remember the funeral? How did you feel about what they did to your father? How did you cope with the way he died?"

I was eager to find out how he had come to terms with life in the shadow of a dead man, but he was a little taken aback by the directness, the urgency of my questions. "Well, it's in the past. What can you do?" he said. There was an awkward silence before he added, "A journalist came to me and wanted me to talk about my feelings about his death, and I told her everything. I can send you a copy of the interview if you like."

I asked him if he found it difficult living up to his father.

"You know, sometimes people come up to me and say, 'You know, your father wouldn't have been proud of you for this,' and I say, 'Stuff Steve!'"

We both laughed, though I was surprised that he referred to his father as Steve. "Did you find it hard coming to terms with your father's death?" I ventured.

"I had some problems when I was younger, but that's in the past now."

"When and how did you come to terms with it?" I pressed.

"When I was about eighteen, nineteen. I got older."

I sensed he was uncomfortable with the question, so I decided to leave it. Before I could put another one to him, *he* asked me a question.

"How is your mum?"

"Oh, she's fine. She's coping well," I replied.

"I only asked because my mother centred me," he said.

I realized that he was answering my question about how he had coped with his father's death. I looked at him and nodded. There was no need for him to elaborate. What was left unsaid was implied by our common experience. Our mothers had centred us, had kept us on an even emotional keel, filling the space vacated by our fathers.

We opened up to each other after that, talking about all kinds of things—how he had spent so much time reading and rereading his father's writing that he really felt he knew his mind. We spoke about his film, his work as a filmmaker, his ambitions to study at Oxford and about politics.

"I gather you've had some problems with the Truth and Reconciliation Commission. Do you think the commission is useful?"

He leaned forward in his chair. "The commission has laid down certain criteria for amnesty," he said with the resignation of someone who has been over the story a few times. "One"—he counted with his index finger—"those applying for amnesty have to admit to their crimes. Two, the crimes have to have been political—that is, they have to show that they were acting under orders. There has to be full disclosure."

I asked him why his family had refused to grant amnesty.

"Because they [Biko's killers] are still saying the same things they said in 1977, only they've polished up their version of events. We do not feel that they have shown any contrition for us to grant them amnesty." There was a hint of annoyance in his voice. He told me that he had just returned from a session of the TRC in Cape Town, and I asked him if he had faced his father's killers.

"Oh, yes, we saw them," he said wearily.

"How did you feel about being in the same room as the men who murdered your father?"

"That Nieuwoudt," he said, narrowing his eyes. "I looked at him. Man, he was cold. He doesn't look like he has a heart."

I was surprised that Nathi was philosophical, almost dispassionate, about his father's killers, but I now understand his attitude as part of the Xhosa philosophy of Ubuntu: you are made human through other people. In other words, your humanity is expressed by your disposition towards other people.

It took the ending of apartheid for Steve Biko, the man who had once been *the* most potent symbol of black resistance in the 1970s, to be widely acknowledged by all the black groups that had struggled against the system. Twenty thousand people turned up to commemorate the twentieth anniversary of Biko's death, including Nelson Mandela who unveiled a statue in his honour in East London, atonement perhaps for not mentioning Biko once in the seven hundred pages of his autobiography. In the rush to forgive old antagonisms and honour the dead, the cemetery where Biko was buried was renamed and declared a national monument. He was also given honorary doctorates from the University of Fort Hare and the University of Venda. I suspect that his father's rehabilitation had helped Nathi achieve peace of mind, a state that I was still seeking and that, I imagined at the time, would come only after I returned to Nigeria to give my father a proper burial.

I saw Nathi's film when I returned to England. *Beacon of Hope* is a moving testament, and I say this with complete prejudice. It is a philosophical film that follows Nathi as he reconstructs a picture of his father through interviews with Steve's friends and family. *Bra Nathi, I know how difficult it is to tread that fine line between finding the man without compromising the myth. I love your film. I'm sure you know that you should never meet your heroes, but stuff that. We need to reclaim our fathers.*

While we were chatting, a massive thunderstorm drenched the city. We just carried on talking through the storm, reading each other's minds and finishing each other's thoughts. Like me, Nathi was the oldest son, and we spoke about the responsibilities and the dilemmas of having to be both son and husband to our widowed mothers.

"Yes," Nathi said nodding, "you're the one who has to make sure the gate is closed and everyone is safely tucked in bed."

I liked the analogy—he had obviously thought deeply about his responsibilities and his life. When he announced that he had another appointment to go to, I was disappointed. We'd been going for three hours and could have carried on talking for another three days. But I was happy to have finally met a kindred spirit, and Nathi suggested I come to a *braai* at his place that weekend.

"You can come and meet my girlfriend and hook up with my people," he said, grinning.

Nathi's people were young black South Africans who were still involved in the Black Consciousness Movement. I would loved to have seen how Biko's political heirs had interpreted the great man's legacy—whether they had recast the movement in their image or remained entirely faithful to Steve Biko's words—but I was already booked on a flight to the Eastern Cape that weekend.

"Well, let's meet again next week when you get back," he suggested. He consulted his diary: he was due in Cape Town for a session of the TRC and then at an event at Fort Hare on behalf of his father.

"Do you still do a lot of running around for your father?" I wondered.

He laughed. We hugged and pumped fists black power style. We didn't managed to meet up that time, but we keep in touch.

By a bizarre coincidence, when I was in the Eastern Cape, I came across the magazine interview he had referred to. In the article, he described being the son of Steve Biko as a "blessing and a serious challenge." He also said, rather touchingly, that "he was happy to share his father because Steve was such a generous man." He went on to confess that he often felt "trapped in his history," and explained why he called his father Steve. "I didn't grow up with Steve, which takes away the immediacy of calling him 'daddy.'"

▼

As I wandered around the Steve Biko Memorial Gardens, I thought about Nathi and his family, about the pain they had endured before Steve Biko was finally accorded his true place in the history of the anti-apartheid struggle. It had taken twenty years for the Biko family to wrest that from their country. As I looked around the cemetery, enjoying the calm and dignity of the place, it occurred to me that Biko's death had not been in vain, and I felt a little reassured that my father would one day get his justice, that his death too would not be in vain.

When I left the cemetery, I took the N2 west towards Grahamstown and Port Elizabeth. I knew where I was headed, but there were no signposts on the road and I was agitated again. I couldn't stop thinking about the words I had seen when I left the cemetery.

When I went to the entrance to sign the visitor's book, it had disappeared. Instead, I ran into the inscription at the front of the graveyard. It is Steve Biko's epitaph, and it simply says:

It is better to die for an idea that will live
than to live for an idea that will die

16

Burma: Running in the Family

▼

As my father's daughter I have a responsibility towards my country.
—AUNG SAN SUU KYI, *Freedom from Fear*

W hat were you doing in Myanmar?"

The question hung in the air between me and the security agent who had just spat it at me. We were standing in the main concourse of Rangoon International Airport, a clapped-out aircraft hangar of a building. A handful of passengers were milling around, waiting to board the early evening flight to Bangkok.

I could almost taste the security agent's breath—a pungent, stale whiff of cigarettes and alcohol. From the way he was glaring at me, I could tell he was a man who *needed* an answer to his question. A bunch of his MIS (military intelligence service) colleagues were huddled in a group a few metres away, watching our tête-à-tête. There were plain-clothes security officers all over the airport. One had his ear glued to a mobile phone, another had his face clamped to my camcorder and a third was circling around us, taking pictures of me with a small, cheap-looking camera with a flash so impressive that it lit up the terminal. It was early evening in Rangoon, and I was beginning to steel myself for a spell in Burma's notorious Insein prison.

There were three possible answers to the agent's question. The official one: "I came to Burma to do some sightseeing." The unofficial one: "I came to interview Aung San Suu Kyi." The third—a little more subtle and perhaps too complicated for the tall, skinny man standing in my face—might have made the newspapers: "The real tragedy of Ken Wiwa's arrest in Burma is that he went there in a suicidal bid to prove himself to his father."

I'd been feeling uneasy about the trip to Burma from the moment I arrived in Bangkok thirty-six hours earlier. In theory, it had seemed like a good idea to interview Aung San Suu Kyi about the challenges of following in a martyred parent's footsteps. But the night before I was due to fly out of Thailand and into Rangoon it occurred to me that I might be asking for trouble.

I suppose it was inevitable, looking back, that I would, sooner or later, put myself into a dangerous situation as I chased after my father's ghost. The epitaph at Steve Biko's grave had stirred up old fears about my authenticity as an activist—although many people had commended me for the way I defended my father, I never felt I deserved the plaudits. Unless you had spent some time in jail, you couldn't consider yourself a *real* activist. I was uncomfortable with all the sympathy after my father died; I felt it was reflected glory and had little to do with me. It's all very well speaking to a roomful of journalists or lobbying a prime minister in nice, comfortable surroundings, but you always wonder whether you would be so bold if your own neck was on the line.

When my father said that the greatest gift of life was to die for your people, I took it as a personal challenge. If death was his gift, then what was mine? Did I have what it took to stand up for what I believed in? When I was in Auckland, a Nigerian activist had suggested that I would never have been as vocal if I had been living in Nigeria. That was the first time I experienced survivor's guilt, and after my father's execution the feeling intensified.

I thought that going to Burma and interviewing Aung San Suu Kyi might clarify these questions for me. Her father is known as the founder of Burma, and he was martyred for that cause; she herself is carrying the torch, following in her father's footsteps as the focus of Burma's opposition to the military junta.

Aung San Suu Kyi has lived all my dilemmas, and far, far more. Like her father before her, she has had to make a "choice" between her country and her family. Although she is free to leave Burma and join her family in exile in Britain, she chooses to remain under virtual house arrest, offering herself as a symbol of resistance and opposition to a vicious military regime.

There was a time when anyone could go to Burma and walk right up to Aung San Suu Kyi's house on University Avenue in Rangoon. Those days were gone by the time I flew in. The MIS had got wise to the attention she received from the foreign visits, and they were now vetting her visitors carefully.

It was difficult to meet Suu, as she is affectionately known, without official approval, but I was determined to do so. My cover wasn't exactly sophisticated. Amnesty International, with the support of the Body Shop, was running a campaign to mark the fiftieth anniversary of the Universal Declaration of Human Rights (UDHR). The object of the campaign was to raise awareness of thirty unknown prisoners of conscience around the world. I volunteered to go to Burma to help publicize the case of two Burmese comedians, U Pa Pa Ley and U Lu Zaw, who had been denied the right to free expression after they were both sentenced to seven years imprisonment and hard labour for telling jokes.

All I had to do was fly into Burma with a camcorder, pretend I was a tourist, film an interview with Suu, then get the hell out of the country before the MIS got wind of my scam. I returned from South Africa on a Thursday at the end of April 1998. I had a couple of hours of training on a Hi-8 camcorder on the Friday, and I flew out to Bangkok on Sunday morning.

No one at the Burmese consulate in Bangkok suspected anything when I strolled in to apply for a tourist visa. I got the visa in less than an hour, and I was feeling pretty good until I settled into my hotel room in downtown Bangkok and started acquainting myself with the junta's appalling human rights record.

Until that evening what I knew about Burma was next to useless. I was at university when I saw the famous footage of Aung San Suu Kyi defying the military junta to address crowds of students in 1988, and I knew she had won the Nobel Peace Prize in 1990. I had done some last-minute research by reading her two books, *Freedom from Fear* and *Voice of Hope*, while I was in South Africa. But as I lay in my hotel room in Bangkok, brushing up on the harsh reality of life in Burma, it dawned on me that my little trip was going to be far more complicated than I had imagined.

The first thing that struck me was that SLORC, the sinister-sounding acronym of the military junta (the State Law and Order Restoration Council), had reinvented itself and was now known as the State Peace and Development Council (SPDC)—the same initials, ironically, as Shell Nigeria. Like SPDC Nigeria, SPDC Burma had gone in for a makeover, renaming the country Myanmar. But all the cosmetic changes couldn't hide the fact that Myanmar was one of the most repressive, authoritarian regimes in the world. Anyone SPDC didn't like the look of was carted off to Insein prison, where inmates were routinely tortured, forced to work in chain-gangs in mind-boggling temperatures and kept in small cells that were originally intended to be used as dog kennels.

Insein was not exclusively reserved for the Burmese either. In 1996 a British businessman, Leo Nichols, was found guilty of passing faxes to Aung San Suu Kyi and sentenced to three years with hard labour. Nichols died in Insein, and an inmate's recollection of a conversation with him remained at the forefront of my mind throughout my short stay in Burma.

"According to Mr. Nichols, he had to stand up for hours during interrogations and was not allowed to sit down or walk around in order to diminish his stiffness and pain. According to the friendly warder, the MIS officers and Mr. Nichols exchanged angry words in English during one of the interrogation sessions in the interrogation room of the Special Prison. He told us that he overheard some MIS officers discussing how to break down his morale and said they were talking about the best ways to give Mr. Nichols a lesson in psychological torture. We also learned about the ruthless determination of his interrogators. Another warder who got on well with us told us that MIS major Soe Nyunt had ordered his men to carry out their duty regardless of the consequences after he read Mr. Nichols's interrogation report. The major said, 'Be tough on him, no matter who he is. I'll take full responsibility if anything happens.'"

▼

The Burmese peninsula had been a British colony right up to the Second World War. It was the scene of some of the war's fiercest fighting as the Japanese attacked the soft underbelly of the British Empire in Asia. In 1942, a group of young Burmese idealists, the Thirty Comrades, went to Japan for military training as part of a fledgling movement to wrest independence from Britain. The thirty were led by Bogoyoke (General) Aung San, Aung San Suu Kyi's father. After switching to the British side, Aung San played a key role in securing Burma's independence in 1948. But he never saw the fruits of his labours: he was mysteriously gunned down in Rangoon in July 1947.

The first government of independent Burma—the country's first and last democratic regime—was overthrown in 1962 by General Ne Win, a close associate of Aung San, who, according to some theories, was behind his assassination. If that's true, then Ne Win's dictatorship was soaked in blood from the start. He earned himself a page in the universal history of infamy in 1988, when he ordered a crackdown that resulted in the massacre of three thousand people. His leadership had slid into the realms of the absurd by then. He ruled by numbers—literally—often with comic and tragic effects: his lucky number is nine; fifty kyat and one hundred kyat notes were replaced by forty-five and ninety kyat denominations. As the economy collapsed, Burma seethed with social unrest and anti-military sentiment. Ne Win consulted his stars. Fearing a prophecy that Burma would be liberated on August 8, 1988 (8.8.88), he ordered the crackdown. The number eight apparently does not sit well with Ne Win.

After a concerted international outcry over the massacre, Ne Win retreated, camouflaging his leadership under the guise of SLORC. The new junta tried to appease the world and buy itself international respectability by holding democratic elections. SLORC went to great but transparent lengths to rig the elections, placing Aung San's daughter, who had returned from exile to find herself leading the opposition National League for Democracy (NLD), under house arrest. The move backfired: the NLD won the election by a landslide. Embarrassed by the opposition's unexpected victory, SLORC cancelled the results, cracked down on the party, imprisoning most of the NLD's delegates, and threw a veil of secrecy over the country.

After seven years, Aung San Suu Kyi was released from house arrest in July 1995. But the junta still refuses to hand over power to the NLD. The SPDC is not about to relinquish its grip on a country that is rich in mineral resources, especially oil and timber. Stigmatized by its illegitimacy and reputation, weakened by trade sanctions, the junta has had to resort to drug trafficking to supplement its income. Burma is widely acknowledged as a major conduit for the international heroin trade, the centre of the so-called Golden Triangle. In January 1996, the U.S. government released a list of twenty-two countries that were co-operating with Washington in the fight against drugs. Only four countries, Burma, Afghanistan, Iran and Nigeria, had been "decertified."

Burma was practically shut off from the outside world after Ne Win seized power, but in 1996, as part of its facelift, SLORC opened up the country to tourists, declaring it a Visit Myanmar Year. Satellite TV was beamed into Burmese homes, the economy was liberalized and a host of five-star hotels went up in downtown Rangoon. Tourists flocked in to visit an achingly beautiful country, but the sudden influx of Western travellers and ideas unnerved the junta. SLORC quickly circled its wagons and turned its back on the world.

Companies that had been seduced with the promise of investment opportunities began to leave after the junta's appalling human-rights record kick-started a disinvestment campaign. The exodus was not a matter of altruism so much as a sign of frustration with a junta whose army of spongers soaked up bribes and demanded large kickbacks that ate into profit margins. The Tatmadaw (military) leaves its fingerprints on virtually every aspect of life in the country. Burma spends 40 per cent of its budget on the military, with as little as 5 per cent going to education. I've never been in a place where the military presence was so palpable and so oppressive.

When I breezed into the country, SPDC was actually experiencing one of its periodic bouts of "contrition." The junta was desperate to salvage its image in the West and entice business back, and it was lobbying the U.S. government to lift restrictions and sanctions on investment. The SPDC had hired two Washington firms, Jefferson Waterman and Bain and Associates, to do a bit of old-fashioned image laundering to spread the message that, contrary to what the economic saboteurs and their agents in the West were saying, Burma was, in fact, a paradise of social freedom and economic opportunity.

▼

I was the only black face in the queue for the Bangkok to Rangoon morning run. All I had to my name were the clothes on my back, a state-of-the-art Hi-8 camcorder and a change of clothing in my backpack as I joined a line of businessmen, hippies, monks and diplomats. By the time the aircraft landed at Rangoon airport, I was tense. I kept reassuring myself that the whole foolishness would be over in thirty-six hours and I would be safely back in Bangkok.

I had been briefed on how to handle Burmese officials, so I handed a fistful of dollars to the woman behind the customs desk, slipping her a generous tip. The SPDC is so desperate for foreign currency that all tourists have to bring three hundred dollars into the country—and have to spend it all too (you weren't allowed to leave Burma with any foreign currency). Three hundred dollars is a lot of money to spend in thirty-six hours in Burma, so the official behind the customs desk got a nice surprise that day.

Once I was past immigration—again no questions asked—I went over to a kiosk to book a hotel room and hire a taxi.

"I want to see all the sights of Rangoon," I explained to the woman behind the counter.

She smiled, snapped her delicate fingers and a young guy scuttled over to me, bowed and offered me his business card. He told me to wait by the kiosk while he went off to fetch me a taxi. It was unbelievably hot—forty-five degrees in the terminal, and as I waited, I examined the card that had been pressed into my hand with a reassuring smile. It told me that my new friend was Tun Min Oo, a licensed tour guide who would "need your contact to pay attention to your special and individual interset [*sic*], time and budget." Tun Min Oo returned a few minutes later and escorted me to a taxi. "My uncle will show you around," he beamed as I climbed in.

There was a commotion on the pavement as an argument broke out between the local airport hustlers and the taxi drivers. My driver got out of the car and another driver took his place. I glanced at Tun Min Oo. He smiled to reassure me, then disappeared into a huddle on the pavement. Another driver broke out of the huddle and swapped places with driver number two. I looked to Tun Min Oo for an explanation of what was going on, but he had disappeared.

"What happened to Tun Min Oo's uncle?" I asked driver number three.

"Yes," he replied helpfully.

"Do you speak English?"

"Yes."

"Are you Tun Min Oo's uncle?"

"Yes, I'm uncle," driver three said unconvincingly.

Later, I learned that everyone in Burma is called uncle. My uncle, driver three, looked harmless enough, with his steel-rimmed glasses, check cotton shirt and *longyi*—the long sarongs that are one of Burma's national costumes.

"Okay, let's go and see some sights," I said.

Tun Min Oo's uncle grunted and we set off. He was a man of few words, which did nothing for my anxiety; my guidebook had suggested I invest some time in the taxi drivers of Rangoon because they are among the most informative people in a country that is generally paranoid about talking to tourists. Whoever wrote the guidebook had obviously not met driver three. I imagined he was an intelligence officer or, more likely, an informant. One in four people in Burma are reputed to be one or the other.

"This is University Avenue," he piped up as we crossed one of Rangoon's main roads in a quiet, tree-lined part of the city. I kept my eyes on the map in my lap as I imagined he was checking out my reaction in the rear-view mirror.

My hotel was practically empty. I saw only one other guest, and I was convinced that he was a security agent or an informant. One in four in Burma . . .

I spent most of the day at the two-thousand-year-old Shwedagon Pagoda, with its six-thousand-carat diamond top, which Kipling described as a "beautiful winking wonder." I spent three hours practising my camcorder skills, filling the tape with shots of lovely old villas and smiling soldiers. "How long are you staying in Yangon?" driver three suddenly asked. We were standing by Lake Inya, watching the setting sun as it bounced off the pagoda.

"Just one day," I replied absentmindedly.

"Why are you doing all this filming?" he wondered.

"Oh, I have some friends in London who need some footage of the Shwedagon Pagoda and when they heard I was in Bangkok, they begged me to come over and take some shots for them."

"Yes?" He smiled.

When we finished sightseeing, I gave him a nice tip and he actually seemed grateful. As he pulled away, it occurred to me that he could have been just an ordinary guy trying to be careful, trying to make an honest living in the kind of society that makes life difficult for honest people.

The next morning, I checked out of the hotel and went to the house where I had arranged to meet Aung San Suu Kyi. As I waited on the verandah at the back, I heard what sounded like a fleet of cars pull into the yard at the front of the house. Next door, dogs started barking furiously; car doors opened and slammed, then I heard voices exchanging greetings. I was straining to pick up the pieces of the conversation when a tiny, delicate woman suddenly appeared on the veranda.

I forget who described bumping into a famous person as "the shock of recognition," that moment when you find yourself comparing the image to the reality.

Someone once described Aung San Suu Kyi as having an "unnerving serenity." She is tiny, barely an inch over five feet tall, and looks so fragile, but she has an enormous presence. She moves quietly, without fuss, seeming almost to glide, yet her whole demeanour suggests steely determination, grace under pressure, an inner resolve and reserves of strength.

She looked like a painted figure on a china vase. She was dressed in a silk Burmese wrap, and was much more beautiful in person than in her photographs. I couldn't believe she was fifty-three years old and the mother of two grown sons. She could easily have passed for someone half her age.

She was accompanied by several older, male figures, whom I soon discovered were members of the NLD. I noticed that she bowed reverentially before the men took their seats, and she made sure they were comfortable before she took a seat next to me. There was some light-hearted banter after the introductions were made. U Tin U, a little wiry old man and the chairman of the NLD, couldn't contain himself when Suu mentioned that Burma's leader, General Than Shwe, had just been voted second to General Abacha in a poll of the world's most brutal dictators. I smiled nervously.

In her book *Voice of Hope*—which is a transcript of conversations between her and the American writer Alan Clements—Clements at one point asks her whether she thinks about her father every day. "Not every day, no. I'm not obsessed by him as some people think I am," she replies.

I began by explaining to her that I was trying to write a book about my father.

"Oh, yes? What is it called?" she asked.

I told her.

"Was he a saint?" She was staring across the lawn, a wry smile on her lips.

"Well, not exactly," I said.

I explained that I wanted to correct all the misconceptions and lies that had been written about him.

"Hmm," she mused. "I've given up talking to journalists about my life. You say one thing, and they go away and write something else." She sounded quietly exasperated. She spoke in a soft English middle-class accent.

Explaining that I was trying to understand my father's legacy, I said: "I'm doubly cursed—or blessed—because I too am called Ken Saro-Wiwa."

She smiled sympathetically, as I described the various transmutations and reincarnations of my name and identity. "We sing the words," I explained. "We say Saaaro-Wee-wah. When I saw your name, I assumed it would probably be something like Aaung Saaan Suuu-Ki."

She complimented me on my pronunciation and wondered whether I was educated in England.

"Yes, but I can still speak my language," I said. "My vocabulary is not all that good, but I float between my two identities."

"It's probably a useful defence against the racism in England," she suggested. "I know my sons have had that problem. Alexander found it difficult to fit in. Kim fitted in much more easily because he can just about pass off as English. He is more like his father."

I mentioned that I had seen pictures of her sons collecting awards on her behalf and told her I had done much the same thing for my father.

"Yes, I regret asking them to do that for me. If I had the chance, I wouldn't do that again. They were much too young."

She spoke candidly about her sons and explained that she had taken a decision with her husband to keep the children out of the spotlight.

"Alexander has got a nice girlfriend now and is studying in a small university. He doesn't feel any pressure there and he doesn't have my name, which is good because he can remain anonymous and do his own thing."

When I told her that I was finding it difficult to resist the temptation to follow in my father's footsteps, she stared out into the garden again. After a short pause, she turned to me and said something I hope I never forget: "Alexander always refused to believe me whenever I told him I did not expect him to follow in my or his grandfather's footsteps."

You have to feel for him. His grandfather is a martyr and his mother won the Nobel Peace Prize. How the hell do you follow that? The struggle that your parents lived and died for has framed your life. It is the family business. It will always be at the back of your mind that you will, one day, have to make a firm decision to pick up the mantle or pass up your birthright.

Aung San Suu Kyi had always known that she would have to face her father's legacy one day. Before she got married, she wrote to her fiancé, advising him that her ultimate destiny was in Burma. "I ask only one thing," she wrote to Dr. Michael Aris. "That should my people need me, you would help me to do my duty by them." She lived in England for sixteen years, raising her sons until her time came in 1988.

She admits she was "gradually drawn into the movement," although ironically she had returned to Burma only to take care of her dying mother when she found herself caught up in her father's struggle.

"Do you think daughters find it easier to follow in their father's footsteps?" I asked.

Suu was the youngest of three children. She had two older brothers (one of whom drowned when he was a child), and I wanted to know why she, and not her brother, had taken up their father's struggle. (Aung San U is a businessman in America and had once been persuaded to return to Burma, but he had an unhappy experience after he was unwittingly used by the junta.)

"Do they?" she asked.

"I'm thinking about Benazir Bhutto, for one."

"I gather she was her father's favourite. That probably helps."

"Were you your father's favourite?"

"Yes. Probably," she said. "Well, I have memories of him coming home and sweeping me off my feet, although I'm not sure if that is a genuine memory or if I've simply been told that story so many times that it has become part of my memory."

In *Voice of Hope*, she explains that her decision to remain in Burma rather than join her family in exile was "a choice, rather than a sacrifice." I might have suggested that where she saw her decision as a choice, I saw it as pre-determined, conditioned by her sense of duty to her parents and her sense of her own place in their history. But back in March 1998, I hadn't yet acquired the understanding of how my father had dealt me my choices, of how children choose their parents.

We broke for lunch and discussed the logistics and possibility of filming Suu at U Tin U's house later that afternoon.

"Will it be safe to film there?" I wondered.

"Oh, they watch my house all the time," U Tin U said, waving his hands in the air dismissively. "It won't be a problem."

"So they will know I've been filming."

"Yes," U Tin U said. A wiry little man, he must have been the original Burmese uncle because *everyone* called him uncle. He had an impish smile and devil-may-care attitude that did nothing to alleviate my fears about a possible confrontation with the MIS. When I wondered whether the MIS would rough me up at the airport, U Tin U couldn't see that there would be a problem, but Suu shifted uneasily. "You've got a British passport, haven't you?" she asked.

"Yes?" I answered, looking to her for reassurance.

"We'd better be honest with Ken," Suu suddenly confessed, exchanging knowing looks around the table. "Let's face it— they're going to give him a hard time because he is black."

We spent the next few minutes making the arrangements to do the filming. U Tin U volunteered to take my backpack and camcorder to his house; I would show up later, just before 5:30 p.m. Suu would come by shortly after, we would do the interview, then she would leave. I would give my future torturers a few minutes to salivate at the prospect of some action, before catching a taxi and racing to the airport. The idea was to get on the 8 p.m. plane and be out of Burma before the MIS cottoned on. It was a foolproof plan.

When I told the taxi driver where I was headed, he did a double take. U Tin U had warned me that taxi drivers often refused to approach his house for fear of reprisals. He was grinning as he told me this. I soon found out the real reason why taxi drivers were afraid to stop at his house: the MIS rents the house opposite so it can keep tabs on the comings and goings. No taxi driver would risk a spell in Insein for a measly fare, even if it was in U.S. dollars.

The taxi driver dropped me a couple of streets away. I had no idea where U Tin U's house was—all the signs and street names were in a Burmese alphabet. I was about to ask someone when I spotted Suu's car coming up behind me. I was relieved until I realized that the car following behind hers was a police car crammed full of security agents. Her car did not stop, but instead turned down another side road and into a compound that was obviously U Tin U's house. The squad car stopped outside the gates. Five plain-clothes security men dressed identically in check cotton shirts and *longyis* jumped out and started speaking into their mobile phones. One of them came running right up to me and started taking pictures. I kept walking towards U Tin U's house, trying to ignore him, but the flash on his camera almost blinded me each time it went off. When I finally made it to U Tin U's house, my heart was racing.

Inside, Suu and U Tin U didn't look concerned.

"Did they see you?" Suu asked.

"Yes," I croaked.

"Oh, well, too bad," she said, shrugging her shoulders. She was grinning as she said this.

I was shaking as I set up the camcorder. Your luck has finally run out, Ken Wiwa, a little voice kept telling me. The acoustics in the room were terrible. You could hear the security men speaking on their mobiles outside in the street. It was about forty-five degrees outside and there was no air conditioning inside. Sweat was streaming off my face and my glasses kept sliding down my nose. I glanced up at Suu. She was sitting on a chair, unconcerned by the fuss and commotion outside. There wasn't even a bead of sweat on her face. When I told her I was ready to start shooting, she calmly took out a purse and dabbed her cheeks and eyebrows, putting on her public face. I began by asking her about human-rights abuses in Burma. She took a deep breath, drew herself up and ignored my question. She went straight to the point she wanted to get across, explaining that the only way to leverage the military out of power in Burma was to apply sanctions against the regime.

I had to ask her to repeat the short interview twice because of the background noise. She didn't complain. Each time she calmly slipped into her political persona and made her statement while I fussed and fretted behind the camera. Then she had to leave for her next appointment. Her people needed her.

As she was about to go, she walked up to me, touched my arm lightly and whispered some words I will never forget:

"Best of luck in everything you do, Ken, because you know, we are one family in all of this."

I froze, stunned at her transformation from political dissident. She had shown me an aspect of martyrs that their children often don't see. I was moved by the tenderness of the gesture. I was staring at my feet, trying to think of something to say in response.

When I looked up she had gone.

▼

"They're going to find the videotapes, aren't they?" I asked U Tin U.

"Oh, they won't do anything to you," he said. "Just search your bags, that's all."

"So they will confiscate the tapes?"

"Probably," he said, smiling.

Much as I liked U Tin U, I just couldn't see the funny side of my predicament. For some reason, I decided I was going to get the tapes out of Burma somehow.

"Don't worry, they're a bunch of cowards," U Tin U offered helpfully. "If they start harassing you, just shout at them." He was still grinning as my taxi pulled away.

Everything went smoothly at first. I was trying to look relaxed as I handed my passport to the immigration officer.

"Where are you from?" the official behind the counter asked, inspecting my passport.

"London," I replied casually.

"Where were you born?"

"Lagos."

"Lagos? Where is that?"

"Nigeria."

"Why are you carrying a British passport?"

"Because I live in London."

"What were you doing in Myanmar?"

"Sightseeing."

He stamped my passport. I was doing mental cartwheels when a customs official in a naval uniform sauntered across, peered over the immigration official's shoulder, glanced at me and back at my passport. I noticed a group of about ten plain-clothes security men gathered in a huddle a few yards behind the immigration counter. They were all watching me.

"Is there a problem?" I said anxiously.

"No problem, sir," the man in the naval uniform said, smiling. He invited me to follow him. He escorted me to a desk and chair in the middle of the terminal. The security men broke out of their huddle and formed a cordon around me. The man in the naval uniform asked me to empty my backpack. I did as I was told.

"What's in this bag?" he asked, pointing to the bag containing the camcorder. He was smiling.

"My video camera," I replied, smiling back at him.

"Can I have a look?" he asked politely.

"Be my guest," I said casually.

It was as hot as an oven in the terminal. He called to one of his agents and instructed him to inspect the camcorder. One of the security men broke out from the group and swaggered over. I leapt out of my chair. "Let me show you how it works," I cried.

"Please, sit down," he insisted.

"No, no. This is an expensive piece of equipment. I don't want *him* messing around with it," I said, pointing to his colleague dismissively. I switched the camera on and scenes of the Shwedagon Pagoda flickered onto the small screen.

"Here, take a look." I said as I offered the camcorder to the agent, who seemed aggrieved by my accusation that he didn't know how to work it. He spent the next hour wandering around the concourse with one eye glued to the viewfinder.

I noticed, from the gleaming brass plate on his chest, that the man in the naval uniform was called Maung Y Maung. He seemed to be the big chief at the airport. He wandered off with my passport. As soon as he left, another security man strode out from the group. It was the agent with the stale breath.

"What are you doing in Myanmar?" His narrow face was as angular and hostile as Maung's was round and friendly.

"Sightseeing," I replied calmly.

"Where are you from?"

"London."

I was amused by the banality of his questioning at first, but "Where are you from?" gets a little tedious after the tenth time. He ordered me to empty my backpack again. He flicked through my clothes with a look of contempt, then ordered me to put them away. I did as I was told. Then he asked me to empty it again.

Maung came back, still clutching my passport. I was relieved to see him.

"Empty your bags," he said casually. He was smiling.

"What are you looking for?" I asked him.

"Why were you filming in Myanmar?"

"You did not declare your camera on your customs immigration form." the other agent suddenly barked at me.

"What?" I exploded. "Since when do you have to declare camcorders on an immigration form?"

He produced my landing card and jabbed his finger at the small print. A smug smile of satisfaction spread across his face. I snatched it out of his hand and inspected it. Sure enough there was a regulation stipulating that all videos and camcorders had to be declared before entering the country. I checked the name and handwriting on the card. It was mine. I was mortified and pleaded with Maung, pointing out that I had made a genuine error.

"Who were you filming?" he asked, smiling.

"Look I haven't done anything wrong, have I? I wouldn't do anything stupid—" I stopped myself just in time. "I want to speak to the British ambassador." I declared, "I haven't done anything wrong, so I'm not answering any more questions until I speak to someone from the embassy." I jabbed my finger into Maung's chest.

"Okay relax." He held up his index finger. "Just one more thing."

I looked at him quizzically. He smiled. "Please follow me," he said, holding out his hand to show me the way.

I hesitated.

"Please," he said, almost pleading. "One more thing."

I followed him, walking past the huddle of security agents and into a backroom in the terminal. There were three men standing in what looked like a cloakroom.

"Take off your shirt," Maung ordered.

I looked him squarely in the eye.

"Just one more thing," he pleaded again, "then you can go."

I peeled off my shirt, and Maung reeled back in horror.

"What is this?" he grimaced, pointing to the scars on my chest and stomach.

"I had an operation," I said, laughing. "I have a pacemaker in here."

He looked horrified. I invited him to touch the scar on my stomach.

"No, it's okay. No problem. You can go now."

As he led me out to the bus that was waiting to take passengers to the plane, he started talking about the World Cup.

"You like Alan Shearer?" he asked.

"No. Nigeria or Brazil," I replied. "I like Ronaldo."

As I stood at the departure gate, Maung waved to me cheerily. "Come and see us again, but next time make sure you follow the rules," he called.

▼

The shakedown at the airport is standard procedure for any foreigner MIS doesn't like the look of, but the week after I left Burma, a British student was arrested in Rangoon on suspicion that he was a "human-rights terrorist." He was sentenced to two years in Insein prison.

I don't know if I was lucky or whether my name saved me but as I flew back to London, I kept thinking about Aung San Suu Kyi desperately trying to convince her son that she didn't expect him to follow in her or his grandfather's footsteps.

17

The Labyrinth
of Solitude

▼

I walk between darkness and light
the night of exile and the shining memory of home
the land I knew is given up to strangers
there in the sunshine do they feel my shadow . . .

—ANONYMOUS, WRITTEN ON A WALL IN THE GAZA STRIP

I was at Amnesty International's head office in London, describing my experiences in Burma, when Sarah Pennington, the head of Amnesty's U.K. section, burst in and handed me a note.

"Channel 4 wants to speak to you," she said breathlessly. "General Abacha's dead. Here's the number."

I was impressed that Channel 4 had managed to track me down. I called home. Olivia answered, then put me on hold to take another call in the study. While she was handling the second call, I could hear my mobile phone ringing somewhere else in the house. Olivia came back to me.

"Hello? Olivia Wiwa."

"It's me!"

"Oh God, it's going crazy here," she gasped. "Channel 4 wants to speak to you. The BBC want to speak to you. CNN—"

"Okay, okay slow down," I said. "I'm still at Amnesty. I'll be home in about forty-five minutes. Just try to hold everyone off, make a few appointments, but make Channel 4 a priority. How did they know I was here?"

"I told them."

Two hours later, I was in Channel 4's huge studio waiting for the evening news to begin. There was no doubt what the day's top story was.

As the program was about to go on air, technicians, producers, journalists and makeup artists were running around the studio, preparing for the live broadcast. I sat next to the presenter, John Snow, observing how live television news is put together. Snow was rehearsing the script on his teleprompter. From time to time, he would turn to me and make small talk.

"Did you have a nice trip here?" he asked.

I was recounting the story of how I heard the news, when Snow suddenly turned away from me and started reading from the teleprompter.

"Nigeria's military strongman General Abacha is dead . . ."

The studio had gone silent. We were live on air. As Snow's voice came in over the signature tune of Channel 4 News, the screen on the desk in front of me showed footage of a small man in military uniform and dark glasses inspecting a parade.

"Good evening. General Sani Abacha, Nigeria's military strongman, is dead . . . in the studio tonight, we have Ken Wiwa . . ."

There was a brief report giving the bare details of Abacha's death then Snow turned to me.

"Ken Wiwa, the man who killed your father is dead. How do you feel tonight?"

I hadn't anticipated Snow's question. I almost panicked as I searched for the appropriate diplomatic but philosophical response. Diplomatic, because that was the persona I had cultivated throughout the campaign to save my father's life. Philosophical, because I was conscious that my reaction could set the tone for what happened next, if not in Nigeria, then at least for our people.

What came out—in the split second between the end of Snow's question and the start of my response—came from the heart.

"I hope my father's legacy outlives General Abacha's terrible legacy to Nigeria."

The day before Abacha died, my cousin Charles had flown in from Chicago, where he had relocated after he escaped from Nigeria. We planned to spend a week catching up and watching the World Cup finals.

Before Charles arrived, I had been drawn into a debate about Nigeria's participation in the World Cup. NADECO, the country's democratic opposition, wanted to embarrass and undermine Abacha's authority by pressuring FIFA to expel Nigeria from the tournament. Abacha had covered himself in reflected glory when the Super Eagles won a gold medal at the 1996 Olympic Games in Atlanta, and NADECO didn't want to give him another opportunity to make political capital out of the soccer team. When I was asked to lend my support to the boycott campaign, I refused, arguing that football was Nigeria's only coherent expression of national identity. If we were genuinely interested in nation building, I believed, we should let the Super Eagles compete in France. I couldn't see how ordinary Nigerians would credit Abacha if we won the World Cup. Sports and politics are never easy bedfellows, as the Super Eagles later proved.

When the tournament began, my loyalties were divided between Nigeria, England and Brazil—Nigeria for obvious reasons, England because it had become my adopted country and Brazil for love of the game. (Anyone who loves *el jogo bono*—the beautiful game—wants Brazil to win the World Cup.)

England started slowly, but Nigeria and Brazil were quickly into their stride. All three qualified for the knockout stages, though. Charles surprised me when he confessed that he wasn't supporting Nigeria. Between matches, he described his experiences in detention and in the refugee camps in neighbouring Benin after he fled Nigeria. Charles is one year older and we are very close, more like brothers than cousins. I used to spend all my holidays in Nigeria with him. In many respects he was my alter ego—I could have been the one on the end of that savage beating that left him unconscious. But for the fact that I was given the opportunity to study abroad, I could have ended up in the squalor of a refugee camp, suffering the pain of being separated from my family. It was hardly surprising after what he told me that Charles didn't care for the Super Eagles. Millions of Nigerians feel the same way about their country. Many are at best cynical and at worst indifferent. There aren't many Nigerians who would be prepared to die for the country. Most see themselves as Ikwere, Ijaw or Ogoni first, and Nigerians second.

General Abacha died on June 3, 1997. His passing marked the beginning of the end of military rule in Nigeria—an era that formally ended two years later with the swearing-in of President Olusegun Obasanjo on May 31, 1999. With Obasanjo's election, Nigeria had in one sense turned a complete revolution, because it was General Obasanjo who in 1979 ended fourteen years of military rule by handing over power to President Shehu Shagari's administration.

There are rumours that Abacha died after taking Viagra to satisfy his lust for Indian prostitutes. Like many Nigerians, however, I suspect he was murdered. At any rate, his death left a vacuum. The Yoruba clamoured for the reinstatement of the June 12 mandate, insisting that their man, Chief Abiola, who had won the annulled elections, should be made president. With Abacha dead it seemed logical—if there can be such a thing in Nigerian politics—that Chief Abiola should fill the vacuum.

But Nigeria is a wonderful place, and there were a few more twists in the tail of this tale.

After Abacha died, rumours circulated that the man who handled the win bonuses for the Super Eagles had decided to help himself to the windfall that Abacha had promised to the team. Whether true or not, the Super Eagles were disillusioned and Denmark thrashed them 5–0. England also went out in the second round, and my allegiance was now fully and much more happily behind the Brazilians.

Thirty minutes before the quarter-final match between Holland and Brazil was due to start, I went for a run. When I returned, Olivia was standing by the door, speaking on my mobile. Every telephone in the flat was ringing. Chief Abiola was dead.

When Abiola died, there were claims that he had refused to accede to the terms of his release from prison—which included renouncing his claim to the presidency. But the official line was that he had died of natural causes. Faced with the understandable anger and scepticism of Abiola's family and supporters, an international team of pathologists eventually went to Nigeria to perform an independent post-mortem. Their verdict was the same—Abiola had died of natural causes. I'm prepared to suspend my disbelief in the face of scientific evidence, but nothing surprises me about Nigerian politics.

After Abacha's death, the soldiers went behind closed doors, and General Abdusalam Abubakar emerged as the new head of state. The UN secretary-general, Kofi Annan, flew to Nigeria along with a host of other diplomats and power-brokers. Where the world's leaders had once been reluctant to intervene in the "internal affairs" of Nigeria, they were now beating a path to Abuja to seek an audience with the nervous career soldier who suddenly found himself in power. So there we were, at a crossroads in history, with the people clamouring to take control of their destiny, and what do the world leaders do? They legitimize military rule.

The events of that summer were a graphic illustration that Africa is a plaything of the West, and a sop to the objectives of multinationals. That the people of the largest and most powerful country in Africa were prevented from deciding their own destiny is an indication of the obstacles blocking Africa's route to self-expression and self-fulfilment.

The political crisis eventually petered out. There was a moment when the military was uncertain and the people could have seized power, but Nigerians have never really had much taste for revolution. The country is too big; there are too many conflicting agendas. The size and diversity of the country is both its weakness and its strength. Still, there was a window of opportunity that summer.

Maybe we were too busy mourning the exit of the Super Eagles. Maybe we have become too cynical, resigned to paralysis, trapped in our history. Maybe we have come to accept that our destiny will always be decided by the people who make decisions in the multinationals that run Nigeria, and by the elites who benefit from those decisions. Imagine what would have happened if Chief Abiola had been released and the Super Eagles had won the World Cup. That might have ushered in a new era for Nigeria. Am I dreaming? Maybe. I suspect that "Maybe" will be Nigeria's epitaph.

In the end, it was business as usual; Nigeria reverted to a military government that, to give it credit, supervised the handing over of power to a civilian administration. But I'd be surprised if we have seen the last military regime in Nigeria. For now, a civilian administration is seen as the most viable instrument for maintaining the balance of terror, keeping the uneasy peace between ethnic groups, protecting vested interests and their lucrative investments.

All my dreams for the summer ended in rude awakenings. France broke my heart when it beat Brazil in the final of the World Cup and Charles flew off to Benin Republic to try to get his wife out of the refugee camp. The events of the summer set me thinking about my future. I was conscious that there were many more experienced and more knowledgeable Nigerians in exile, yet I was the name and the face that the world's media came to for an analysis of the situation there. Was I going to remain in exile forever, cut adrift from home and the rest of my family? Was I going to spend the rest of my life talking about a country that was receding further and further into the depths of my memory?

The writer Chinua Achebe reckons that an African in exile faces conflicting forces. "These forces have a certain dangerous potency; dangerous because a man might perish there [abroad] wrestling with multi-headed spirits, but also he might be lucky and return to his people with the boon of prophetic vision."

I got my prophetic vision that summer. Once journalists stopped calling on me to comment on the situation in Nigeria, I settled down to do some serious reading. I read voraciously. I discovered John Edgar Wideman, James Baldwin, Richard Wright, Frantz Fanon, Octavio Paz, Michael Ondaatje and Ralph Ellison. Just as you never see the same river twice, you never read the same book. I began to reread books with greater insight. I reread Chinua Achebe, Ben Okri, Nadine Gordimer, Arthur Koestler, Kafka and Conrad. I dipped into Camus, Soyinka, André Brink and Gabriel García Márquez. I discovered that the best books, the best writers, can be read on several levels—on the superficial level of plot, as well as on a deeper level offering motivation and psychological insight. I imagine my father would have been looking down on me with a wry smile when he realized that his son had finally discovered the joys of reading. The more books I read, the more I was excited. I was "trembling on the verge of a great discovery," as Baldwin described the time he spent wandering around Paris before he found the inspiration to write *Go Tell It on the Mountain*.

When I heard a voice urging me to read James Joyce's *Portrait of the Artist as a Young Man*, I gladly gave in to it. Wondering why Joyce had named his character Stephen Dedalus, I decided to look up the myth of Icarus and Daedalus.

Daedalus, the father of Icarus, fashions wings for himself and his son so that they may escape from King Minos's labyrinth. Daedalus warns Icarus not to fly too close to the sun, but he disobeys his father. When the sun melts the wax on his wings, Icarus plunges into the sea.

I began to see that my father, like Daedalus, had given his son wings with which to escape. Ken Saro-Wiwa could not free himself to tell the story of our hell in Nigeria's labyrinth, but by sending me to study abroad, he had given me the wings to fly. He hadn't been able to reach or influence a wider audience with his writing, but in dying for his people he had scripted the most compelling story of his life. And it was my duty, my destiny, to tell his story to those who were waiting to hear about Ken Saro-Wiwa and the Ogoni.

After Joyce, I went back to reread my father. As I was reading the letters he had written to me from detention, I found the words that gave me the purpose and direction that had always been missing in my life:

Knowing what you want out of life is the real thing. Once you are clear, you can work towards it and make alterations where necessary. You must have ambitions, goals. I don't see you with your education scratching around on the fringes of British society. You should use the advantages which your British experience has offered you to promote your African/Ogoniness. And don't feel intimidated by my "success." I do not demand, will never demand, the same of you. I repeat: I'm not trying to build a dynasty. Be yourself. You can . . . [unclear] a success in even a little way, in one little field, you will have satisfied me. I cannot

recommend the sort of life I've lived to any of my children. It's been too
dizzying, too controversial. But it was my destiny. I hope you relax,
build a good family and help our people when you can. But always
write. You have a good style. . . . .

How liberating that passage was. I couldn't understand how I
had managed to miss the significance of it back in 1994. As I
looked back over my life—my childhood memories, coming to
England, the campaign to save my father's life, my experiences
in South Africa and in Burma—the jigsaw was almost complete.

The final piece fell into place as I was driving in my car one
day. My mind went back, for some reason, to a meeting I had
with the Argentinian-Canadian writer Alberto Manguel. As I
crossed over London's Putney Bridge, I remembered Manguel's
reaction when I explained that I was going to interview Aung
San Suu Kyi and Nelson Mandela in a quest to find and understand my father.

He got up from his chair and walked over to a shelf of books
behind me. He pulled out an old hardback from his library. I can
still see him now, standing by the shelf in the corridor of his flat in
London, reading an extract from Jorge Luis Borges's *Labyrinths*.

Manguel's genius is his understanding of what words and stories can offer us. That afternoon, he read me the story about a
man who goes around the world, searching for his father. He
never finds his father, but when he returns from his travels, he
sits down to recall the places he has been, the faces he has seen
and all the stories he has heard.

As he looks back over his travels, he realizes that the map of
his journey has traced the outline of his own face.

18

Home . . .

▼

"Lie there, brave hunter. Lie there, poor man, far from the tax gatherers,
the big liars. You have paid the final tax to Oyeoku and your god. Lie
there and watch us slowly live this death in life, our life a burden and a
terror. But see us smile like sunshine, sing like the cricket through it all.
And join us at the feast of the new yam; celebrate with us, brave
ancestor, the feast of the maidens fresh from the fatting rooms. Then
watch us succumb at the touch of nature, watch us die a happy death.
Farewell . . . what else is there to say?
—KEN SARO-WIWA, *A Forest of Flowers*

He was buried on Easter Monday, 2000. On the eve of the funeral, mourners gathered in the family compound on a humid night at the end of the dry season in Bane to observe an all-night vigil and the traditional wake-keeping. There was a strange atmosphere around the compound and a soft, warm breeze whispering through the trees in the forest carried rumours of rain.

Inside my father's bungalow, in the long, rectangular room where I had caught up with my father on my trip home seven years earlier, the scene was like a ship marooned in the middle of an ocean on a dark night. Candles threw long shadows against the walls and ceiling; people were clustered in small groups, whispering in low, hushed voices as workmen rushed around trying to connect the electricity supply to the generator at the back of the house.

Outside, women sang tributes to Ken Saro-Wiwa, the soft haunting melody of their voices wafting in on the breeze along with the smell of roast yam, of jellof rice and fried plantains. A steady stream of people flowed through the house. Some came to offer their condolences, some to watch or observe the vigil. Some came to drink and eat and talk.

I was sitting in a quiet spot by a window, watching the scenes, keeping an eye on the weather, hoping that the rain would hold off for another day, when I caught my father staring at me from a table across the room.

He seemed so alive, and I saw the familiar look of disapproval in his eyes.

As I stared at him, I thought I discerned the look of someone who knew that his life would end violently. I saw a man who seemed to be contemplating the possibility that martyrdom might just be a merciful and heroic release from the rigours of living, and I found myself thinking about the last few seconds of his life. . . .

As I stared at his picture that night, I was looking for a glimpse, behind the tired, sad eyes, of the man who had always been so full of life, the man who always saw the humour in any situation, who never lost faith in even the most irredeemable reprobate. I was looking for assurance, for some sign that everything was going to be fine in the morning.

A fork of lightning snaked across the sky. And as the storm moved in over the village, trees swayed and sighed in the wind, bats flitted across the opaque sky and the sound of croaking frogs echoed in the forest. For the next hour, there were spectacular bursts of thunder and lightning. Then the rains came.

▼

I returned home on April 15, 2000. The journey back had begun in May 1999, when I wrote a letter to President Obasanjo, requesting, in the spirit of reconciliation and celebration of democracy, that the new government return my father's remains and those of the other eight executed Ogoni to their families for a proper burial. I had no idea that this simple request would later cause so much rancour.

President Obasanjo had no hesitation in granting the request. That should have been the beginning of the end of the saga, but in Nigeria things are never straightforward. Stories rarely have neat conclusions and happy endings.

According to Ogoni traditions, I, as my father's Saro (first son), am the chief mourner, and it is my duty and responsibility to bury him. I took up the challenge, calling members of the Gbenedorbi clan to a meeting in Chicago in September. Many of those who were exiled in North America after my father was executed came, and my uncle Letam flew in from Nigeria to observe our deliberations and report back home. Although it was safe for me to return to Nigeria, I wanted to delay that moment for a little longer. I had just moved my family to Canada, and I wanted to establish myself there before tackling whatever Nigeria and my people would throw at me. At the family meeting, we decided that the funeral should take place sometime in early 2000, and I sent a message back home asking my grandfather, Papa, to set the exact date. As I headed back to Toronto, I acknowledged that it was only a matter of time before I would have to face a journey I had been both consciously and unconsciously avoiding for eight years.

▼

When I landed at Port Harcourt airport six months later, I walked into a crowd of about a thousand of our people who had come to welcome me home. A giant Ogoni flag bearing a picture of my father was unfurled behind me as a supporter stepped forward to read his final statement to the tribunal:

"My lord, we all stand before history. I and my colleagues are not the only ones on trial. . . . I predict that the scene here will be played and replayed by generations yet unborn. Some have already cast themselves in the role of villains, some are tragic victims, some still have a chance to redeem themselves. The choice is for individuals. . . ."

As my father's words echoed into the warm evening air, I looked into the faces in front of me and wondered how many of them felt his words as keenly as I did. The sun had set on Port Harcourt, and my father's shadow was already looming over me.

When I left the airport, I was followed by a convoy of minibuses filled with ecstatic Ogoni who had come to witness the reincarnation of Ken Saro-Wiwa. It was too late that night to go to the village, where my grandparents were waiting for me. I later gathered that the road back there had been lined with people who had spent the whole day waiting to get a glimpse of me. I also disappointed the large crowd that had gathered outside my father's bungalow. Instead, I went to Simaseng Place, the home in Port Harcourt. When I arrived there, Nene came out to meet me. She had travelled ahead of me to prepare the ground for my return. She was relieved to see me safely home, after fretting all day because my flight from London to Lagos was diverted by a huge thunderstorm as we came in to land. She advised me to say a few words to the assembled crowd, so I stood on the steps of my father's house and addressed them in Khana. I thanked them for my reception and apologized for being late. I excused myself, explaining that I was tired after the long journey; inside the house there were more people waiting to welcome me. I acknowledged the half-familiar faces of friends and relatives before escaping upstairs.

Alone in the darkness of my father's study, the emotions came pouring out: regret; anger, happiness, sadness; tears of grief, and of relief at having finally made it home.

Nothing had been touched. The study was exactly as I remembered it, except that the venetian blind had been replaced by curtains. On the table facing the window were old newspapers, copies of *The Economist* and *Time* magazine, a rack of pipes, letters and a stack of the Ogoni bill of rights. When I ran my hand along the bookshelves, a thick coat of dust came off on my fingers. It was as if the room had been sealed on May 21, 1994.

That small room, about eight feet by six, in an en suite annexe of his bedroom is where the Ken Saro-Wiwa that the world knows was conceived. That room was where he researched and planned his life; it was in there that he saw an Ogoni star in the sky telling him to abandon his writing and lead his people to the promised land. He was always beavering away in there, and I imagined it was his escape from us. He would listen to the news from the BBC World Service or Voice of America on his short-wave radio, and I would be in my room at the end of the corridor with my door open so that I could hear the cricket or football scores from England. When the sports report came on, he would turn up the radio.

As I stood in the study that night, I contemplated the length of that corridor—how short it was and how little it would have taken for one of us to cross it. And yet—and *yet*—we were always on the same wavelength, our minds in tune. We communicated easily through the sports report, but we were unable, unwilling, even afraid, to walk the ten metres and cross the threshold of the doors between us.

The lightbulb was dead and it was dark and uncomfortably humid in the study, but the smell of the damp, moulding carpet and the whiff of old paperbacks was reassuring. I used to spend hours in my father's study, but only when he had gone to the office. As I squinted at the bookshelves, I saw some familiar titles. I noticed that we had a lot of books in common. Most of my favourite authors were in there: García Márquez, Salman Rushdie, Michael Ondaatje, Ngugi Wa Thiongo, Ben Okri, Wole Soyinka, Nadine Gordimer. Some of the books were mine too—such as the anthology of New Journalism I had lost a few years before. I felt at home in there. In that small space I connected with my father; everything that was in it was his, mine, ours. The yellowing paperbacks, the letters. These, more than anything else, are the most precious things my father has left me. When I finally collapsed into my old bed that night, I fell into a deep, contented sleep.

The next morning, my mother and I set out for the village. We stopped at Bori as usual, but my grandfather wasn't there. He was in the village, where he had retreated after my father's execution.

When I reached the outskirts of the village, I got out and walked the last stretch to the family compound. Just before I reached Zongo'Gbo, one of Bane's nine districts, people came flocking out to welcome me back. The look on those faces reminded me of just how much my father meant to them. It was as if our people had been orphaned by my father's execution. They just wanted to touch me, as if that would bring them closer to their spiritual father.

"Saro kenule naa wah."

"Ehn. Ye tua tua naa wah."

"Chai. Ah bee ye tee."

"Is that his first son? Yes. That's the first. Wonderful! He looks like his father. I kept hearing that same whispered exchange wherever I went.

It became clear that while I had conceived of my return as a private, intimate and personal journey, our people saw it as something bigger. My homecoming was a political, symbolic, even communal ritual. No one was interested in Ken Wiwa. As far as they were concerned, I was Ken Saro-Wiwa, *Jr.*, my father's son.

A week before I arrived, a MOSOP activist had sent me an e-mail advising me of the kind of reception awaiting me. "The Ogoni people will come to the airport to receive you. The people intend to do this as a symbol of their respect for Ken, as if he were the one returning home from prison."

In the face of such huge and unwarranted expectations, how could I possibly explain who Ken Wiwa was? How could I tell the people that while I appreciated the reception, appreciated that many of them had exhausted their emotional and financial resources to welcome me back, I would have preferred to come home on my own terms? It had taken me three years to arrive at my understanding of his death and what that meant to me, but I couldn't expect them to make that journey in two weeks. They were not ready; they were still coming to terms with the death of their father.

Meeting my grandparents helped me to put my return in perspective.

I was relieved to find that Papa was still fit and well. The old man was finally settling down into old age—his last child, Gibson, my uncle, was now seven years old, and he seems to be Papa's last. Papa beamed like a little boy when he saw me. It had never occurred to me that I could make the old man so happy. But it was when I saw Mama that I began to appreciate what my homecoming was all about.

I was distressed at how frail she was. She looked much older than I remembered. There was nothing to her, just skin and bone. When I walked into her house, she was sitting in her usual seat opposite the door, her right hand propping up her chin sadly. She stared at me for a few seconds, then suddenly, as the shock gave way to recognition, she got up and embraced me, squeezing me tightly. She looked up at me with tears in her milky, yellowing eyes and whispered that she wasn't going to cry any more now that she had seen me. And that was when I began to appreciate that my homecoming was as much for those I had left behind as it was for me.

Going home to bury Ken Saro-Wiwa was never going to be a simple, private affair. The political had to be accounted for, and there was already a dispute about who had the right to bury him. The battle for Ken Saro-Wiwa's body had been raging in the local newspapers for three months.

After the family meeting in Chicago, we had decided to take up an offer from the Boston-based Physicians for Human Rights (PHR) to help identity and exhume my father's remains. By the time a pathologist from the PHR arrived in Nigeria in January, however, the intricacies of Ogoni politics had coughed up a dispute that ultimately prevented us from getting his remains at all.

The origins of the dispute are convoluted, but the essence of it is that MOSOP, or at least one of the many factions within MOSOP, felt it should handle Ken Saro-Wiwa's burial. A faction of MOSOP felt that because he had been executed with eight others, the Ogoni martyrs should be buried together in a public and political ceremony. I had some sympathy for that view, but my priority was to ensure that my father's will, in which he is explicit about his burial rites, was honoured. "I shall be buried in the Ogoni National Cemetery in Bori," he wrote, "or where that is not available, in a simple grave and without elaborate ceremony in the family compound at Bane. I shall be buried with my gold pipe and a copy of each of the following books: *On a Darkling Plain* and *Pita Dumbrock's Prison*."

My father had clearly set out two scenarios. In the first— burial in the Ogoni National Cemetery—he wanted to be honoured if our people had achieved a measure of self-determination. In his definition, self-determination meant when Nigeria became a true federation of nations, with Ogoni as an autonomous but integral part of the larger whole. The second scenario was a tacit acknowledgement that our political goals might not have been achieved in his lifetime; that being the case, he wanted to be buried in the private family compound in Bane.

And so, given that an Ogoni national cemetery remains one of my father's pipedreams, we decided to bury him in a simple ceremony.

I imagine he wanted a private ceremony because he had lived a political life in the service of his people and he wanted to return to the family he had sacrificed for the cause. He wanted us, his family, to have the last rites.

There was another reason my father wanted a simple ceremony: he had always been dismissive of the kind of lavish funerals Nigerians enjoy. In one of his columns he wrote about "burial carnivals" which he considered "a waste and an unnessary show-off." The idea that the living would go to the extent of bankrupting themselves to commit the dead to the ground offended his sensibilities.

At any rate, when the PHR representative arrived in Nigeria in January to carry out my father's exhumation, he walked into an argument over who had the rights to Ken Saro-Wiwa's body. After two weeks of negotiations between the family and MOSOP, the representative left Nigeria without exhuming the body.

Dr. Bill Haglund is a forensic anthropologist based in Cyprus. We have never met—communicating only by e-mail and on the phone—but I gather he is a brusque, larger-than-life character, schooled in some of the world's hell-holes, exhuming mass graves in places like Bosnia and Rwanda. I laughed when he confessed to me during a telephone call after he returned from Nigeria that he had never encountered such a complicated situation in his professional life. He spent a week shuttling between the state government, various MOSOP factions, and the families of the Ogoni nine, trying to conclude what he imagined would be the simple task of identifying Ken Saro-Wiwa's remains. He told me that he was fed so many different stories until he was officially informed that the consent of all nine families was needed before any exhumation could take place.

The families could not agree because eight of the nine had been advised that the Saro-Wiwa family had attracted all the global attention since the executions, and that we were trying to corner the sympathy market and exclude the other families by going it alone.

The "debate" began on the Internet and spilled over and into the international media with stories in the *New York Times* and the *Observer*. There was a flurry of accusations and counter-accusations; I publicly denounced a MOSOP burial committee which had arrogated itself the task of burying my father without consulting me. The widow of one of the martyrs countered with a statement alleging that I was acting under the influence of a MOSOP faction, and suggested that I had done nothing but benefit from the cause.

I was enraged; my mind was made up. I had given up my father to the struggle, and he had given his life to the people. I was determined to reclaim what was left of my father for myself. But aside from internal Ogoni politics, there were the wider political and legal implications of burying Ken Saro-Wiwa.

When it was clear we might not even get my father's body, we appealed to President Obasanjo. I had just got home after a dinner in honour of Desmond Tutu at the University of Toronto one Thursday night in February 2000 when my mother called from London and informed me that we had a meeting with President Obasanjo on the following Monday morning. Two days later, on the evening of February 20, I was sitting on a British Airways flight at Lagos airport. Two hours later, at about 9 p.m., I was standing outside the new international airport at Abuja. Three days later, I was back in Toronto.

It all happened so fast, and the only thing that stands out about my first trip back to Nigeria in seven years was the moment when I walked into the meeting with the president.

Obasanjo was courteous, statesmanlike and sympathetic to our cause. But though the presidential heart and mind were willing, it was clear that there were all kinds of factors complicating the retrieval of Ken Saro-Wiwa's bones. The rest is a haze of fleeting memories.

I have to choose my words carefully here, because retrieving my father's bones is an ongoing concern and what I say may affect the situation. Let me try to explain it philosophically.

The conspiracy to execute Ken Saro-Wiwa involved many people who are still at large, and who still exercise undue influence in the corridors of power. And these people would rather not stir up old, contentious bones. At the heart of it is the old problem of how victims and oppressors can co-exist when there has been no mechanism for legal redress. People are afraid of the implications of releasing Ken Saro-Wiwa's bones for several reasons. First, it would give my father the honour that those who killed him are determined to ensure he does not have. Second, it seems that returning his bones not only would be an admission that he was innocent, but also would open up the possibility of legal redress for his killing. Third, apart from the fact that Ken Saro-Wiwa pricked consciences and stood on too many powerful toes, there is still the issue of four Ogoni chiefs killed in May 1994. The families of the four were never given their remains. My father was ostensibly killed in retribution for their deaths, and our family was never given his remains. An eye for an eye, a tooth for a tooth . . .

So we're all square. Let bygones be bygones, forget the past and let's move forward to reconciliation. I am all for moving forward, but how can you have reconciliation without restitution? How can you ask people to forgive *and* forget?

In Chile they tried a blanket amnesty, which created a society in which victims and oppressors are condemned to live in a climate of fear, retribution and mutual suspicion. In South Africa, the Truth and Reconciliation Commission insisted on full disclosure as a precondition for granting amnesty, hoping this would break the vicious cycle of violence and recrimination.

But truth is relative, and our people have been traumatized. The past is dead but the future is struggling to be born and as long as the convulsions of 1993–95 remain unresolved, the community will never be at ease with itself. Positions are hardening; the air over Ogoni has been soured by the whiff of betrayal. It will be difficult but not impossible to hammer out a truth that satisfies everyone and enables the community to move forward.

When I went to see Dr. Peter Odili, the governor of Rivers State, a week before my father's funeral, I told him that I was ready to help the reconciliation process, that we needed to move on, that my family needed to go ahead with a funeral with or without the bones. Then I made a formal request for my father's remains. I cannot disclose the details of his response, and negotiations are still ongoing, but when my father's coffin was lowered into his grave, it contained two copies of his books and his gold pipe, as he requested.

▼

On the morning of the funeral, my grandfather and two of my uncles woke me to fill my father's casket. I had almost observed the full night's vigil, but my chronic lack of sleep during that week caught up with me in the early hours.

At 10:30 a.m., my sister Zina led the procession out of my father's bungalow, carrying a cross of hibiscus flowers she had gathered from the forest that morning. Behind the pallbearers, Zina's twin, Noo, carried a picture of my father. I followed behind, leading the rest of the family on the short walk to the Anglican church behind the family compound.

The crowds, already ten deep, kept a respectful distance as we entered the church for an inter-denominational service. Despite frequent interruptions from the crowd massed restively outside, the service went smoothly. The church was packed with members of the Gbenedorbi clan. In all there were about three hundred in the congregation, give or take the one hundred or so uninvited guests who had gate-crashed in the Nigerian tradition.

After the service, the procession followed a narrow dirt track to the one-acre plot of land that had been donated to the family by the village. The route was lined with people straining to get a glimpse of the coffin. As the procession turned into a cleared field, the crowd followed behind and massed on the fringes to observe the last rites. Such is the people's love and respect for my father that nothing was going to stop them from getting a glimpse of his burial, despite the efforts of security officers to keep them back.

In the middle of a freshly ploughed field was a six-metre concrete tomb lined with white ceramic tiles. As the coffin was lowered into my father's tomb, the ground began to shake and I realized that the crowd was swarming to the edge of the grave. I braced myself for the impact, and for a terrible moment I was convinced we would be swept into my father's grave. There were scuffles and arguments as people fought to get a glimpse of the coffin. When the crowd eventually settled, the archdeacon gave the final orations, but I could barely hear him above the commotion. When he gave me a signal, "Ashes to ashes, dust to dust," I shovelled three small clumps of earth onto the coffin and said a quick, silent prayer. I retreated from the scene, pushing my way through the crowd to return to my father's house, where I collapsed on his bed. I'd been in Nigeria for two weeks, but it felt like years. That afternoon, I just wanted to close my eyes, go to sleep and wake up in Canada.

Felix and Olivia had not come out to Nigeria with me. Olivia was eight months pregnant and was therefore not allowed to fly. The day I left them behind in Toronto, I feared I might never see them again. As my taxi pulled away, I held on to the picture of Felix standing at the front door waving goodbye, blissfully unaware of where his father was headed. When he disappeared back into the house, I wondered how I was going to decide between my obligation to my father and my duty to my family. I knew deep down that I would be back with them. And as I lay on my father's bed that afternoon, I was already back in Canada, far from the crowds queuing outside my father's house, waiting to offer their condolences.

I flew out of Nigeria a week after the funeral.

As I left Africa, I knew I would have to come back. I can never leave Africa. It is in my blood, in my face, in my name. I always imagined I would be free the moment my father's coffin was lowered into his grave, but as Lagos disappeared beneath the plane I was conscious that there was still so much to do, that I was leaving with so much unresolved. I stared out of my window, the scenes at my father's graveside occupying my thoughts. I felt I had been cheated of something. But how could I resent our people for wanting to be a part of his funeral? After all, he was their father too. As I drifted off, I just wished I had been allowed a chance, a private moment, to say goodbye.

Postscript

▼

Dear Jeje,

   Someone once told me that when your father dies, he takes a little bit of you with him and leaves a little bit of himself in you. I've been trying to work out what you took and what you left, trying to establish where you end and where I begin. This is the final chapter in that process, and I still don't know where you end but I now know that I began on the night Felix was born and asked me a simple question.

   When he was delivered, the midwife handed him to me. I wasn't expecting to get the first look, so I was completely unprepared. I'm sure you know how hard it is to describe your emotions when you see your son for the first time. You have anticipated the moment, tried to imagine what it will feel like, yet when it comes, it still takes you by surprise.

   We stared at each other. I didn't know what to do or say. I suppose I was looking for signs of me in him, trying to confirm that he was my son. He looked as surprised as I was, but he had this intense, precocious little frown on his face. The question was in his eyes: "Who are you?"

I didn't understand why at the time, but that frown unnerved me, and it was months before I was able to look him squarely in the eyes.

"Is it a boy?" Olivia's excited voice interrupted our first discussion.

"Erm, yes it is," I replied and handed him over without even checking.

Mother and son took to each other with an uncomplicated affection. I must admit I felt a twinge of jealousy. As I watched the doctor and midwife fussing over my family, I felt I was intruding on an intimate moment. I slipped out of the room to make the announcements.

Nene was fast asleep in a waiting room outside the delivery ward. She took the news in her waking stride and told me she had just seen Felix in a dream. I smiled. I felt so proud as I led her into the delivery room. When she saw her grandson's little face, she melted and I saw her lovely smile for the first time in years. She stood by the bed, stroking Felix's head with such tenderness that I cried. It really was a bittersweet moment because I would have given anything for you and Tedum to be in that room with us.

Olivia and I chatted into the early hours, staring at the small human being we had brought into the world. I was pensive when I finally drove home. My thoughts drifted back to the moment Felix and I had our first conversation and it occurred to me that I didn't have an answer to my son's first question.

I couldn't sleep that night. I paced around, trying to make sense of the scattered thoughts swirling in my brain. I sat down at my computer and sent out some e-mails. I can't remember what I wrote, but it was something about waking from a bad dream to find that the sun was shining and birds were still singing in the trees.

It's been more than three years now since that night, but it feels more like eighty-six because I have relived two lives since then—yours and mine.

I was just thinking that all this should be private, but I realize that you of all people would understand. That's the way it's always been with us: the personal is political. We sold our privacy to the public a long time ago. Anyway, to put you in the picture, I am in good spirits, and for once in my life I really feel I know where I am going. I'm lucky that I have been able to spend so much time with Felix, but it's been a mixed bless-ing because I've mostly been locked away in this room, writing, trying to find an answer to his first question. I am writing this from my study, which is in an annexe of my bedroom in our home in Toronto. There are pictures of Felix, Suanu (your second grandson), Olivia, Nene and Tedum on my desk and on the walls. None of you, I'm afraid. I still get a little anxious when I catch you staring at me. I hope that feeling goes if and when I ever feel I've done you proud. Yet I don't need a picture of you in here, because I can sense you all around me anyway. I am looking at my fingers as I type and I'm still amazed at how familiar they are, how they bend at the same angles, how they peck at the keyboard just as yours used to do. Stubby little Wiwa fingers these.

I've noticed that my face is changing too. Jeje, I am getting old, you know. It amazes me to think that I am five years older than you were when I was born. And yet I still think of myself as your son, a boy, hardly a man and a father. But the evidence on my face is unmistakable: look how I've put on weight! Because I've been fairly sedentary for the first time in my life, my face is fuller, a few more chins downstairs, and upstairs the hairline has already begun its inevitable retreat. I'm watching out for the moment I take a good, long look in the mirror and have to accept that the man staring back at me looks like my father.

If these eighty-six years have taught me anything, though, it is this: it is not just through physical appearance that parents reveal themselves in their children. I still maintain that I don't look exactly like you— there are enough traces of Nene in me to assuage those fears—but there are subtler signs of you in me—like this study, for instance. There are the obvious items, such as the shelf of your books, but there are also the cabinets crammed full of documents in a neat filing system and the venetian blinds that must have subliminally reminded me of the ones in your study when they chose me. Nene once saw me beavering away in here, and she said, "Junior, you're just like your father, you know?" She was smiling to herself as she said this. It was a coy, girlish smile, as if she was remembering the young man she fell in love with. The thing is, our lives do seem to be following an eerily similar trajectory. Our stories overlap and complement each other. Chinua Achebe once wrote that each generation regenerates the circumstances that created the previous generation.

I suspect a genetic instruction behind our narratives, adding and subtracting, writing a new chapter to the Gbenedorbi saga whenever one chapter comes to an end.

My story, the struggle to find the beginning to my own chapter, is almost complete now, and I hope that in narrating mine, I have helped to tell a little bit of yours. I hope—in fact, I know—you would approve of the functionality of that, but there have been so many distractions. The interest in you and the struggle has been phenomenal. I seem to spend my life answering enquiries about you. The irony is that every time I throw myself into the task, I understand and appreciate you a little more.

I am fairly diligent when the mood takes me, but it is a thankless task. There are times when I feel as if I'm chasing my tail. It comes at me from all angles: by post, e-mail, telephone and fax. It started with the condolences, hundreds of them; letters, cards and faxes from every corner of the world. It was humbling and reassuring to see just how much you meant to people. I responded to all of them—just as you had always advised me to do. But that was in the first flush of enthusiasm. The letters, faxes, requests and proposals kept coming, and even though the influx has slowed, it hasn't stopped and probably never will.

I don't resent the imposition any more, though. No, handling the by-products of your life has become something of a labour of love for me. Managing your legacies is a full-time job, but I see myself as an unpaid volunteer, bonded by blood and inspired by both love and my determination to honour and keep your memory alive.

I am conscious when I survey the mountains of paper in this room that buried in there are some of my own documents—stray pieces, but poignant reminders nevertheless that I have a life of my own. Every now and again, I hear the most important reminder loitering outside the door, trying to grab my attention. Your grandson has an uncomplicated and irresistible way of getting that attention—he just barges in and demands it.

I just hope he doesn't have to remind me too often of the day he came in here and I ignored him. He stood by the door, watching me trying to fulfil my duty to you. I could see him out of the corner of my eye as I typed away. When I didn't acknowledge him he turned around and walked out quietly. My heart sank. I slumped back in my chair. He came back a few minutes later, though, and this time, I turned to face him as soon as he walked in. He had that intense, precocious little frown on his face, the same question in his eyes. I smiled at him and held his gaze. His eyes lit up and he ran into my arms, shouting: "Daddeee!"

Jeje, rest in peace.

Your son

Acknowledgments

▼

I had so many collaborators and conspirators that a fair acknowledgement would probably be longer than the book. To cut a long story short, I'd just like to preface a few. First and foremost are the half-million Ogoni heroes. Without their sacrifices, enthusiasm and support, there would never have been a Ken Saro-Wiwa. Then there are the nameless and faceless millions in Nigeria, in Africa and around the world who also helped my father tell our story. Thanks to all of you for your support, and my own thanks to those of you who made it this far. You're now a part of our struggle.

I must mention a few people who helped to make me what I am, who read and encouraged, who gave me a nudge from time to time and who offered me insights I cherish: Evan Solomon, William Boyd, Gavin Grant, Roger Alton, John Vidal, Natasha Hassan, Paul Webster, Maureen Issacson, Joanna Pachner, Rebecca Fox, Alan Rusbridger, George Alagiah, Frances Alagiah, Heike Fabig, Geoffrey Allibone, Ken Wareham, Clement

Adibe, Mike Mullvihill, Angus Choi, Glenn Ellis, Kay Bishop, First Direct plc, Richard Goldman, Rhoda Goldman (RIP), Barry Kumbe, Jordana Friedman, Professor Claude Ake (RIP), Diana Morant, Kofi Agyemang, John Sutton, George Irish, Sister Majella McCarron, Isobel Harry, the Rascals, Duane Silverstein, Jonathan Smith, Jennifer Barclay, June Cutforth, Hilary Stanley, Dionne Brand, Desmond Martin, Anelyn De Luna, Nicholas Claxton, Glennys Kinnock, Michael Mouland, Noelle Zitzer, Nikki Barrett, Valerie Ahwee, Father Ken Bowler and Scott Greathead. My sincerest apologies to anyone I have "forgotten."

Thank God for my parents, Jeje and Nene, whom I chose wisely. My humble and grateful thanks to my brothers and sisters, Gian, Zina, Noo, Tedum, Singto, Adele and Kwame, because while I hog the limelight, I always remind myself that so much of this is also about them and for them.

I owe so much to Cristina Barchi, who had the original idea for this book way back in the dark days of December 1995. Thank you Mark Johnston for believing in me, for nurturing the seed and for friendship and trust. And thank you to Master John Fraser, the staff and the Quadrangle Society at Massey College, University of Toronto, where I was a much-indulged writer-in-residence and an associate of the Southam Fellowship in 1999.

A special thanks to my agents, Bruce Westwood at Westwood Creative Artists and Derek Johns at AP Watt, who, in their very different ways, kept me sane, kept me solvent and kept me on the road.

Dear Alberto Manguel. Thank you for teaching me how to read. Thank you, Doris Jahnsen, for spotting the outline of my face. And my thanks to my publisher and editor in England, Bill Scott-Kerr. Your enthusiasm and instinctive understanding of where this story had to go gave me the extra push I needed to finish it.

I don't know enough ways to thank my editor, Louise Dennys, but she was my interpreter and my guide. You taught me so much about writing, Louise, and you handled this with such tender care, such brilliant insight, that I think your legendary reputation is actually underestimated.

The last word is for the three people without whom Ken Saro-Wiwa would never have made sense to me and this book would never have been written: Olivia Wiwa, Felix Saro-Wiwa and a little, little man called Suanu Saro-Wiwa.

Born in Nigeria and educated in England, Ken Wiwa now contributes to newspapers, including *The Globe and Mail,* the *National Post,* the *Ottawa Citizen, The Toronto Star, The Guardian, Sunday Telegraph,* the *Independent,* the *Independent on Sunday* and the *Observer.* Internationally his journalism has appeared in South Africa, Holland, Germany and Spain and in a weekly column for *Vanguard* in Nigeria. Ken was also Internet editor for *The Guardian* for nearly two years. He now lives in Canada with his family and is Senior Resident Writer at Massey College in the University of Toronto.